Reimagining Educational Justice in the Face of Opposition

Reimagining Educational Justice in the Face of Opposition

Altheria Caldera, PhD

BLOOMSBURY ACADEMIC
NEW YORK • LONDON • OXFORD • NEW DELHI • SYDNEY

BLOOMSBURY ACADEMIC
Bloomsbury Publishing Inc, 1359 Broadway, New York, NY 10018, USA
Bloomsbury Publishing Plc, 50 Bedford Square, London, WC1B 3DP, UK
Bloomsbury Publishing Ireland, 29 Earlsfort Terrace, Dublin 2, D02 AY28, Ireland

BLOOMSBURY, BLOOMSBURY ACADEMIC and the Diana logo are
trademarks of Bloomsbury Publishing Plc

First published in the United States of America 2026

Copyright © Altheria Caldera, 2026

Cover design by Kathi Ha
Cover image © iStock.com/melitas

All rights reserved. No part of this publication may be: i) reproduced or transmitted in any form, electronic or mechanical, including photocopying, recording or by means of any information storage or retrieval system without prior permission in writing from the publishers; or ii) used or reproduced in any way for the training, development or operation of artificial intelligence (AI) technologies, including generative AI technologies. The rights holders expressly reserve this publication from the text and data mining exception as per Article 4(3) of the Digital Single Market Directive (EU) 2019/790.

Bloomsbury Publishing Inc does not have any control over, or responsibility for, any third-party websites referred to or in this book. All internet addresses given in this book were correct at the time of going to press. The author and publisher regret any inconvenience caused if addresses have changed or sites have ceased to exist, but can accept no responsibility for any such changes.

Library of Congress Cataloging-in-Publication Data is available

ISBN: HB: 979-8-216-38107-5
PB: 979-8-216-38106-8
ePDF: 979-8-216-38104-4
eBook: 979-8-216-38103-7

Typeset by Integra Software Services Pvt. Ltd.
Printed and bound in the United States of America

For product safety related questions contact productsafety@bloomsbury.com.

To find out more about our authors and books visit www.bloomsbury.com
and sign up for our newsletters.

*I dedicate this book
to the justice workers upon whose shoulders I stand,
to those whose lives have been irrevocably diminished because
of white supremacy, to the Black feminists whose theorizing,
teaching, and activism inspired and informed my work,
to my teachers, professors, and mentors, for helping me develop
the skills needed to write a book, to my ancestors, from whom
I inherited determination and resilience, to my family and friends
in Sumter County, Alabama, who will always be home to me,
May this book represent a portion of the honor you deserve.
Ubuntu.*

Contents

List of Figures xi
List of Tables xii
Foreword xiii
Preface: How I Came to Care for and Cultivate Trees xv
Acknowledgments xxii

Introduction 1
Who This Book Is For 3
A Note About Language 5

Part I Centuries in the Making: Planting Trees in Poisoned Soil

1 Soiled: A Society Rooted in White Supremacy 9
Hidden Under Our Feet 10
Contamination Through Colonization 11
Whiteness as Social Identity 11
Origins of White Supremacy 13
Definition of White Supremacy 15
The Birth of a Nation and a National Identity 17
One Oppressive System, Many Forms of Oppression 23
Forms of Systemic Oppression Rooted in White Supremacy 25

2 Planting Trees: The Resistance to White Supremacy 31
Planting Trees: Reconstruction Era (Late 1800s) 32
Planting Trees: Civil Rights Era (1950s–1960s) 33
Interconnections but No Solidarity 39

Planting Trees: Civil Rights Act of 1964 and Beyond 40
Schools and Society 46

3 Bearing Fruit: The Evolution of Schooling for Students of Color 49
The First Schools of Social Reproduction 49
Early Schooling for Students of Color 50
The Disruption 58

Part II The Blighting of the Fruit

4 Leading Up to the Blighting 71
Widespread Commitment to Racial Justice or Something Else? 72
Black Lives Matter (BLM) 73
BLM and the Covid-19 Pandemic 75
Race/Ethnicity-Centered Curricula 75
The Backlash 76

5 Blighting the Fruit: Opposition to CRT and DEI 79
Critical Race Theory (CRT) 80
CRT and Social & Emotional Learning (SEL) 87
Diversity, Equity, and Inclusion (DEI) 90
Conclusion 100

6 Blighting the Fruit: Attacks Against Other Minoritized Students 103
LGBTQIA+ Students 103
Students Who Are Religious Minorities 109
Students of Color, Students with Disabilities, and LGBTQIA+ Students 110
Immigrant and Emergent Bilingual Students 112

7 Harmful Lies and Ideologies 117
Lies They Tell Others 118
Lies They Tell Themselves 119
Conclusion 132

Part III Healing the Trees

8 Healing the Trees Through (Critical) Introspection 135
Knowledge That Matters 135
The Role of Bias 138
Doing the Work 139
Me and White Supremacy 143
Healing the Trees 145

9 Healing the Trees Through Institutionalizing 147
What Is Education Policy? 148
Love and Justice 149
My Policy (Dis)Engagement 150
Policymaking 152
Healing the Trees 154

10 Healing the Trees Through Inclusivity and Intersectionality 157
An Anecdote 157
My Journey to Viewing Justice Through the Lens of Inclusivity 158
Encountering Black Feminist Theory 160
Justice for All Students 162
About Antiracism 164
Healing the Trees 166
About Identity 168

11 Healing the Trees Through Insurgency 169
Don't Ask Questions 170
Teaching When the World Is on Fire: Reimagining the Purpose of Schooling 172
Healing the Trees 178

12 Healing the Trees Through (Radical) Imagination 181
Afrofuturism 183
A Radical Imagination 184
Using Artificial Intelligence to Imagine 185
Healing the Trees 188

Conclusion: Make a Career of Humanity 191
On Differences 191
To Humanize? 192

References 196
Index 219
Author's Biography 235

Figures

1.1 Imperialist White Supremacist Capitalist Cisheteropatriarchy Links to a Range of Systemic Oppression 28
5.1 Increase in Anti-CRT Legislation Since 2020 86
6.1 Data from Trans Legislation Tracker Showing the Rise in Anti-Trans Bills 106

Tables

1.1   Examples of Policies, Laws, Court Decisions, and Practices That Granted Systemic Advantages to Whites 21
1.2   Legalization of Citizenship for "Others" 22
2.1   Legislative and Judicial Milestones 43
6.1   Discriminatory 2025 Executive Orders That Impact Schooling 114
8.1   Framework for Critical Introspection, Part I 140
8.2   Framework for Critical Introspection, Part II 141
8.3   Framework for Critical Introspection, Part III 142
10.1 Student Identities Privileged and Victimized by White Supremacy 163
11.1 Insurgent Education 178
12.1 Improvement or Justice? 183

Foreword

It is a profound honor to write this foreword for Dr. Altheria Caldera, a teacher, researcher, and advocate whose work does not simply inform, but transforms. With experience as a classroom teacher, college professor, community member, entrepreneur, and policy reformer, her unique experiences and expertise are truly one of a kind, making her uniquely suited to write the book that is before you. What truly distinguishes Dr. Caldera's writing is how she communicates with a clarity and conviction that pierces through noise. I've found her to consistently invite readers into a sacred kind of discomfort, one that is necessary for growth, healing, and justice. I have no doubt that you will find her voice is at once fierce and generous, vulnerable and unflinching. Reading her work, you don't just learn; you remember what matters, and you're inspired to do your part.

I met Dr. Caldera when we were both assistant professors at a regional university in Texas. We both worked in the same department, but it would take some time before we met. What stood out to me was her commitment to critical consciousness and our mutual professional and personal connections with the Black and Latinx communities. We both had intuited and experienced the simultaneous distinct and interlocking ways our communities have experienced injustice and how we could learn from and lean on one another as we forged our paths forward. We eventually coauthored several articles and a book chapter together. The most illustrative of our journeys was the article "Being a Conduit and Culprit of White Language Supremacy," a deeply personal and political duo autohistoria-teoría. We vulnerably name and lay bare how we had internalized and at times reproduced linguistic oppression in ourselves and our communities, and how we hoped to reflexively move forward. Writing that piece required trust, excavation, and tenderness—qualities that Dr. Caldera brings not only to her scholarship, but to every space she inhabits.

Since that time, Dr. Caldera has continued her work as an educator, scholar, and advocate in additional capacities, refining and extending her skills for even more communities and at wider scales. Our paths would diverge and later cross again with our joint work at the Reading League. This new work continues in that spirit. With characteristic depth and accessibility, Dr. Caldera explores how race, language, place, and power are inextricably intertwined. She reminds us that the educational work we do is not neutral. It is laced with histories and futures. And in this book, she refuses to sidestep the complexity. She names the pain. She refuses the lie of perfection. She models what it means to critique the systems that have harmed us, even as we remain committed to creating something more just in their wake.

But what sets her apart is not only her analytical brilliance, it is her spirit. Her writing is filled with *coraje* (courage) and *cariño* (care). She brings her whole self to the page: scholar, teacher, Black southern woman, and spiritual being. She draws from the wisdom of her people and from the truths etched in her own bodymindspirit. As a result, her words resonate on frequencies beyond the academic. They speak to our bones.

This book is also in conversation with a larger tradition of women of color feminist thinkers (Anzaldúa, Lorde, hooks, and many others) who insist that the personal is political and the emotional is epistemological. Dr. Caldera builds on this lineage while making it her own. What keeps me *boquiabierta* (mouth agape) is how she simultaneously communicates so comprehensively and approachably, how she outlines and connects historical facts with personal vulnerability. Dr. Altheria Caldera's work speaks directly to the growing movement among educators of color who are refusing burnout, cynicism, or despair as a badge of honor and instead choosing healing, sustainability, and joy as radical acts of resistance.

In these pages, readers will find an offering that functions as a mirror, a map, and a call. Dr. Caldera does not promise easy answers. Instead, she offers questions that return us to ourselves. She invites us to be honest about the roles we play in the histories we acknowledge, the languages we privilege, and the silences we keep. And then she invites us to choose differently. With intention, integrity, and love.

As you turn each page, may you read slowly. May you pause often. May you feel held. And may you walk away not only with insight, but with a renewed sense of purpose.

This book is a gift. So is its author.

—Alexandra Babino, PhD,
Associate Professor, Literacy and Language,
Texas Woman's University,
Coauthor of *Radicalizing Literacies and Languaging* (2020) and *Latina Pedagogies of Care* (in press)

Preface: How I Came to Care for and Cultivate Trees

I love trees. I mean, I really love trees. Maybe I should have been an arborist. Maybe I am an arborist, of sorts. Trees are majestic, powerful, and beautiful—simultaneously representing the past (the planting), present (today's reaping), and future (tomorrow's reaping by others). When I'm among trees, I'm deeply reverent. Still. For me, woodlands, groves, orchards, and forests are places of contemplation, reflection, and dreaming. As one of my favorite authors Indigenous (Potawatomi) botanist, scholar, and best-selling author, Robin Wall Kimmerer (2013), surmised, planting trees is an act of faith. But it is also an act of hope, hope that something life sustaining and beautiful will one day exist where there are currently voids. Planting trees reflects hope that tomorrow's landscape will be different from today's. It seems fitting, then, that I'd use trees as an analogy to convey my ideas about educational justice.

I don't remember a lot from eighth grade, but I remember having to memorize the Preamble to the U.S. Constitution. I can still recite it today. While some readers may see the Preamble as aspirational, Dr. Martin Luther King Jr. regarded it and the Constitution that follows as a promise. In this case, "establish Justice" is one of the first promises made by the founders. In his "I Have a Dream" speech, King (1963a) claimed that America has defaulted on this "promissory note to which every American was to fall heir." For many generations, our progenitors worked to ensure that the United States fulfills the "promissory note." I describe their work as *tree planting*. Their tree planting was motivated by a singular goal—that their descendants would live in a society marked by fairness.

Two songs associated with the civil rights movement in the U.S. South remind me of the faith and hope embedded in tree planting—the gospel song "We Shall Overcome" and Sam Cooke's soulful "A Change Is Gonna Come." This faith and hope was also encapsulated in a motto that inspired the United Farm Workers movement—"Si, se puede!" translated to English as "Yes, we can!" Tree planters sought to change the social, political, and economic landscape of a country conceived with justice as a foundational ideal. I, too, am a tree planter standing upon the shoulders of generations of justice workers who came before me. The pursuit of justice has guided my professional work for nearly twenty years.

As far back as I can remember, I've cared about people. As a child, I was described as "sweet" and "kindhearted." But these attributes didn't make me a justice worker. My justice work didn't truly start until 2007 when I taught my first diversity course. As we Generation Xers tend to lament these days, it seems unimaginable that this was almost twenty years ago. At the time, I was a full-time Texas community college instructor teaching education courses in an Associate of Arts in Teaching (AAT) program that our college had begun offering a few years prior. Although the AAT does not result in a teaching certification, it does allow community college students—many of whom are Black and Latino(x) first-generation students—to explore the teaching profession and to earn their first transferable credits in education by completing two discipline-specific courses that I developed and taught: Introduction to the Teaching Profession (EDUC 1301) and Introduction to Special Populations (EDUC 22301). Students saw Special Populations as "the diversity course." The course description read as follows:

> An enriched, integrated pre-service course and content experience that provides an overview of schooling and classrooms from the perspectives of language, gender, socioeconomic status, ethnic and academic diversity, and equity with an emphasis on factors that facilitate learning.

My charge was to teach my students—all prospective teachers—about race, ethnicity, gender, socioeconomic status, religion, and other factors that shape cultural identity. As reflected in the course description, I would help them understand diversity and equity in education. Thinking back on this course offering, I'm surprised that conservative-led Texas would require it. I now wonder how long it, and other diversity courses in teacher education, will be required, or even offered, considering Texas's recent restrictions on DEI in higher education (more on this in Chapter 5).

Throughout this book, I'll make confessions about my work. I think it's important that you as readers see that becoming a justice worker is a journey traveled imperfectly. "We make the way by walking" (Horton, 1990). Here's my first confession. It's an understatement to say that I was not equipped to teach Special Populations when it was handed to me. I am a Black woman from rural Alabama, born a few years after schools in my county were desegregated. With roots in the U.S. South—arguably the birthplace of the movements for racial equality in the United States—I was familiar with *equality*, which I understood as treating individuals the same, or equally. But *equity*, the focus of Special Populations, was a new concept for me. Throughout my adult life, I had not thought deeply about equality and had never thought about equity. For many years, I had believed, perhaps naively, that life is about choices. "The choices we make determine the life we live" was my motto. I believed that if people weren't successful, it was because of personal failures and individual shortcomings. I believed that the civil rights movement of the 1960s had mostly relieved us, Black people, of oppression. If someone had asked me if I had ever experienced racism, not knowing the three forms of racism (internalized, interpersonal, and institutional), I would likely have said no.

A senior colleague at the community college where I worked, a Black man with enough age to be my father, frequently tried to convince me to believe otherwise. He advised me to be aware of the ways racism showed up on our campus. I would respectfully listen but immediately dismiss his "dated" advice. I thought that Mr. Davis made too big of a deal out of race. I didn't see any evidence of racism on my campus. I was not seeing the world through critical eyes. I was not awake. I was not asking the right questions.

My early years as a teacher were mainly spent in classrooms with Black and Latino(x) students, but I never thought deeply about how racism might shape their education. I earned a Master of Education, along with a teaching certification in 1998, without taking a single diversity course. The only "difference" for which I was formally trained was "exceptional learners," or students with special needs. Now, as a community college instructor, I was on the verge of simultaneously teaching and learning about diversity in education.

Most professors would likely acknowledge that they learn a lot preparing to teach a new course, but the learning I experienced was nothing short of life changing. Although I had been a public school teacher for several years, I had never dedicated time to learning about justice, or more accurately, injustice, in education. Sure, I had witnessed disparate student outcomes, but I had attributed those outcomes to their "broken" families and poor neighborhoods, from which I was there to save them. Through my reading the word and reading the world (Freire, 1985), I was learning that certain populations of students were underachieving not because of familial or cultural deficits, but because of inequitable schooling policies and practices. Assessments were biased. Discipline policies were discriminatory. Urban schools were underfunded. Teachers of Black and Latino(x) students were underprepared. And resources for English language learners (now more appropriately called emergent bilinguals[1]) were limited. Curricula centered white culture and marginalized ethnic cultures, and more. Whoosh!

Don't judge me. The idea of schools being instruments of oppression is far more readily accepted today, but this was in 2007. Just imagine. The face of the U.S. presidency was still all white. President Obama's presidency, which ushered in renewed conversations about race in the United States, was still a year away. MySpace was the most popular networking site. Facebook was only three years old and was still mainly limited to use by college students. Trayvon Martin was in second grade, "woke" was years away from entering mainstream vernacular, #BlackLivesMatter was not a controversial hashtag, former NFL quarterback Colin Kaepernick had not coupled patriotism with protest by kneeling during the national anthem, and widespread adoption of diversity statements by institutions of higher education was still more than a decade away. No TikTok teachers were creating social justice content. Times were truly different.

In my studies to prepare to teach Special Populations, I learned from Myles Horton and Paulo Freire (1990, p. 180) that "the educator has the duty of not being neutral." As a new teacher educator, I could not continue the neutrality, this blindness, that I brought to my work. I needed to shed light on the violence that Black and Hispanic students, LGBTQIA+ (lesbian, gay, bisexual, transsexual, queer, intersex, and asexual + others) students, emergent bilinguals, students who were religious minorities, and students from economically disadvantaged backgrounds, among others, were experiencing in schools. There was an achievement gap (later conceptualized by Gloria Ladson-Billings (2006) from a justice perspective as an opportunity gap), and students from families and communities like mine were on the lower end of this gap. I wanted my preservice teachers to be aware of existing conditions, to know that they could be effective teachers of minoritized students, and to be committed to educational justice.

Knowing that Special Populations was likely the only diversity course my students would be required to take as part of their teacher preparation, I was determined to make it meaningful. I was positioned to impact the teachers who would teach marginalized students, teachers who could help these students be academically successful or contribute to their failure. To this day, I feel the weight of this responsibility as a teacher educator. Thus, I began a justice-centered learning journey that I'm still on today.

Around the same time that I began teaching this course, I met a veteran educator, Dr. Danna Diaz, who had been doing racial equity work as an education administrator for many years. I worked summers in her office at the school district, where she created initiatives to improve the high school completion rates for students of color, and learned from her mentorship. Through this summer work, I received training at the local YWCA to be a Dialogue on Race facilitator. The YMCA director who trained me, Marcy Paul, was a Jewish woman whose equity simulations were eye opening. I still remember one of those simulations. Marcy divided us into groups of two and gave each group a bag of supplies with which we were to build the biggest house we could build. (She paired me with another Black woman.) My partner and I intently worked on building our house and were proud of what we had constructed. When time was up, we looked around and noticed that everyone's house was bigger than ours. Marcy asked, "Why do you think the other groups' houses are bigger than yours?" Someone answered for us, "Because we had more supplies." Another person added, "And our supplies were better." Marcy then asked, "What if I told you that in our society, some communities are behind from the start because they don't have the resources and support that other groups have?" She helped us to see how systems were designed to advantage some and disadvantage others. Through this experience, I began to understand that structural inequities had enabled many of my white colleagues to participate in study-abroad experiences during college, to graduate from college without student loan debt, and to become homeowners in their twenties. They'd had advantages, like access to resources and opportunities, that I had not had. I learned so much from working alongside Marcy and Danna, who became mentors. Additionally, I was also fortunate to be mentored by the president of the community college where I worked. As president of "the Black campus," which was one of five campuses in our community college district, Dr. Ernest Thomas fought for equitable resources for our students and insisted on a diverse faculty to match our diverse student population. His unwavering commitment to do what was just for the students of our campus inspired me to do the same in my work.

I engaged in professional development opportunities related to my new interest, which was becoming a commitment. I attended a Teaching for Change Conference with the theme "Taking Teaching to the Edge" and the International Women's Peace Conference that focused on "Education and Peace." I remember attending a session at the University of North

Texas's (UNT) Diversity and Equity Conference that inspired my political activism. I learned from Toni Medellin, an attorney and Chicana civil rights activist, how education policy shapes school practices. Sadly, after more than two decades of hosting its Diversity and Equity Conference, UNT will not host a conference in 2024 and has dissolved its diversity office to comply with Texas's new anti-DEI law that took effect on January 1, 2024 (Runnels, 2023).

Still, I had more questions than answers and felt that I needed formal education. These questions about how to improve opportunities and outcomes for marginalized students led me to pursue a PhD in curriculum studies. Curriculum studies (CS) is a field in which scholars, among other things, interrogate the sociopolitical issues that impact schooling. We ask questions about learning and teaching, practices and policies, and curriculum and philosophy. And some CS scholars, like myself, critically examine these factors through the lens of race, class, and gender. Earning a graduate certificate in women and gender studies while studying for my PhD equipped me to examine how individuals and communities experience oppression as a result of holding socially constructed identities. I used my developing knowledge to write editorials for a popular blog, *For Harriet*, that centered Black women and Black womanhood. I was a cultural critic who wrote about socioeconomics, race, gender, colorism, motherhood, cultural appropriation, and more—all by centering the experiences of Black women. Doing this work strengthened my ability to recognize how systemic oppression shows up in the lives of Black women and helped me to extrapolate my findings to other marginalized groups.

After graduating from doctoral school, I returned to my role as a teacher educator, but this time I worked at a university, teaching in-service teachers in a graduate program in curriculum and instruction in rural Northeast Texas. The course that I taught most frequently was Diversity and Equity in Education. This time I was ready to teach "the diversity course." Prepared. Equipped. Ready to continue learning and teaching. I view teaching and learning as inextricably linked, so I learned from the wealth of experiences my students, who were practicing teachers, brought to our class. I learned from their curiosities, resistance, emotions, and perspectives. Later, I was recruited to teach part time in an online graduate program in antiracist education at the University of North Carolina, Charlotte. In this program, I taught courses like Race and Education, Equity in Education, and History and Psychology of Racism. Over the years, I've also mentored doctoral candidates writing dissertations on race-related topics in education. To deepen my capacity to teach and mentor educators, I attended conferences like the American Education Studies Association Annual Conference, the Critical Race Studies in Education Annual Conference, and the National Women's Studies Association Annual Conference. I was also selected to join the Teacher Educators of Color Convening sponsored by the Institute for Teachers of Color Committed to Racial Justice.

Since teaching my first diversity course in 2007, I've become a scholar who has conducted research studies on race, gender, socioeconomic status, language, and the intersections among them. I have given dozens of academic presentations and written dozens of articles and book chapters on equity in education. As a diversity, equity, and inclusion consultant, I've given keynote speeches, facilitated workshops, and delivered many presentations internationally and nationally. One of the reasons that I enjoy and appreciate teaching and facilitating is that it simultaneously postures me as a learner. But this learning doesn't happen by osmosis. I am a deeply reflective practitioner who continues to think and grow from my work.

I came to care for and cultivate trees—to advance educational justice—because I care about humanity. I care about children, especially. Schools from prekindergarten through higher education should be places that liberate, inspire, support, and affirm all students, but too often this is not the case for students at the margins.

I am an arborist, of sorts. And this book is a tree, of sorts, written in faith and hope that it will help readers make schools and society more just.

Note

1 See "Words Matter—The Case for Shifting to 'Emergent Bilinguals'" by Araceli Garcia at https://www.idra.org/resource-center/words-matter-the-case-for-shifting-to-emergent-bilingual/

Acknowledgments

I am deeply grateful for the love, support, and encouragement of my spouse, Francisco Javier Caldera Reveles, who has been my office mate, dialogue partner, and cheerleader. You have pushed my thinking and often seen more potential in me than I see in myself. And to my stepchildren, Lizi and Francisco, and stepgranddaughter, Arianna, thank you for engaging in many conversations about injustice that help me to see your points of view. I appreciate your support.

Throughout this process, I've been fortunate to have critical readers whose keen insight and broad, interdisciplinary knowledge have made this work sharper and stronger. Dr. Monica Lugo's expertise about sociological aspects of immigration and illegality on the southern border, Dr. Alexandra Babino's deep knowledge of bilingual education and linguistic imperialism, Dr. Ernest Thomas's lived experiences as an activist and academic knowledge about the sociology of race and African American studies, Dr. Kurk Gayle's inspiring work as a justice-centered teacher, Dr. Carla Wilson's remarkable competence in multicultural feminist studies, Toni Medellin's, Esq., insight into the Chicano movement in Texas, and Ryan Buggy's adeptness at writing have impacted this book in immeasurable ways.

I always say that I am surrounded by the most wonderful circle of friends. And I mean it. My friends make me feel like I can change the world! Javita, Lizdelia, Adena, Michelle, Katrina, Tamika, Andrea, Cessilye, Gigi, Beth, Meg, Gabby, and Susan, you are true jewels. I wish I could list every friend who has encouraged me on this journey. I love you real big! To my students, colleagues in academia, and consulting clients, I learn and grow from working with you. I'm exceptionally thankful to Dr. Maria Murray and The Reading League, who have allowed me to learn and grow with them as their Diversity, Equity, Inclusion, and Belonging consultant for the past three years.

The trees. Throughout the day and at the end of a long day of writing, I made a point of surrounding myself with trees. And, somehow, through the touching, hugging, and being near, they guided, uplifted, and energized me. I am forever grateful for the trees.

Last, I'm writing this as my two dogs fight for space in my lap. My pups, Koko and Kanela, have been a necessary distraction from writing, comfort when I'm distressed, and a source of laughter when I need to lighten up. I am very grateful to be their mom.

Introduction

I was inspired to write this book in response to the "culture wars" that made their way into American education during the early 2020s. Instead of attenuating, the culture wars have strengthened in recent months, with the 2025 Trump administration ushering in attacks on educational justice with renewed fervor. "Culture wars" are defined as conflicts between groups based on ideological beliefs. Schooling is at the epicenter of these conflicts. This should not come as a surprise, as schools are the primary institution responsible for creating citizens who make decisions about our democracy.

I was an education policy fellow in Texas from 2020 to 2021 and experienced firsthand the first round of assaults on schooling waged and won by the Right through what became known as "anti-CRT" legislation. The second round of assaults would come two years later in 2023, with a focus on dismantling DEI (diversity, equity, and inclusion). Now, in year one of the 2025 Trump administration, the CRT and DEI attacks have melded into one to form the most egregious assaults on educational justice in the last sixty years. As a university professor who's a teacher educator working to prepare preservice teachers for pre-K (PK)–12 classrooms, I have a vested interest in both schooling sectors. The attacks were directly related to my life's work—helping to ensure that education majors are empowered to serve marginalized P-16 students effectively and humanely.

I wanted to draw upon the expertise I had gained as a public school teacher, college professor, education policy fellow, antiracism scholar, Black feminist thinker, and DEI consultant to help educators understand what the deluge of purposely complicated anti-CRT and anti-DEI policies meant for schools, teachers, students, and their families. Most importantly, I wanted to offer insight on how to move past these attacks. It was important to me that I write a book that helped readers see the connections between all forms of systemic oppression in schools; consequently, although I have been primarily an antiracist scholar, this book is not just about freedom from racial oppression for racially minoritized students. Pursuit of freedom for all students who have been disenfranchised by unjust policies and practices is its goal. A second priority was to equip readers with the knowledge necessary to reimagine the pursuit of educational justice.

As I began to examine the current iteration of attacks (the present) and offer ideas for reimagining educational justice (the future), I recognized the need to look back. It was important to uncover how schooling has become what it is today. In doing so, readers would realize that justice workers have been fighting to make schools more just for centuries, that the recent attacks aren't as new as some think they are, and that white supremacy is our common enemy. Consequently, I included a social, political, and historical analysis that explores the colonial roots of society and schools.

I conveyed the book's main ideas by drawing upon the analogy of trees—the planting, the blighting of fruit, and the healing. Part I focuses on the precarious nature of tree planting, beginning with a focus on the soil. In this section, I review how justice workers have advanced equity in educational policy for many decades (tree planting). Justice workers were the activists, students, parents, policy advocates, organizational members and leaders, educators, and everyone who worked with and for marginalized students and their families. I use the word "workers" deliberately to draw attention to the fact that justice only comes about when we work for it, not when we dream about it, not when we seek it, but when we work for it. I considered the term "justice warrior," but it evokes fantastical images of imaginary characters with swords, not the human beings who sometimes put their lives on the line for justice. The term "workers" also connects me to the generations of working-class people whose labor was exploited in the building of the United States. Tracing the socio-political-historical evolution of justice work on behalf of marginalized peoples serves at least four purposes: (1) it demonstrates how, since its founding, U.S. society has been defined, in part, by the systemic oppression of certain populations and how the schooling of these groups has been shaped by this marginalization; (2) it provides models of resistance for today's justice workers; (3) it shows the links between multiple expressions of oppression; and (4) it shows how systemic oppression has been codified through laws and policies.

Part II shifts to the blighting of the fruit. As I write this book, states are passing laws that undermine the tree planting of the previous decades.

This onslaught has intensified under the second Trump administration. Blighting is the perfect description of these assaults. The chapters in this section illuminate the most horrific present-day threats to educational justice, which are exacerbated by long-standing inequities related to school funding and segregation (Sciarra, 2023). The attacks over the last five years have been orchestrated by opponents whose ideologies and actions are regressive, assaultive, and discriminative. Drawing upon skills I gained as an education policy fellow, I analyze the present-day assaults upon students of color, LGBTQIA+ students, religious minorities, emergent bilinguals, and immigrant students by dissecting Supreme Court policies, executive orders, and federal and state laws. This section explains the restrictions, how they aim to destroy decades of progress toward educational equity, and the ideologies that undergird them.

The central idea of Part III is the healing of trees that were planted by justice workers in white supremacist soil. In this section, I describe how justice workers can heal trees rooted in white supremacy through principled work, which is explained through the six Is: introspection, inclusivity/intersectionality, institutionality, insurgence, and imagination. When educators rigorously and genuinely shape their practice around the six Is, schools can become democratic institutions that serve all students effectively. This is my reimagining of the pursuit for educational justice.

Distinct features of this book are the in-depth historical analyses of education-related and education-adjacent policies before and after the civil rights movements of the 1950s and 1960s; the study of present-day opposition to educational justice, along with the ideologies that inform it; the connections between the assaults on PK–12 and higher education; and the insight that I offer to justice workers on how to uproot the trees of white supremacy, based on more than a decade of experience working with and on behalf of marginalized students. Perhaps the most important feature is my elucidation of the social psychology of white supremacy, which includes an explanation of how white supremacy leads to all forms of systemic oppression.

Who This Book Is For

In my career as a professor, I work with preservice and in-service teachers. Naturally, I wrote this book with this audience in mind. I imagine how powerful their work would be if informed by the ideas put forth in these 12 chapters. At the same time, I felt like I was writing to all who work in pursuit of educational justice. Individuals who want to ensure that all students are treated impartially, fairly, reasonably, and humanely. This book is my offering of support to justice workers who are committed to this goal. You may be wondering if you are (or can become) a justice worker.

- If you are a teacher, instructor, or professor who aims to make your classroom more inclusive and equitable, you are a justice worker.
- If you are a school leader who wants to improve outcomes for all students at your school, and/or institution, you are a justice worker.
- If you are a community member or religious leader who's trying to transform schools to address the needs of marginalized students in your community, you are a justice worker.
- If you work at or lead an education-related or education-adjacent organization that seeks to make sure communities served by your organization are represented fairly in your work, you are a justice worker.
- If you are an education policy advocate or policymaker who's concerned about making sure that the voices of marginalized communities are honored and reflected in school policy, you are a justice worker.
- If you are a scholar/researcher who asks questions about underserved and underresourced communities, you are a justice worker.
- If you are a preservice teacher who wants to make sure that your teaching practice will honor the cultural backgrounds of your students, you are a justice worker.
- If you are a parent who is raising your child(ren) to respect the dignity of all peoples, you are a justice worker.
- If you are a graduate student with interests in social justice, critical pedagogy, and/or antiracism, you are a justice worker.
- If you are a DEI administrator, specialist, or consultant, you are a justice worker.
- If you are an advocate who speaks up for the disenfranchised students at your child's school, you are a justice worker.

I want anyone who sees themselves as a worker advancing educational justice to deepen their knowledge around diversity, equity, and inclusion. I want to inspire those whose light for justice has grown dim to recommit to the work that beckons them. I want to help self-doubters feel empowered with the knowledge to do the justice work to which they are compelled. I want everyone who's leading others in DEI work to be able to do so in affirming, responsible ways that don't cause further harm—to individuals or the movement. I want every reader to be brave enough to take the risks that justice work entails. Ultimately, I want this book to be a supportive friend and knowledgeable guide to those who imagine a just society and are brave enough to work toward it. You may feel uncomfortable at times, but you will always be safe. You won't be attacked, but your beliefs may be. You won't be blamed, but you will be assigned responsibility for your words and actions. You may feel alone as you read, but thousands of other readers are taking this journey with you. I feel immensely grateful to be able to share my love, knowledge and wisdom with you.

In his 1963 "Letter from a Birmingham Jail," Dr. King wrote about interrelatedness: "We are caught in an inescapable network of mutuality, tied in a single garment of destiny. Whatever affects one directly affects all indirectly" (King, 1963b, p. 3). These words stay close to my heart, as do those from civil rights activist Fannie Lou Hamer in a 1971 speech. Though she was denied access to schooling past sixth grade, Hamer has been described as having "remarkable rhetorical abilities" (Brooks & Houck, 2011, p. xiii). Her words are my compass in my justice work and inspire the theme of solidarity I hope this book conveys:

> Now, we've got to have some changes in this country. And not only changes for the black man, and only changes for the black woman, but the changes we have to have in this country are going to be for liberation of all people—because nobody's free until everybody's free.
> (in Brooks & Houck, 2011, p. 136)

I wrote this book because I want schools to be liberatory spaces for all students. I want everybody to be free.

A Note About Language

Using precise language to describe individuals and groups is hard, for language often fails to easily capture nuance and can lead to confusion, reduction, and oversimplification. Like Chicana feminist theorist Gloria Anzaldua, "I struggle with naming without fragmenting, without excluding" (Anzaldua, 2009, p. 166), I'd like to clarify how I use certain terminology.

1 I use *people of color* to mean nonwhite people. In the United States, this group includes Native Americans, African Americans, Hispanic/Latino(x) Americans, and Asian Americans/Pacific Islanders. I want

to point out, however, that there are wide intragroup differences within each of the stated groups and that each group experiences white supremacist violence distinctly.

2 I use *Hispanic/Latino(x)* realizing that the labels are problematic for individuals who prefer to identify themselves by country of origin, such as Mexican Americans, or other attributes. This is also true for Asian Americans/Pacific Islanders.

3 I use the terms *Black* and *African American* interchangeably to describe people of African descent in the United States.

4 I use *white* to describe people who have European ancestry, though I acknowledge that Europeans have intragroup differences in histories, cultures, and positioning on the white hierarchy.

Please read with these definitions in mind.

Questions to Ponder

1. What do you hope to learn from reading this book?
2. In what ways might your existing beliefs and knowledge be challenged?

Part I

Centuries in the Making: Planting Trees in Poisoned Soil

Central questions answered: What socio-historical-political factors gave rise to the need for the movement for educational justice, and how did justice workers respond to these factors?

1
Soiled: A Society Rooted in White Supremacy

Educational justice can be defined as fairness in access, resources, and opportunity that results from dismantling systemic barriers and creating intentional pathways in schooling for historically and currently marginalized students. It is an aspiration that faces ardent opposition. Several terms have been used to describe the recent Trump conservative attacks on educational justice. The descriptions *troubling, perilous, regressive*, and *unprecedented* come to mind. For the most part, the first three terms capture the essence of these attacks, but *unprecedented* is historically inaccurate. As egregious as the current attacks are, educational justice has been a centuries-long struggle for marginalized groups in the United States. What this version of attacks offers—with its direct threats on once-secured rights—is the opportunity to reimagine ways to attain educational justice and envision, perhaps for the first time, what justice for all marginalized communities might look like in schools.

Part I of this book traces the origins and development of the movement for educational justice, in part to illustrate that withholding and restricting education of some students, while prioritizing and privileging the education of others, is customary and systematic in a nation that prides itself on democracy. Without the "tree planting" of justice workers whose actions moved society toward justice, schooling in the United States would likely be much as it was upon its inception. I define *tree planting* as the individual and collective actions undertaken to build a democratic society. We plant trees through advocacy, activism, organizing, boycotting, theorizing, voting, teaching, tutoring, lawmaking, registering to vote, mentoring, volunteering, and more. This tree planting has been centuries in the making. Before delving into this historical planting of trees (Chapters 2 and 3), I start this examination in Chapter 1 by looking at the soil in which the trees were planted. Wohlleben (2015, p. 86) declared, "Without soil, there would be no forests, because trees must have somewhere to put down its roots." For that reason, this examination starts by looking at what lies beneath, or what's hidden under our feet.

Hidden Under Our Feet

I recently moved to rural Georgia, where I live on a pecan orchard. Shortly after moving to Pigan Place, the name we gave to our property to honor the Native people who once occupied this land (Wall Kimmerer, 2013), I called the local extension office to ask for information on caring for the trees. The agent I spoke with advised, "The first thing you need to do is have your soil tested." She went on, "The soil composition profoundly determines the condition of the trees." As I continued to prepare to take care of Pigan Place, I learned that the trees' root systems transport water, nutrients, and more to the branches, leaves, and eventual fruit, or pecans in our case. Roots are the source of provision and protection. Consequently, the soil, being the anchor for the trees' roots, should be the starting point in any examination of trees, even symbolic trees. Collins, Newman, and Jun (2023, p. 20) conveyed this point about roots in *Global White Supremacy: Anti-Blackness and the University as Colonizer*:

> Tree roots absorb soil, minerals, and water to generate the trunk, branches, leaves, and fruit that are visible above the ground. In a similar way, the historical roots/strands provide insights into the contemporary fruits of settler colonialism and White supremacy.

Before examining the trees and fruits, it is essential to inspect the soil that nourishes their roots. Wall Kimmerer (2013) reminded readers, "The land is the real teacher. All we need as students is mindfulness" (p. 222).

Two books have been immensely beneficial as I have simultaneously studied tree planting and justice. Coincidentally but significantly, both books have "hidden" in their titles: *The Hidden Roots of White Supremacy and the Path to a Shared American Future* (Jones, 2023) and *The Hidden Life of Trees: What They Feel, How They Communicate* (Wohlleben, 2015). Wohlleben theorized that "we know only a tiny fraction of what there is to know about the complex life that busies itself under our feet" (p. 85). I've become intrigued by the sophisticated root systems and organisms that remain hidden until we dig beneath what we see above ground. The central aim of this chapter is to study the roots, work that is crucial to understanding the current attacks in education. The next section examines the soil, or more precisely, the contamination of the land.

Contamination Through Colonization

Indigenous peoples worldwide are known to have deep connections to the land. In fact, Booth (2003) quotes a Native American saying: "We are the land." This sacred relationship between humans and the environment is characteristic of Native Americans, a term to describe the many tribes that were the first peoples to occupy the land now known as the United States of America. This point was poignantly conveyed by Wall Kimmerer (2013):

> In the settler mind, land was property, real estate, capital, or natural resources. But to our people, it was everything: identity, the connection to our ancestors, the home of our nonhuman kinfolk, or pharmacy, our library, the source of all that sustained us.
>
> (p. 17)

Because they saw themselves as environmental stewards—not owners—they took care of the soil and the vegetation that grew from it. Europeans, however, would soon dominate and contaminate the land, literally and figuratively, that Native Americans had cared for and protected for millennia. (The current Land Back movement intends to repair past and current European abuse of the land by restoring it to the Indigenous people who have the knowledge and desire to promote sustainable practices that have the potential to mitigate the negative impact of centuries of mismanagement.)

Before delving into contamination through European colonization, it is important to establish an understanding of two related terms—*whiteness* and *white supremacy*.

Whiteness as Social Identity

The concept of whiteness is elusive because of the way meanings shift over time, the fluidity of boundaries, and the lens through which identity is viewed (Bush, 2004). On a basic level, whiteness is a social construction of race that refers to European cultures, traditions, and customs. Bush offered, "Being white has generally been associated with ancestry from the European continent, the denial of African blood, and boundaries that have shifted during different periods in history to include or exclude various groups" (p. 15). Whiteness and blackness are often seen as antithetical. To be white, one must not be Black. Cancelmo and Mueller (2019) clarified that *whiteness* refers to a structural position, a racialized social identity that is placed in a superior position to other races in a system of racial hierarchy. Moreover, whiteness is the existence of a white racial identity that is unmarked and invisible, standard and default, and too often unquestioned and unchallenged. Without intentional interrogation, one can easily assume that "whiteness," as a social position, is just the order of things—a concept known as *white normativity*—when the truth is that U.S. society has been constructed to center whiteness. Consequently, whiteness carries with it power, privilege, and advantages that are denied to nonwhite, or racialized, others, which helps to explain why many nonwhite individuals and groups seek white proximity. In seeking white proximity, nonwhite people align themselves with white cultural values and standards to experience the privileges granted to white people. They may even engage in cultural assimilation, losing aspects of their own culture to adopt traits of the dominant white culture. They seek to find favor within an oppressive system rather than aiming to dismantle it.

In some cases, however, *whiteness* is used synonymously with *white supremacy*, as in this co-constructed definition created by a professor and her doctoral students:

> Whiteness is a hegemonic system that perpetuates certain dominant ideologies about who receives power and privilege. Whiteness maintains itself in cultures through power dynamics within language, religion, class, race relations, sexual orientation, etc.
>
> (Carter et al., 2007, p. 152)

Given this definition, one can see that *whiteness* is sometimes used to describe the ways Europeans have been positioned to dominate non-Western societies and, importantly, the ways that their values and beliefs have dictated laws and policies. In my work, I use *whiteness* when referring to white identity and *white supremacy* when describing the system of domination. Tracing the origins of white supremacy can help uncover its mechanisms.

Origins of White Supremacy

White supremacy can be traced to the 15th century and the Catholic Church's granting of territorial sovereignty to Christian monarchs through its papal decrees. The language used by Pope Nicholas V in 1452 fueled the invasion of Portuguese colonizers and the subsequent enslavement of Indigenous Africans. Pope Nicolas VI encouraged them to "capture, vanquish, and subdue all... pagans and other enemies of Christ... to reduce their persons to perpetual slavery... and... to take away all their possessions and property" (Friends Committee on National Legislation, 2020). Pope Alexander VI, in 1492, perpetuated this legacy by granting the same colonizing authority to Spain: "All islands and mainlands found and to be found, discovered and to be discovered, towards the west and south... from the Arctic pole... to the Antarctic pole.... And we... appoint... you and your said heirs... lords of them with full and free power, authority, and jurisdiction of every kind" (Friends Committee on National Legislation, 2020). Collectively, these decrees and others became codified in the Doctrine of Discovery. Driven by these policies, European colonizers saw themselves as (1) divinely ordained to control non-Christian lands and (2) justified in wielding systemic violence upon Indigenous peoples in order to seize these lands. Jones (2023) explained that knowledge of the doctrine has been hidden:

> Its absence from the historical canon of predominantly white academic institutions is testimony to its continued cultural power. While the Doctrine of Discovery has escaped scrutiny by most white scholars and theologians, Indigenous people and African Americans have long been testifying to these Christian roots of white supremacy, while dying from and living with their damaging effects.
>
> (pp. 17–18)

The Doctrine of Discovery must be revealed, as it was a main catalyst behind global white supremacy.

Global white supremacist ideology led to the invasion and subsequent domination of much of the non-Western world—the continents of Africa, North America, South America, parts of Asia, and Oceania. Collins, Newman, and Jun (2023) distinguished the ways Europeans dominated many parts of the world:

> European imperialism was distinctly different from previous forms of domination in the world. It was larger in size, scope, longevity, stratification,

and organization.... When combined with conquests by the United States through the early twentieth century, most of the globe was impacted by colonialism.

(p. 22)

Although the Christian (Catholic) faith sanctioned colonization, religion was not the sole mechanism. According to Collins, Newman, and Jun (2023), there were five tools of European imperialism: religion, empire, appetite for conquest, science, and capitalism/economy. These interwoven tools, wielded distinctly by different European colonial powers, made way for the spread of white supremacy. The mission was straightforward— "discover, claim, conquer, and tame the corners of the earth" (Collins, Newman, & Jun, 2023, p. 35). Interestingly, explorers (colonizers) used their writing and art to depict Indigenous peoples throughout Asia, Africa, and the Americas as not just different from but inferior to Europeans, creating a racial hierarchy that would last for centuries. These portrayals led to narratives that were used to justify natives' subjugation (Riley, 1984; Morgan, 1997). Moreover, European technological advancements—guns, compasses, the telegraph, and steamships—aided their dominance.

For the Americas specifically, it's important to point out the role infectious diseases brought from the Old World to the New (to Europeans) World played in Europeans' ability to dispossess Indigenous peoples. Said differently, it can be concluded that infectious diseases were an inadvertent tool of invasion used to spread white supremacy. It is estimated that up to 95% of the Native American population, who were immunologically defenseless against the germs and viruses that caused infectious diseases, were decimated within the first 100–150 years following Columbus's arrival in 1492 (Nunn & Qian, 2010). Even though nationalists emphasize the supposed benefits of the Columbian Exchange, the devastation and violence European colonists inflicted upon Native peoples is indefensible.

Even though the North American colonies, in what would become the United States of America, gained independence from Great Britain during the Revolutionary period (late 1700s) and were no longer under European control, leaders in this newly formed country maintained their colonizers' beliefs in white supremacy. Specifically, the beliefs enshrined in the Doctrine of Discovery emerged in the 1800s within the North American context—same beliefs, new term: *Manifest Destiny*. Manifest Destiny is a moral concept catapulted by a belief that God had ordained the United States to expand westward to the Pacific Ocean. Driven by

Manifest Destiny, the United States overtook Native American lands, and the law supported this theft. In *Johnson v. McIntosh* (1823),[1] the Supreme Court declared that the United States had the right to Indian land and that Native Americans could be only occupants. This is one of the earliest examples of white supremacy being institutionalized in the U.S.

Definition of White Supremacy

White supremacy can be defined as

> a political, economic and cultural system in which whites overwhelmingly control power and material resources, conscious and unconscious ideas of white superiority and entitlement are widespread, and relations of white dominance and non-white subordination are daily reenacted across a broad array of institutions and social settings.
>
> (Ansley, 1997/2015, p. 592)

As a belief system, it is the belief that white people and everything associated with European culture are superior to other peoples and cultures. The enforcement of this belief system is not limited to the United States. This superiority complex drove European explorers to usurp control over the peoples they encountered.

> White supremacy is a global, transnational, and imperial phenomenon. It has been widely transmitted through time and space in ways that are often difficult to name. The fruits of Whiteness that emerged from the fertile soils of Europe produced a now centuries-long stretch of dominance.
>
> (Collins, Newman, & Jun, 2023)

Gillborn (2005) asserted that the real danger of white supremacy is the "taken-for-granted routine privileging of white interests that goes unremarked in the political mainstream" (p. 485). To be clear, white supremacy as a belief system is not upheld by only white people. Though benefiting white and white-adjacent people, it is sustained, mostly unknowingly, by people of all races. This "system" was institutionalized with the nation's recognized founding, but white supremacist and racist ideology had long fueled European colonizers' actions and predated the signing of the Declaration of Independence in 1776. The nation, then, was birthed in white supremacist soil, and every tree planted in this soil has been polluted, even the trees planted by justice workers. Before the nation was even born, the founding fathers had already contaminated the soil with white supremacy, which would act as fertilizer to bolster the formation of what would become the United States of America. In *Stamped from the Beginning*, Ibram X. Kendi surmised that early British settlers "carried racist ideas to America"—ideas about Black inferiority and white superiority, or white supremacy (Kendi, 2016, p. 6). White supremacist ideology is evident in the ways European colonizers, namely the French, Spanish, Portuguese, Dutch, and British, justified their conquest of Asia, Africa, and the Americas. But it is also evidenced by the ways Europeans, who saw themselves as moral and intellectual authorities, usurped power and authority and established their will upon nonwhite populations.

Though nationalists argue that the official birth of the United States was the adoption of the Declaration of Independence on July 4, 1776, others contend that the birth began centuries before the celebrated independence from Great Britain. For example, Nikole Hannah-Jones (Hannah-Jones, Roper, Silverman, & Silverstein, 2021), in *The 1619 Project*, challenged readers to reframe this history by acknowledging that European colonizers had already begun establishing the country when the first enslaved Africans were forcefully brought to Virginia in the 17th century. To go back further into the birth of the nation, it's important to point out that the enslavement of Africans was made possible because of the violent conquest of Native Americans by Europeans in the late 15th century. Nevertheless, many "patriots" prefer to celebrate what they see as the country's valor in the mid-1700s, while ignoring its inglorious past that can be traced to the late 1400s—a past that is rooted in "mass racial violence" (Jones, 2023, p. 25) Hence, it is evident that the United States underwent a birthing period that spanned hundreds of years. This period was not only characterized by Eurocentrism and white supremacy, but it was also defined by brutality and violence that are the hallmarks of European colonization.

In writing about equity in writing instruction, Asao B. Inoue (2022, p. 5) clarified his use of *white supremacy*:

> Let me pause for a moment and explain why I will be using the terms, "white supremacy" and "white language supremacy," since I know they can be triggers for many, especially white people. I use these terms compassionately as a way to help teachers of all political stripes confront their whiteness and stay in the discomfort that the term generates . . . When we associate the things we hold dear with something like white supremacy, it can sound like an attack on your person. It can be uncomfortable. Yes, I want you to feel

uncomfortable because it can help you feel the problem, not intellectualize it, or see it, or hear it. You need to feel it if you want to change systems.

I, too, would like to explain why I use the term white supremacy despite the discomfort it might cause and why understanding it is integral to educational justice.

Admittedly, the term *white supremacy* can be inflammatory, polarizing, and undoubtedly offensive to some readers because of its connotations. For many, the concept is reminiscent of hate groups and extremists, like the Ku Klux Klansmen that terrorized southern Blacks during the mid-20th century. Others might envision today's white nationalists and neo-Nazis protesting in Charlottesville against the removal of a Robert E. Lee statue or storming the nation's capital on January 6, 2021. Layla Saad (2020, p. 13) reminded us, however, to think beyond the imagery and emotions the term can evoke: "This idea that white supremacy only applies to the so-called 'bad ones' is both incorrect and dangerous because it reinforces the idea that white supremacy is an ideology that is only upheld by a fringe group of white people." Due to its pervasive nature and detrimental effects on education, those committed to educational justice should become deeply familiar with the term and be able to use it with dexterity.

The Birth of a Nation and a National Identity

As with European imperialism, American imperialism was driven by white supremacist beliefs, religious compulsion, and economic aims, but was also rooted in American exceptionalism, the belief that the United States is distinct from, superior to, and a model for other countries. In its desire for dominance, the United States, through military conquest and economic exploitation, purchased Louisiana, seized Mexican land throughout the Southwest and West, annexed Hawaii, acquired Puerto Rico, and more. Once colonized herself, the United States became a colonizer and a competitor to European colonists. U.S. imperialism was seen as a moral obligation by some. Poet Rudyard Kipling described it as "the white man's burden," as he urged the U.S. government to take control of the Philippines (Kipling, 1899). White savorism, the colonial belief that white people must rescue non-white people from their own supposed helplessness and that non-white people need the benevolence of white people to solve their problems, can be seen in some 21st-century white educators.

In the United States that was forming, colonizers driven by capitalistic aspirations saw nonwhite peoples as subjects to be controlled and owned and saw themselves as conquerors and owners destined to dominate. Consequently, they inflicted brutality and violence upon Native Americans who were the original inhabitants of the land and Africans who had been forcibly brought to and enslaved in the burgeoning country. Benjamin (2022, p. 107) encapsulated this capitalistic violence uniquely inflicted upon Native Americans and Black Americans:

> European colonists unleashed smallpox on the Indigenous people of North America, demonstrating the genocidal effects of infectious disease. Intertwined with this long history of settler colonialism and native genocide is the transformation of human beings into property, or chattel, in law and custom. Enslaved Africans were not simply exploited to enrich plantocracy—they themselves were the riches. Human beings were bought and sold. They were reduced to capital, assets, goods, things.

Yet the founders put forth governing foundational documents that espoused principles of freedom, democracy, and egalitarianism. In the Declaration of Independence, they wrote, "We hold these truths to be self-evident, that all men are created equal, that they are endowed by their Creator with certain unalienable Rights, that among these are Life, Liberty and the pursuit of Happiness," but excluded nonwhite humans from their imperialist imagination. In other words, the nation was born rooted in white supremacy because ideas around whiteness and lesser others were deeply entrenched in the psyches of European colonizers and their descendants, who were the nation's founders. In essence, the foundations of the "New (to Europeans) World" were white accumulation, native dispossession, and forced labor (Benjamin, 2022). As the founders were building the country, they were simultaneously creating a "caste" system that was based upon white supremacist ideology. Isabel Wilkerson (2020, p. 23) defined the U.S. caste system as "an internalized ranking, unspoken, unnamed, unacknowledged by everyday citizens even as they go about their lives adhering to it and acting upon it subconsciously to this day." Those who created the caste, not surprisingly, placed themselves at the top, and "everyone else would rank in descending order on the basis of their proximity to those deemed most superior" (p. 28).

Identity in the United States is built largely around race, with its institutions functioning on racism, creating "an apartheid-like system" (Benjamin, 2022, p. 104). Consequently, white Americans historically have had the greatest access to resources, have been afforded the most opportunities, have wielded most of the power to determine the distribution of resources, and have been inherently assigned civil rights promised by the U.S. Constitution. Laws, policies, and court decisions enshrined white hegemony (dominance), creating a disparate society with enduring binaries that shape much of our thinking around identity and positioning, all of which could be dismantled by the destruction of white supremacy:

- colonized/colonizer
- people of the Global South/people of the Global North
- oppressed/oppressor
- victim/victimizer
- disenfranchised/privileged
- subjugated/dominant
- minorities/majority
- marginalized/centered
- people of color/white
- Black, Indigenous, and other People of Color (BIPOC)/white
- immigrant/citizen
- English learner/English speaker
- object/subject
- disempowered/empowered
- others/those who belong

A classification that aims to reverse the existing social structure by reflecting the composition of the worldwide population is *people of the global majority* (PGM). This designation is used to refer collectively to people who are not white, signaling that people of African, Asian, Indigenous, and Latin American descent are the global majority. Social identity is contextual, multifaceted, and shifting; consequently, rigidly positioning oneself in either column can be problematic.

It is important to recognize, as the following list indicates, that white supremacy is not limited to racial identification and that racism isn't the only manifestation of white supremacist oppression. Racism, according to Vaught (2011, p. 10), is a "mechanism of White supremacy," operating within the larger system of oppression. Within this larger system of oppression, white supremacy determines who's in and who's out when it comes to nationality, language, sexuality, and more. White supremacy is wide-reaching, exerting all manner of systemic oppression fueled by the belief that "European civilization and western Christianity are superior to all other cultures, races, and religions" (Jones, 2023, p. 14). Resultantly, white supremacy extends its privileges and entitlements to tangential, or closely associated, social identities in addition to white racial identity, those being the following:

- male
- heterosexual
- Christian
- middle-class/wealthy
- English-speaking
- able-bodied and mentally sound
- native-born (ironically, not including Indigenous peoples)

This constellation of identities has led to a national identity that aims to paint a picture of what it means to be American. (Consider the "founding fathers" and the face of the U.S. presidency as evidence of this national identity.) I like to think of this as the quintessential white identity. Those who hold the quintessential white identity sit at the top of the social hierarchy and, consequently, haven't had to fight to have civil rights extended to them. As a matter of fact, the Naturalization Act of 1790 ensured citizenship and the rights that accompany it only to free white persons and their posterity. Senator Jefferson Davis (1860, as cited in Kendi, 2016, p. 208) announced directly, "This Government was not founded by negroes nor for negroes but by white for white men." Moreover, the Bill of Rights of the U.S. Constitution, which outlined civil rights, was written with this population as automatic grantees. Colker (2022) argued that the Constitution has "helped further white supremacy" during every era. This hoarding of power and privilege supports the establishment of a white ethnocracy instead of a multicultural democracy. This legalization of privilege to some and denial to others has led to generational disparities in access to resources and opportunities. Shining the spotlight on the ways white supremacy has been embedded in the structure of institutions is necessary for dismantling white supremacy. Table 1.1 outlines several structural advantages that were granted to white men by default, implied, or explicitly stated. There are innumerable others. I urge you to think about the ways white men benefited and others suffered politically, socially, and economically, and the enduring effects of these acts of injustice.

Table 1.1 Examples of Policies, Laws, Court Decisions, and Practices That Granted Systemic Advantages to Whites

The Bill of Rights of the U.S. Constitution (1787)	By default, granted fundamental rights and liberties to white men.
Naturalization Act of 1790	Granted citizenship only to free white persons and their children.
Schooling	Only white children were allowed to attend the nation's earliest schools. Consequently, only whites could realize all the benefits of a formal education.
Jim Crow laws (1877–1960s)	Enforced racial segregation in institutions, resulting in white people having access to better public facilities, employment opportunities, and more. Legalized discrimination and inequality.
Sharecropping/tenant farming (late 1800s)	A post–Civil War agricultural system involving a contractual agreement between mostly Black farmers who rented land from white landowners and paying them in cash or with a portion of crops. It established wealth for landowners and oftentimes resulted in insurmountable debt for Black farmers due to exploitative practices. Economic servitude.
Redlining (1930s–1960s)	A practice of refusing to insure mortgages in Black neighborhoods by the Federal Housing Administration and the Home Owners' Loan Corporation. Neighborhoods were color coded to indicate, among other things, race and socioeconomic status, with Black neighborhoods being coded red. Led to residential segregation.
Restrictive housing covenants (1930s)	Clauses in deeds that limited Black people from buying or living in certain houses. Led to residential segregation.
G.I. Bill (1944)	Guaranteed benefits like low-interest home loans for World War II veterans but excluded Black soldiers from these benefits. As a result, many Black families have had little access to building generational wealth through home ownership.
Black codes (1865)	Laws that restricted the rights of formerly enslaved African Americans. These laws limited where they could work, restricted them from testifying against whites in court, and dictated the kind of property they could own.

Homestead Act (1862) federal land giveaways	Allowed American citizens to claim 160 acres of public land in the West. This act mainly benefited white settlers and disadvantaged Native Americans and Black Americans.
Wagner Act (1935)	Gave employees the right to organize (unions) but excluded agricultural and domestic workers, who were mostly Latino(x), Asian, and Black, leaving them unprotected from workplace exploitation.

On the other hand, individuals who do not own these social identities have been positioned in varying places within the margins. Said differently, they are victims of "othering," which, according to powell and Menendian (2024), is more than simply interpersonal bigotry. Rather, othering is "the expression of broad prejudice in law, culture, and norms, and the condition of group subordination and marginality" (p. 19) that prevents full membership in society. Table 1.2 indicates when "others" were allowed citizenship.

It is crucial to highlight that citizenship is a social construction (defined and maintained by those with power), with criteria for inclusion and exclusion that shift over time. Often weaponized against people of color, citizenship continues to be a negotiated and renegotiated identity, as is evident by Trump's 2025 goal of repealing the 14th Amendment that grants birthright citizenship. This is especially true of Mexican Americans. Neither Black, nor white, they are often suspended between legal/illegal, citizen/noncitizen, importable/deportable, naturalized/native-born. (*See Molina's How Race Is Made in America.*) In his review of Black citizenship in 1921, Black historian Carter G. Woodson (1921, p. 1) observed, "The citizenship

Table 1.2 Legalization of Citizenship for "Others"

"Others"	Legal Action	Year
Mexican American	Treaty of Guadalupe Hidalgo (allowed Mexicans in the lands that were formerly Mexico to become U.S. citizens)	1848
Black Americans	14th Amendment (granted citizenship to all persons born or naturalized in the U.S., regardless of race—birthright citizenship)	1868
Native Americans	Indian Citizenship Act (granted citizenship to Native Americans born within the U.S.)	1924
Chinese Americans	Repeal of the Chinese Exclusion Act (allowed Chinese to become naturalized citizens and increased the immigration quota for Chinese)	1943

of the Negro in this country is a fiction." This description doesn't just pertain to "the Negro." Laila Lalami (2020, p. 22) described individuals who do not hold the national identity as "conditional citizens" and explained the exclusive and often elusive nature of citizenship:

> Millions of people in this country live with the terrible reality that their relationships to the state is at least partly determined by the color of their skin, the nature of their creed, their gender identity, or their national origin. American citizenship was created in the image of the man who wrote the Declaration of Independence.... It took centuries of struggle, some of it violent and bloody, for this philosophy to be disrupted, but it has not yet been fully dismantled.

Conditional citizens have been denied civil rights and have suffered a myriad of intersecting forms of state-sanctioned discrimination codified by laws that limit full citizenship. Significant to note as well is that conditional citizens are rarely marginalized due to a single facet of identity. Instead, their statuses are impacted by membership in intersecting social identity groups, for example, a gay Asian immigrant whose home language is Korean. Consequently, the forms of discrimination listed in this chapter, though listed separately, should be seen as distinct yet interdependent. Just as social identity is an intersection, so too is the resulting discrimination. Conclusively, from its inception, the U.S. has been a country that granted and denied rights based on social identity. That social identity still drives policymaking (and resistance) should come as no surprise.

One Oppressive System, Many Forms of Oppression

As early as 1892, Black feminists emphasized the importance of recognizing that Black women's freedom was tied to race and gender (Cooper, 1988). According to Beal (2008), Black women faced "double jeopardy" due to race and gender, while Jones (in McDuffie, 2011) and Davis (1981) argued that they face "triple oppression" because of race, gender, and class. These ideas are also central to Chicana/Latina feminist theory: "Chicana/Latina feminism aims at dismantling systems of oppression based on race, ethnicity, class, gender, sexuality, and other structures that sustain domination over women, particularly those of Latin descent" (Peña et al, 2023). Resisting an additive approach to analyses of oppression, Crenshaw (1991) and Collins (2000) contended that systems of power—like racism, sexism, and classism—are not separate and should not be isolated one by one. Instead, multiple forms of oppression operate simultaneously and interlock, forming a matrix of domination that grants different levels of power and oppression based on multiple, overlapping social identities. bell hooks (2000) theorized that these multiple forms of oppression had one root cause. To this end, she introduced the term *imperialist white supremacist capitalist patriarchy* (p. 46) to name the single oppressive system that marginalized and dominated many social identities and privileged others. It might be helpful to unpack this term by examining the following concepts that underpin this idea:

- *European imperialism*: the forceful expansion of the European empire into territories occupied by Indigenous peoples. Imperialism is accomplished mainly by military force (militarism), religious persuasion (Christian theism), and economic manipulation (capitalism).
- *European colonialism*: the violent establishment of colonies throughout Asia, Africa, and the Americas by Europeans, starting in the 15th century and lasting until the 20th century.
- *Settler colonialism*: the displacement, repression, and genocide of Indigenous peoples in order to replace Indigenous populations with European settler groups.
- *Capitalism/racial capitalism*: an economic system characterized by the buying and selling of goods and services for profit and the accumulation of capital through the exploitation of labor. Capitalism was formed and has been maintained by the exploitation of racialized groups, resulting in the economic advancement of white people.
- *Patriarchy*: a socio-political-economic system in which men are empowered to control and dominate societal institutions, and women are denied access to such power.

Nichols (2022) explains hooks's use of the term:

> When bell hooks writes, as she famously does, of "white supremacist capitalist patriarchy", or "imperialist white supremacist capitalist patriarchy", she employs the list as a powerful way of evoking an integrated system in which a range of forms of oppression work together in tandem: each one intensifies the effects of the others in one unified direction.
>
> (p. 263)

hooks later added a descriptor to the term "patriarchy," resulting in more precise terminology—*imperialist white supremacist capitalist cisheteropatriarchy* (bell hooks Center, 2023). Whereas patriarchy privileges men in general, cisheteropatriarchy is the sociopolitical structure that grants power and authority to cisgender, heterosexual men. This term recognizes that gay and transgender men are often excluded from this power structure. Identifying this "range of forms of oppression" is integral to dismantling white supremacy. The list below delineates forms of oppression that are rooted in imperialist white supremacist capitalist cisheteropatriarchy.

Forms of Systemic Oppression Rooted in White Supremacy

- *Ableism*: discrimination against those with disabilities (physical and mental); belief that nondisabled people are superior and that disabled individuals offer little to no value in a capitalistic economy.
- *Ageism*: bias against individuals based on age.
- *Anti-atheism*: prejudice against atheists, rooted in the belief that Christianity is the only right and true religion.
- *Anti-Semitism*: prejudice against Jews and/or people of Jewish descent, rooted in the belief that Christianity is the only right and true religion.
- *Aporophobia*: systemic prejudice or aversion to the poor.
- *Cisgenderism*: bias against transgender or gender nonconforming individuals stemming from the prioritizing of cisgender identities, or gender identities that align with the sex an individual was assigned at birth.
- *Classism*: bias against people for belonging to a particular social class or position, namely, people who have been economically disadvantaged through capitalistic exploitation, causing them to occupy a lower class; oppression of the working class.
- *Casteism*: discrimination and marginalization because of one's inclusion in a particular caste, similar to classism.
- *Childism*: prejudice and systemic injustice against children, which can lead to abuse, neglect, and the marginalization of children's needs and rights.

- *Colorism*: bias against people with darker skin tones, usually by members of the same race. This bias stems from the glorification of lighter, European-like skin tones.
- *Elitism*: bias against those who are not a part of the upper class (elite) in terms of education, wealth, job status, and other factors that impact social standing.
- *Ethnocentrism*: using one's own culture as the standard by which other cultural practices and beliefs are judged.
- *Eurocentrism*: having a European (mainly Western European) worldview that leads to the centering of European culture and history.
- *Family structurism*: prejudice against those who do not hold membership in a Standard North American Family (SNAF). SNAF characteristics include a being White, married, opposite-sex, monogamous couple who embodies traditional gender roles, biological children, middle-class neighborhood, and home ownership.
- *Fatphobia*: unfair treatment of individuals with big bodies, rooted in European beauty standards and perceptions of laziness and idleness.
- *Gender binarism*: the assumption that there are only two genders and that one of these genders is assigned to individuals at birth, which leads to discrimination against nonbinary people and those whose gender does not align with the sex they were assigned at birth also genderism.
- *Heterosexism*: the assumption that heterosexuality is the normal, right, or default sexual orientation; discrimination or bias against individuals who are LGBTQIA+. Also homophobia.
- *Islamophobia*: prejudice against Muslims (those practicing Islam), rooted in the belief that Christianity is the only right and true religion.
- *Linguicism*: discrimination based on language and languaging practices, based on the idea that some languages, mainly Western European languages, are superior to others. This belief is known as white language supremacy.
- *Misogyny*: hatred, contempt, and devaluation of women. Also, *misogynoir*, which is hatred specifically toward Black women.
- *Nativism*: valuing the interests of native-born inhabitants over immigrants; enforcing socially constructed laws about citizenship and legality, resulting in discrimination against those viewed as outsiders.
- *Neuroablism*: discrimination against individuals who are neurodivergent (those with ADHD, dyslexia, autism, and more).

- *Neuronormativity*: marginalization of neurodivergent individuals, or individuals whose minds do not function in neurotypical ways.
- *Racism*: prejudice based on socially constructed racial categories. Racism can be enacted institutionally, individually, and internally. Each of the four racialized minorities in the United States suffers from distinct forms of racism.
  - *Anti-Black racism*: stems from a belief in the supposed inferiority and inhumanity of people of African descent.
  - *Anti-Asian racism*: rooted in stereotypes, linked to nativism and xenophobia.
  - *Anti-Latino(x) racism*: often overlaps with linguicism, classism, and xenophobia.
  - *Anti–Native American racism*: often manifests as erasure, isolation, and challenges to sovereignty.
- *Sanism*: discrimination against individuals with mental disorders, like schizophrenia, bipolar disorder, anxiety, and major depressive disorder.
- *Sexism*: discrimination against individuals of a certain gender based on the belief that one gender, usually women, is inferior to another, usually men.
- *Texturism*: discrimination against people with coarse, kinky, or afro hair. This bias stems from the association of straight hair with European beauty standards.
- *Xenophobia*: fear, prejudice, or dislike for those seen as foreign or strange; hostility toward immigrants.

It is not always obvious how imperialist white supremacist capitalist cisheteropatriarchy creates these forms of oppression. Two examples might be helpful. An imperialist white supremacist capitalist cisheteropatriarchy worldview—spread through religion-fueled colonization—determined how institutions, like families, operate and how individuals function within them. Because these views were seen as the divine order, rules were immutable and led to a rigid social order that dictated family structure, marital expectations, and gender roles. Resultantly, individuals whose identities do not align with white supremacist norms, such as those who are LGBTQIA+, face gender binarism, heterosexism, and family structurism. To explain further, capitalism ushered in values around individualism, productivity, competition, control of natural resources, and labor, replacing Indigenous beliefs about community, stewardship, sustainability, and collective well-being. Capitalistic approaches to labor, exceedingly extractive in nature, have yielded systematic disenfranchisement of the working class and individuals with disabilities. These examples illustrate that it is myopic to see racism as the only result of white supremacist oppression. Figure 1.1 shows how imperialist white supremacist capitalist cisheteropatriarchy can be linked to a range of systemic oppressions. *Systemic*, in this case, describes the way oppression is perpetuated, not through individuals but through institutions and structures (embedded in societal policies and practices).

hooks taught that regardless of the form of oppression and the ways they intersect, the "ideological ground" is the same (cited in Hill Collins,

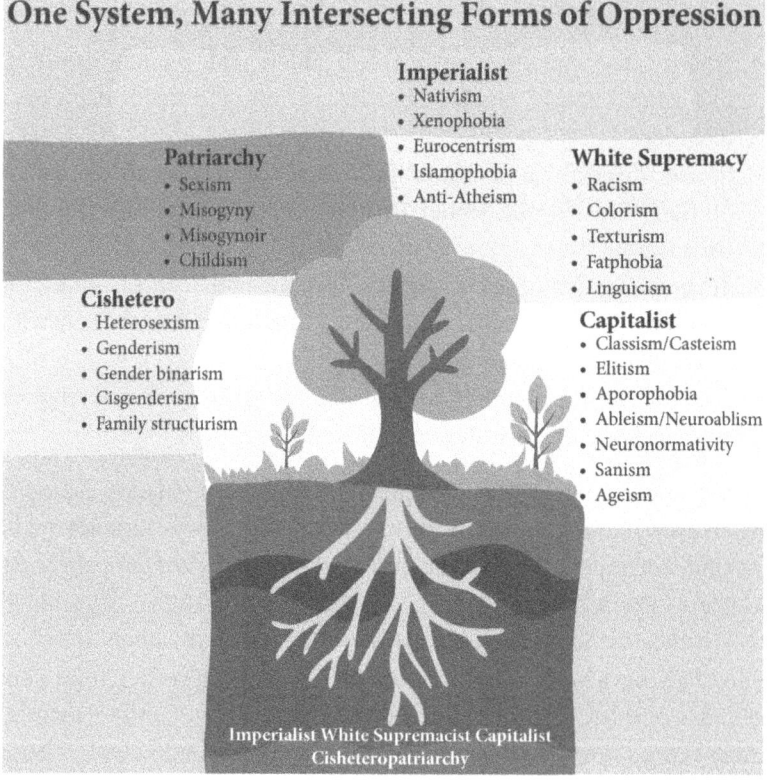

Figure 1.1 Imperialist White Supremacist Capitalist Cisheteropatriarchy Links to a Range of Systemic Oppression.

1990). Said differently, as a belief system driven by notions of inferiority and superiority, imperialist white supremacist capitalist cisheteropatriarchy leads to all forms of systemic oppression. Consequently, purifying American soil of imperialist white supremacist capitalist cisheteropatriarchy would lead to the destruction of each of these forms of oppression. But the opposite is true as well. If we don't purify the soil of imperialist white supremacist capitalist cisheteropatriarchy,

- Racism will be a permanent part of society.
- Sexism will be a permanent part of society.
- Heterosexism will be a permanent part of society.
- Linguicism will be a permanent part of society.
- Ableism will be a permanent part of society.
- Classism will be a permanent part of society.

I hope you get the point. Understanding the impact of this single source of systemic oppression is essential to reimagining educational justice. Another analogy might be helpful. If oppression is a social-political-economic ecosystem consisting of interrelated parts, imperialist white supremacist capitalist cisheteropatriarchy is the central force flowing among the parts. Freedom is only possible when the center is destroyed. Although I abbreviate the term *imperialist white supremacist capitalist cisheteropatriarchy* to *white supremacy* throughout the course of this book, I hope you'll keep at the forefront of your thinking the complete term for this violent, powerful, far-reaching system of oppression.

You might be wondering why a book that purports to focus on educational justice begins with few mentions of schooling but rather with a sociological treatise that centers white supremacy. This grounding is necessary to help build an understanding of what led to the need for social justice and educational justice. Bettina L. Love (2019) stressed the urgency around understanding the system that leads to educational injustice: "We cannot create a new educational system for all with a lack of understanding of what cripples our current system" (p. 89). I wrote this chapter to help build this understanding of what has crippled our current system: white supremacy. A decade ago, Warren (2014) emphasized the need for an educational justice movement, not just to reform but to transform schools and break the cycle of injustice in which low-income children of color are at the epicenter. His appraisal is even more urgent today. The educational justice movement must have at its center a shared commitment to purify the soil of the violent, oppressive system of white supremacy, because none of us is free until all of us are free.

Questions to Ponder

1. What impact has European colonization had on you individually? Your community? In what ways have you decolonized?
2. How do you feel about using the term *white supremacy* in discussions about educational justice? Is there another word that you'd prefer?
3. What connections, other than the ones in the illustration, can you make between white supremacy and the forms of oppression listed in this chapter? How might you redesign the illustration?
4. How do expressions of white supremacy show up in your school? Your community?
5. How might the opposition challenge the ideas put forth in this chapter? What evidence might support/refute their claims?

Note

[1] Johnson & Graham's Lessee v. McIntosh (1823), 21 U.S. 543.

2

Planting Trees: The Resistance to White Supremacy

As established in Chapter 1, white supremacy was infused into the soil of a society yet forming, creating a powerful and enduring caste that permeated every societal structure. Isabel Wilkerson (2020) defined this caste in *Caste: The Origins of Our Discontents*:

> A caste system is an artificial construction, a fixed and embedded ranking of human value that sets the presumed supremacy of one group against the presumed inferiority of other groups on the basis of ancestry and often immutable traits, traits that would be neutral in the abstract but are ascribed life-and-death meaning.
>
> (p. 17)

Though this caste system is formidable, its victims have sought to subvert it from the beginning. It's important to recognize that "historically oppressed and multiply-marginalized people are not simply victims of colonization, capitalism, cisheteronormativity, or ableism—they have agency and are always resisting subjugation" (Camangian & Cariaga, 2021, p. 904). In other words, oppressed peoples don't just acquiesce when treated inhumanely. They and their co-conspirators dissent. Dissension, despite what some would like us to believe, is a key function of citizens in a democracy and is a defining feature of justice work. Their fight for unconditional citizenship was (and is) a fight for equality of rights under the Constitution. I think specifically of Native American tribes' grassroots resistance to British rule in Pontiac's Rebellion in the 1760s (Virginia, 2023). Nat Turner also launched a valiant rebellion against slavery in 1831 (Encyclopedia Virginia, n.d.). This history reminds us that the twenty-first-century pursuit of justice is not new; it is part of a trajectory of counter-hegemonic actions begun by people whose lives and destinies were prescribed by European hegemony.

This inquiry into tree planting has a lengthy historical trajectory that begins with the Reconstruction Era. A deep and broad chronographic framing is necessary to illustrate how the country's oppressed people pursued justice, or planted trees, for a century before modern-day civil rights movements. For this reason, I begin with three cases that were judged by the Supreme Court during Reconstruction—the time after the Civil War when leaders sought to redefine and reestablish the country.

Planting Trees: Reconstruction Era (Late 1800s)

The question of citizenship was a defining one during the Reconstruction Era (and remains one in 2025). In the 1857 Supreme Court case *Scott v. Sandford*,[1] Dred Scott sued for his and his family's freedom from slavery. The Court decided against Scott because, according to the Court, enslaved people were not citizens of the United States and, therefore, could not expect any protection from the federal government or the courts. It was only after the 14th Amendment to the U.S. Constitution passed in 1868 that formerly enslaved Black people and all individuals born in the United States were granted citizenship. In another citizenship case, *Elk v. Wilkins* (1884),[2] the Supreme Court ruled that John Elk, born on an Indian reservation, was not a citizen of the United States. These cases set a precedent for people of color using the courts to demand citizenship rights as Americans. They also show how the racialization of citizenship is used to deny civil rights to people of color, even those born in the United States. More than a hundred years after these 19th-century cases, former President Barack Obama and former Vice President Kamala Harris, both multiethnic with immigrant parents, had their citizenship and legitimacy as Americans questioned through racist lies and innuendo, which resembled the arguments used in the past to exclude people of color from full participation in our democracy.

Another 19th-century case, *Plessy v. Ferguson* (1896),[3] was a fight to desegregate train cars in Louisiana after Homer A. Plessy, a mixed-race man, was arrested for boarding a train car designated for whites. Plessy believed that his constitutional rights, granted by the equal protection clause of the 14th Amendment, had been violated. The Court ruled against Plessy, concretizing the "separate but equal" doctrine that further legitimized Jim Crow laws enacted throughout the U.S. South. Though the Supreme Court decided against civil rights for Black Americans and Native Americans in all three cases, Dred Scott, John Elk, and Homer Plessy provided shoulders upon which future justice workers would stand in the court of law. They planted trees. As is evident here, struggles for equal rights and inclusion are centuries old, having begun long before the modern civil rights era.

Planting Trees: Civil Rights Era (1950s–1960s)

Efforts by oppressed groups toward making the United States more just peaked during the civil rights movements of the 1950s and 1960s. I use "movements" instead of "movement" because several distinct movements for civil rights emerged during this period. The spread of these movements throughout the United States, and the world, can be understood through the symbolism of trees. Wall Kimmerer (2013, p. 20) taught that "the trees in a forest are often interconnected by subterranean networks." They live in what Wohlleben (2015, p. 11) called a "symbiotic community." During the civil rights movements, trees were planted and roots were spreading and strengthening each other, but they were never united with a common goal of liberation for all. Still, these movements were immeasurably complex and robust catalysts for social change; consequently, it is impossible to give the justice movements and the justice workers the analysis they deserve. Suffice it to say, however, the civil rights movements described in the next section, which were movements for social justice, are, at the core, struggles to achieve full citizenship, which means experiencing all the civil and social rights and freedoms to which they are entitled but have been historically denied. It is important to notice which groups were forced to mount resistance to government-sanctioned oppression, but it's perhaps more significant to point out the one group that did not, the ones who experienced all the rights of citizenship by default—white, heterosexual, cisgender, Christian, English-speaking men.

Civil Rights Movement (African Americans)

The most prominent movement for civil rights was led largely by Black folks and their allies in the U.S. South. Banks (2013, p. 73) noted the role that African Americans played in advancing justice:

> African Americans began a quest for their rights in the United States that was unprecedented in their history. Sometimes in strident voices and salient public action, they demanded that various institutions within American society respond to their quest for social, political, economic, and educational rights and possibilities that had been denied, lost, and betrayed for more than three centuries.

The year 1955 was pivotal for the development of the civil rights movement in the South. Two major events accelerated the growth and momentum of this movement against white supremacy. First, in August, was the brutal murder of 14-year-old Chicagoan, Emmett Till, in Money, Mississippi, followed four months later by the refusal of Ms. Rosa Parks to give up her bus seat in Montgomery, Alabama. Ms. Mamie Till-Mobley's (mother of Emmett) refusal to hide his mutilated body ignited public awareness of the macabre nature of white supremacy. Second, Rosa Parks's act of defiance by refusing to give up her seat in a whites-only section of a public bus was the impetus for the Montgomery bus boycott that took place from 1955 to 1956. The boycott was recognized as the first mass civil rights mobilization and led to the U.S. Supreme Court ruling that segregation on public buses is unconstitutional (The Martin Luther King, Jr. Research and Education Institute, n.d.).

Educational justice was a central focus of this movement. In *McLaurin v. Oklahoma State Regents for Higher Education* (1950),[4] the Court ruled in favor of George McLaurin, who accused the University of Oklahoma of discriminatory treatment (separating him from his peers in university facilities). Similarly, in the early 1950s, the NAACP organized several court cases across the country and consolidated them with the case filed by Linda Brown's family, leading to *Brown v. Topeka Board of Education* (1954).[5] In this landmark case, the Court decided that schools that segregate Black students from white students are inherently unequal and, therefore, unconstitutional, and ordered schools to desegregate at once, or "with all deliberate speed." (The *Brown* decision was a reversal of the *Plessy* ruling of 1896 upholding segregation.) In writing the Court's opinion, Chief Justice Earl Warren justified its decision:

> Segregation of white and colored children in public schools has a detrimental effect upon the colored children. The impact is greater when it has the sanction of the law, for the policy of separating the races is usually interpreted as denoting the inferiority of the negro group. A sense of inferiority affects the motivation of a child to learn. Segregation with the sanction of law, therefore, has a tendency to [retard] the educational and mental development of negro children and to deprive them of some of the benefits they would receive in a racial[ly] integrated school system.
>
> (*Brown v. Board*, 1954)

Even after *Brown*, however, many Black families and communities had to sue their local school districts to force them to comply with the ruling. It wasn't until the 1970s that many states and local school districts began to desegregate.

Voting was another major civil rights issue. Hampered by poll taxes, literacy tests, violence, and intimidation, Black people in the South were not free to vote. Congress passed the Civil Rights Act of 1957, which focused primarily on addressing the systemic barriers preventing African Americans from registering and voting. This legislation was weak, leading African Americans to continue to fight for the right to vote. The NAACP established field offices and hired organizers to help Black people exercise their voting rights. Civil rights activist Medgar Evers was assassinated in Mississippi in 1963, in part because of his efforts to register Black voters. Moreover, the goal of the Selma-to-Montgomery marches in 1965 was to secure voting rights for African Americans.

In 1960, activists in North Carolina launched what became the sit-in movement to protest discriminatory treatment at lunch counters. Around this same time, in 1961, the Congress for Racial Equality (CORE) organized the Freedom Rides movement to challenge segregation on interstate buses and in bus terminals by riding through the South with white activists/allies. Another event was the March on Washington for Jobs and Freedom on August 23, 1963, conceptualized by A. Philip Randolph and chiefly organized by Bayard Rustin. It is estimated that up to 250,000 African Americans and their supporters participated in a demonstration in the nation's capital to demand economic justice.

Activism for civil rights for African Americans was not confined to the South. The Watts riots in California, an urban explosion that many white people saw as an expression of anger by unruly Blacks, were, according to the Kerner Commission, a presidentially appointed panel, actually fueled by systemic racism and poverty. Noteworthy as well is the Black power movement that sprang up during the mid-1960s and lasted throughout the 1970s. Inspired by Stokely Carmichael, president of the Student Nonviolent Coordinating Committee (SNCC), the Black power movement advocated for Black nationalism and self-reliance and took issue with the nonviolent approaches exercised by those involved in the civil rights movement in the South. Black power ideology, which was met with much controversy, was evident in groups across the United States, like the Black Panthers and the Black Liberation Party.

The monumental work by African Americans in the South (and beyond), which led to the passing of the Civil Rights Act of 1965, usually takes center stage in conversations about the civil rights movement of the 1950s and 1960s. However, it is important to recognize that other racialized groups were also fighting for civil rights in different parts of the United States.

Civil Rights Movement (Mexican Americans)

The doctrine of white domination has not been exclusive to African Americans. Mexican Americans (also *Chicanos*, a cultural and political term chosen by Mexicans born in the United States, especially those in the Southwest) in the western and southwestern United States were active in their own struggle, known as the Chicano movement (also El Movimiento). In 1929, the League of United Latin American Citizens (LULAC) was formed in Corpus Christi, Texas. The purpose of LULAC was to address the civil rights of Mexican Americans, mainly to improve unfair migrant working conditions and fight for school desegregation. In 1947, Mexican American parents and families won a federal lawsuit against California school districts that had segregated Mexican American children from white children. In *Mendez et al. v. Westminster* (1947),[6] for the first time, evidence was introduced in court proving that school segregation harmed minority children, which became a central argument in the *Brown* case in 1954. The federal court decided

> the equal protection of the laws pertaining to the public school system in California is not provided by furnishing in separate schools the same technical facilities, textbooks and courses of instruction to children of

Mexican ancestry that are available to the other public school children regardless of their ancestry. A paramount requisite in the American system of public education is social equality. It must be open to all children by unified school association regardless of lineage.

(*Mendez v. Westminster*, 1947)

Another court case sought to redress wrongs done to Mexican American students in Texas. The Driscoll Consolidated Independent School District had systemically tracked and retained students with Spanish last names in first grade, for three years in some cases, and segregated them from their white peers. The district claimed that these practices were needed due to language barriers. Families of the Mexican American students sued the school district. The U.S. district court ruled, in *Hernandez v. Driscoll CISD* (1956),[7] that the school district was guilty of racial discrimination against Mexican American students. Dr. Enrique Alemán Jr., a professor who codirected *Stolen Education* (2014)—a film that chronicles the experiences of Mexican students and families that attended schools in Driscoll—expressed, "The case was really about racial oppression, the maintaining of a racial hierarchy" (Zinn Education Project, 2025).

In 1968, in what has been described as "one of the largest student protests in United States history" more than 15,000 students participated in a walkout in East Los Angeles to demand access to education during a time when they were being relegated to substandard curricula that disregarded their culture (Library of Congress, n.d., para. 4). In Crystal City, Texas, a similar walkout involving more than 2,000 students took place in December 1969 to stand against discrimination against Mexican Americans in Crystal City schools. These demonstrations, like many others in the U.S. South, were led by students. Frustrated with marginalization in schools, these student activists insisted on schooling that was fair and equitable to Mexican American students. They were justice workers—tree planters.

Three years after the 1963 March on Washington, Cesar Chavez, Dolores Huerta, and their team organized a 250-mile march with thousands of demonstrators from Delano, California, to Sacramento, the state capital, to bring attention to the plight of Mexican American farmworkers. Their work built on decades of farmworker activism that included the struggle to end the Bracero Program, which exploited Mexican farmworkers who had been brought to the United States to fill labor shortages in agriculture. The purpose of the farmworkers movement, which led to the founding of the United Farm Workers (UFW) in 1966, was to defend the rights of mostly

Mexican American farmworkers who were being exploited by having to work under horrible conditions and for low wages. Filipino farmworkers, previously unionized as the Agricultural Workers Organizing Committee (AWOC), organized with Chicanos. These alliances planted the seed for La Raza Unida Party to sprout and increase Mexican American participation in the American political arena.

Civil Rights Movement (Asian Americans)

Inspired by the activism of the Black power movement, Asian Americans also began a civil rights movement, "yellow power," that lasted through the 1960s and 1970s. (While the term *yellow power* was embraced by some Asian Americans, others found that it reinforced negative stereotypes.) Uyematsu (1969) wrote "The Emergence of Yellow Power in America," a foundational essay that challenged stereotypes, addressed internalized racism, and urged self-definition.

Reflecting on the movement, Uyematsu (2022, p. 265) elucidated,

> I saw the emerging Asian American/Yellow Power movement as part of the ongoing civil rights struggles which had begun in the 1950s. We were inspired by Black activists such as the Black Panthers, Angela Davis, and Malcolm X. We also saw our young movement joining international ones against colonialism and imperialism.
>
> (p. 265)

The purpose of yellow power was mainly to address issues of identity, as Asian Americans experienced a "token acceptance of white America" (Uyematsu, p. 9) because of how well they had assimilated. Their activism brought about changes in the following areas: ethnic studies programs in universities, an end to the Vietnam War, and reparations for Japanese Americans forced into internment camps during World War II.

Civil Rights Movement (Native Americans)

Similarly, Native Americans, inspired by a spirit of Indian nationalism, ushered in "red power" in the 1960s to promote recognition of their federal rights and tribal sovereignty. After decades of assimilation, Native American activists advocated for the reclamation of Indigenous identity. This movement was led by groups like the National Indian Youth Council and the American Indian Movement (AIM), founded in Minnesota under the leadership of Russell Means (McKenzie-Jones, 2023). AIM activists participated in the Siege of Wounded Knee, a 71-day occupation of Wounded Knee, South Dakota, to protest, in part, U.S. treaty failures (McKenzie-Jones, 2023). One of the most well known actions during the red power movement was the 10-month occupation of Alcatraz Island, with the goal of reclaiming this land based on the Treaty of Fort Laramie, which stated that Native Americans could claim unused federal land (Johnson, n.d.; McKenzie-Jones, 2023). This period of Native American history is known as the "Self-Determination Era." Their efforts led to the passage of the Indian Civil Rights Act of 1968.

Gender- and Sexuality-Based Movements

Beyond movements for civil rights for minoritized racial and ethnic groups, white women launched the women's rights movement. Built upon the women's rights activism that led to the first women's rights convention in 1848, the 1960s women's rights movement mainly had as its goals reproductive rights, equality in the workplace, and freedom from limited gender roles. Additionally, the gay liberation movement, a movement to bring about the liberation of gay and lesbian people, can be traced to the Stonewall riots in 1969. The Stonewall riots occurred as a result of a police raid of the Stonewall Inn, one of the few bar establishments in Greenwich Village (NYC) that welcomed openly gay people. Moreover, individuals who held multiple marginalized identities sometimes struggled to be seen in single identity-focused movements. Sitting at the intersection of both racial and gender inequality, Black women ushered in the Black feminist movement for Black women who did not feel adequately represented by the civil rights movement or the women's rights movement. Similarly, Chicano feminists critiqued the Chicano movement because of its patriarchal structures and marginalization of women. Black lesbians had to fight for representation in the Black feminist movement and the gay liberation movement.

Interconnections but No Solidarity

Although these movements were interconnected, they were mostly distinct movements that aimed to advance justice for each group. The existence of separate movements instead of a single, unified movement may be attributed to the failure to recognize and unite against the common enemy that inflicted violence upon each group—white supremacy. Evidence of these separate struggles for civil rights is found in the deluge of laws and rulings that are enumerated in the next section. Black people wanted freedom from anti-Black racism. Speakers of languages other than English sought freedom from linguicism. Women demanded freedom from sexism. Immigrants fought against xenophobia. In all this tree planting, nobody paid attention to the soil. In other words, in their separate movements, they had failed to see that the trees they were planting were being planted in white supremacist soil.

Planting Trees: Civil Rights Act of 1964 and Beyond

Despite the failure to unify, justice workers' efforts were nothing short of heroic and brought about the codification of civil rights by the Civil Rights Act of 1964, which prohibited discrimination based on race, color, religion, sex, or national origin. The movement continued even after the Civil Rights Act was signed in 1964, as activists continued to demand voting rights, bringing out the passing of the Voting Rights Act (1965), later weakened by the Supreme Court in 2013 in a decision that eliminated the requirement for states to get federal approval to change voting laws. In other words, the Supreme Court's decision removed federal oversight of states' voting laws.

This section examines landmark laws and judicial rulings that were spurred by the Civil Rights Act of 1964 (except for the Equal Pay Act that was passed in 1963). The Civil Rights Act of 1964, and all the efforts of justice workers that led to it, were insufficient in addressing all the injustices suffered by marginalized populations. However, it catapulted several other issues to the forefront of the nation's consciousness, resulting in legislation and judicial rulings that were integral in advancing diversity, equity, and inclusion for historically oppressed groups. I call the 1960s and 1970s "the justice decades," as they represent a period of monumental movement toward justice. Here's a list of the most impactful justice-oriented milestones, several of which moved the country toward increased educational justice, specifically. Given that the nation's prior laws had created unconditional citizens who were not entitled to equal treatment, these milestones focused heavily on bringing about equal treatment under the law, as one might expect. This focus on *equality*, or sameness, however, would later be unfairly manipulated by Trump conservatives (those who adhere to the Make America Great Again—MAGA[8]—ideology), who use the rhetoric of sameness to protect, presumably, white citizens from discrimination. Though I endeavored to include the most significant legislation and decisions, the list is regrettably nonexhaustive.

Justice-Oriented Milestones

- **1963:** The Equal Pay Act prohibited discrimination, based on sex, in pay between employees performing the same work.
- **1964:** The Civil Rights Act outlawed discrimination based on race, color, religion, sex, or national origin. It ended segregation in public places and made employment discrimination illegal.
- **1965:** The Voting Rights Act prohibited discrimination in voting based on race, color, or language minority status.
- **1965:** The Immigration and Nationality Act overhauled the immigration system that had restricted the number of people from outside Western Europe eligible to settle in the United States and created new opportunities for immigrants from Asian nations.
- **1965:** The Higher Education Act expanded federal support for higher education institutions and financial aid for students pursuing postsecondary education.
- **1967:** The Age Discrimination in Employment Act (ADEA) protects certain applicants and employees 40 years of age and older from discrimination based on age in hiring, promotion, discharge, compensation, or terms, conditions, or privileges of employment.
- **1967:** *Loving v. Virginia* legalized interracial marriage, representing the freedom to marry granted by the Constitution.
- **1968:** The Bilingual Education Act (BEA) provided federal grants to school districts to establish educational programs for children with limited English-speaking ability.
- **1968:** The Indian Civil Rights Act (ICRA) extended Constitutional rights to Native Americans.
- **1972:** The Equal Employment Opportunity Act sought to combat employment discrimination based on race, color, religion, gender,

or national origin by extending the coverage of Title VII of the Civil Rights Act of 1964 to previously exempt employers with 15 or more employees.
- **1972:** Title IX of the Education Amendments prohibits sex discrimination in all aspects of education programs that receive federal support.
- **1973:** *Roe v. Wade* protected women's right to terminate an early pregnancy, giving them the right to have an abortion.
- **1974:** In *Lau v. Nichols*, the Supreme Court ruled that students who require additional English instruction to succeed in school have a right to those services, improving access and opportunity for students who do not speak English.
- **1975:** The Individuals with Disabilities Education Act (IDEA) is a law that makes available a free appropriate public education to eligible children with disabilities throughout the nation and ensures special education and related services to those children.
- **1975:** The Indian Self-Determination and Education Assistance Act (ISDEAA) gave tribes greater autonomy by granting them the right to take responsibility for carrying-out their own services, such as education and healthcare."
- **1978:** The Supreme Court case *Regents of the University of California v. Bakke* ruled that affirmative action programs can be used to achieve diversity in higher education.
- **1978:** The American Indian Religious Freedom Act preserves the rights of American Indians to practice traditional religious beliefs.

In more recent years:

- **1982:** The U.S. Supreme Court case of *Plyler v. Doe* made it possible for undocumented children to enroll in Texas public schools.
- **1990:** The Americans with Disabilities Act (ADA) is passed, prohibiting discrimination against differently-abled persons in all areas of public life, including employment, education, transportation, and public accommodations.
- **1990:** The Native American Languages Act is a federal policy that allows Native American languages to be used in classroom instruction.
- **2009:** The Matthew Shepard and James Byrd, Jr. Hate Crimes Prevention Act criminalized willfully causing bodily injury when the crime was committed because of the actual or perceived race,

color, religion, national origin, disability, gender, gender identity, and/or sexuality of any person.
- **2010:** The Senate overturned the "Don't Ask, Don't Tell" policy, thus allowing gay and lesbian military members to serve openly in the armed forces.
- **2012:** Deferred Action for Childhood Arrivals (DACA) is a deferred action policy implemented by the Obama administration and formalized by the Biden administration that is aimed at protecting undocumented immigrants who came to the United States as children.
- **2022:** The Respect for Marriage Act provides statutory authority for same-sex and interracial marriages (removing the provision for marriage to be between a woman and a man).

These milestones can be seen as attempts to establish "freedom from" and "freedom to" for populations that had been disenfranchised by unjust laws. These marginalized populations are those who are not native-born white, heterosexual, English-speaking, able-bodied, mentally sound, Christian men. Consequently, as conditional citizens, they've had to demand equal rights, as is reflected in Table 2.1.

Table 2.1 Legislative and Judicial Milestones

Milestones	Freedom from	Freedom (Entitled) to
Equal Pay Act	Sex (gender) discrimination in pay	Get paid equally (women)
Civil Rights Act	Discriminatory hiring and segregation in public places	Not face discrimination in hiring and not be segregated from whites
Voting Rights Act	Voting discrimination	Vote despite race/language
Immigration and Nationality Act	Immigration restrictions	Immigrate to the U.S. (Asians, Eastern Europeans, and persons from Latin America)
Higher Education Act	Lack of access to higher education for low-income students	Pursue higher education for low-income students
Age Discrimination in Employment Act	Age discrimination in employment	Employment regardless of age
Loving v. Virginia	Marriage constraints based on race (miscegenation laws)	Marry interracially

Bilingual Education Act	English-only instruction	Learn in their home language(s)
Indian Civil Rights Act	Exclusion based on citizenship status	Have the same constitutional rights as other citizens
Equal Employment Opportunity Act	Employment discrimination	Work in discrimination-free environments
Title IX	Sex (gender) discrimination in schools	Learn in sex discrimination–free schools
Roe v. Wade	Forced childbearing	Choose to terminate a pregnancy
Lau v. Nichols	Education without language supports	Education with language supports
Individuals with Disabilities Education Act	Inappropriate education	An appropriate education, with related services
ISDEAA	Control of tribal services by the federal government	Self govern
Regents of the University of California v. Bakke	Rejection based on merit alone	Acceptance based on race in higher education (holistic consideration)
American Indian Religious Freedom Act	Bans on religious practices	Practice traditional religions
Plyler v. Doe	Exclusion based on citizenship status	Attend schools regardless of citizenship status
Americans with Disabilities Act	Discrimination based on disabilities	Access to and fair treatment in all public facilities
Native American Languages Act	Discrimination based on language	Receive instruction in Native American languages
Matthew Shepard and James Byrd, Jr., Hate Crimes Prevention Act	Being subjected to identity-based violence	Live without unprosecuted identity-based violence
Overturned the "Don't Ask, Don't Tell" policy	Hiding sexual orientation in the military	Serve openly in the military
Deferred Action for Childhood Arrivals (DACA)	Work bans based on documentation	Work legally in the U.S., with limitations
Respect for Marriage Act	Marriage constraints based on sexuality	Marry regardless of sexuality

Conclusively, federal policies and judicial rulings provided access to schooling and, theoretically, protection from discrimination for marginalized students, like girls, students of color, students with disabilities, immigrants, and English language learners. Federal agencies were established to ensure that states comply with these civil rights laws and rulings and to support states in implementing evidentiary policies and practices. Hannah-Jones (2025) summarized the history of historically marginalized groups and civil rights. For historically marginalized groups,

> the right to be treated as equal citizens, to be treated fairly by the government, private companies and individuals, has for most of the history of this country not been guaranteed. These rights needed to be codified and enforced precisely because the deprivation of those rights was codified and enforced for almost as long as this country existed. When in the past the federal government stopped enforcing these laws, those rights have always deteriorated.
>
> (para. 13)

As civil rights are deteriorating under the 2025 Trump administration, justice workers must ready themselves to reimagine the movement for educational justice.

Months of Observation[9]

Moreover, progress toward justice would also take the form of designated months of observation for marginalized groups. Between 1986 and 1990, several minoritized groups were recognized with a designated month:

- **1986:** Congress passed Public Law 99-244, which designated February 1986 as National Black (Afro-American) History Month.
- **1987:** Congress passed Public Law 100-9, designating March as Women's History Month.
- **1988:** Congress passed Public Law 100-402, establishing the 30-day period starting on September 15 and ending on October 15 as Hispanic Heritage Month.
- **1990:** Congress passed and President George H. W. Bush signed into law a joint resolution designating November as National American Indian Heritage Month (also known as Native American Indian Month).
- **1990:** President George H. W. Bush issued Proclamation No. 6130 designating May 1990 as Asian/Pacific American Heritage Month.

- **1999:** President Bill Clinton declared June Gay and Lesbian Pride Month. In 2009, President Barack Obama declared June LGBT Pride Month. On June 1, 2021, President Joe Biden declared June LGBTQ Pride Month (though not formally codified by law).

Similarly, in 2021, President Joe Biden made Juneteenth (June 19)—commemorating the day that enslaved Black people in Galveston, Texas, found out they were free—a federal holiday. These "heroes and holidays" observations alone are insufficient attempts at diversity, equity, and inclusion. Their curricular marginalization reflects white dominance. Still, it can be argued that they make way for centering racialized groups in ways that rarely happen otherwise. As justice workers reimagine educational justice, our visions should include teaching and learning that deliberately incorporate critical examinations of marginalized histories, cultures, and experiences into the mainstream curriculum throughout the year.

I return to the tree analogy and the words of Wall Kimmerer in *Braiding Sweetgrass* (2013, p. 15) as a reminder of the importance of a coalesced justice movement that can be more potent when it draws from or leans upon the work of others also doing justice work:

> If one tree fruits, they all fruit—there are no soloists. Not one tree in a grove, but the whole grove; not one grove in the forest, but every grove; all across the county and all across the state. The trees act not as individuals, but somehow as a collective. Exactly how they do this, we don't yet know. But what we see is the power of unity: What happens to one happens to us all. We can starve together or feast together. All flourishing is mutual.

Schools and Society

This chapter focuses largely on the pursuit of justice in the country as a whole. There is a reason for this focus. Schools and society are inextricably entwined; consequently, educational justice is deeply connected to the broader struggle for social justice. Moreover, school policies are often a reflection of societal policies. Awareness of the socio-political-historical context of education is pivotal to understanding why certain student populations and their families experience inequitable schooling. Zaretta Hammond (2015) reminded educators in *Culturally Responsive Teaching and the Brain* that we must be "knowledgeable about the larger social, political, and economic conditions that create inequitable education outcomes" (p. 21). Understanding the dynamic interplay between social, political, and cultural factors gives educators a holistic view of factors that impact student success and development. Outlined in his ecological systems theory, Bronfenbrenner (1979) proposed that complex, interrelated environmental, cultural, and social systems shape children's development. Similarly, Duncan-Andrade (2022) described the relationship between schools and society in terms of ecosystems in which both the classroom and school micro-ecosystems "reflect the ecosystem of the community and the broader society." He went on to say that "the forces of each layer of these social ecosystems impinge on one another in both directions.... This interconnectedness shows up every day in every school and every classroom" (p. 56). As an example, learning about federal immigration policies can shed light on student demographic trends and reveal how issues of citizenship and language impact the schooling experiences of immigrant students and their families. Consequently, any attempts to advance equity in education must address the broader socio-historical-political context of schooling. Moreover, educational institutions play a major role in creating society. Said differently, "schools and colleges do not just reproduce culture, they shape the new society that is coming into existence" (Connell, 2012, p. 681). This is one of the reasons why educational justice is paramount.

Although educational justice is the focus of this book, the examination in this chapter includes the struggle for social justice, generally, to illustrate the conditions under which schooling began, evolved, and devolved. These conditions were characterized by white supremacy, as it was embedded in the soil of our developing country. Legal interventions were necessary to counter the discriminatory, inequitable, and exclusionary treatment of minoritized populations and were possible because of the diligence, sacrifice, and ingenuity of justice workers, many of whom preferred to "die fighting against injustice than to die like a dog or rat in a trap" (Wells, in Duster, 2013, p. 53). Our foreparents were planting trees, and these trees were bearing fruit, which is evidenced by the ways marginalized communities began being afforded more opportunities and access than ever before. Still, the work, even the establishment of schooling for students of color, was precarious due to justice workers' failure to recognize that the soil in which they were planting was poisoned by white supremacy. This is the focus of Chapter 3.

> *Questions to Ponder*
>
> 1. What connections can you make between the forms of oppression in Chapter 1 and the legislative and judicial milestones listed in this chapter?
> 2. How would you summarize the various movements for civil rights?
> 3. Are cultural holidays relevant for educators and students today? Why or why not?
> 4. How might this chapter look from the opposition's point of view? What critiques might be valid/invalid?

Notes

1. Dred Scott v. Sandford, 60 U.S. (19 How.) 393 (1856).
2. Elk v. Wilkins, 112 U.S. 94 (1884).
3. Plessy v. Ferguson, 163 U.S. 537 (1896).
4. McLaurin v. Oklahoma State Regents, 339 U.S. 637 (1950).
5. Brown v. Board of Education, 347 U.S. 483 (1954).
6. Mendez v. Westminster, 64 F. Supp. 544 (S.D. Cal. 1946).
7. Hernandez v. Driscoll Consolidated Independent School District, 347 U.S. 475 (1954).
8. MAGA is a right-wing, identity-based movement fueled by white nationalism, xenophobia, racism, gender binarism, and homophobia. It is characterized by authoritarianism and fascism (Parker & Blum, 2025).
9. Department of Defense Secretary Pete Hegseth announced in January 2025 that the DoD, which includes the armed forces, would not recognize cultural or gender identity months in January 2025.

3

Bearing Fruit: The Evolution of Schooling for Students of Color

The focus of this book is educational justice for all students victimized by white supremacy. At the same time, this chapter homes in on the racist experiences of students of color in their early schooling experiences. This narrowing is necessary for at least two reasons: (1) The conservative attacks on educational justice mainly focus on race, and to a lesser extent gender and sexuality. This historical overview provides the background for understanding the racist attacks during the 2020s. (2) As this chapter will illustrate, racism has been the most codified (established by law) form of oppression in schools. Race, more than any other factor, has determined who has access and opportunity in schools.

The First Schools of Social Reproduction

Schools, as reflections and reproductions of society, are castes that restrict the academic success of students of color. Said differently, schools are "social mirrors" (Duncan-Andrade, 2022, p. 4). Although social inequities don't originate in schools, they often appear in and are frequently exacerbated by schools. Educational ethnographer Sabina E. Vaught (2011) concluded from her research that white supremacy is entrenched in contemporary public schooling, which is unsurprising given the context in which the first schools were formed. Duncan-Andrade (2022, p. 3) deduced that public education "was built to be unequal and segregated" by its very design. The first schools aligned with white supremacist social mores and political norms. The Boston Latin School (founded in 1635) and the Mather School (founded in 1639) served only white males and had curricula that emphasized the humanities, namely Western European classics, and religion. These schools existed to prepare white boys for postsecondary studies and careers in leadership and ministry. With a singular focus and homogenous student body, these first schools were Eurocentric and exclusive. Graduates attended the (white) Ivy League colleges for postsecondary education. Early schools and Ivy League universities were rooted in whiteness, or European values, beliefs, and practices. Formal education was denied to people of color for centuries after it was available to white boys, setting the foundation for long-standing inequities between white people and people of color that would be impossible to erase. Early schools for students of color, planted in white supremacist soil, reproduced an unjust society. It's important to examine this historical legacy.

Early Schooling for Students of Color

Because of today's compulsory schooling laws, some might be surprised to learn that education is not a right guaranteed by the U.S. Constitution. While education may not be a "fundamental right" under the Constitution, the equal protection clause of the 14th Amendment (1868) requires that when a state establishes a public school system, no child living in that state may be denied equal access to schooling. It is this clause that made education available to freed African Americans who began attending schools during Reconstruction in the late 1800s and that later made it possible for undocumented students to attend public schools.[1] Though the student population of schools gradually became more racially diverse through 19th- and 20th-century through federal policies and court decisions that granted access to students of color, the functioning of schools remained much as it had always been when the first schools for white boys opened in the United States: Eurocentric. White supremacy, then and now, is the headmaster, even in schools that serve mostly students of color and that are led by educators of color. Too often unexamined, whiteness influenced the following components of early schools designed to serve students of color:

- Funding: financial resources allotted to schools
- Research: what knowledge is valuable and how it is produced
- Curricula: what students learn
- Pedagogy: how teachers teach (instructional methods)
- Resources: materials teachers use
- Discipline: behavioral expectations of students
- Assessment: how teachers measure learning
- Languaging practices: communication standards
- Philosophy: the purpose of schooling
- Lifestyle expectations: ideal teachers, parents, and families

The sections below provide a glimpse into the realities of these early schools, illustrating the impact of white supremacy. This historical examination is important because it helps educators "recognize that today's conditions… are connected to a larger history that cannot be ignored" (Howard, 2024, p. 16).

Native American Students: The Nation's First Peoples

Native Americans educated their own children before the European colonial invasion. Their teachings emphasized the relationship between humans and nature and centered on survival as a group. Knowledge was passed down from elders to children through oral tradition. However, the newly formed country's early leaders, white men, viewed Native Americans in terms of what they supposedly lacked—formal government, schools, and spiritual values—causing mischaracterizations of Native peoples as "savage" and "uncivilized." To address this perceived lack of civilization, the U.S. government enacted the Indian Civilization Fund Act (1819) to fund missionaries and church leaders, in partnership with the federal government, to establish schools for Native American children. The resolute purpose of these boarding, or reservation, schools was to "kill the Indian [in him] and save the man" (Pratt, 1892), a purpose that was to be accomplished by inculcating in Native Americans white, Christian, capitalistic values. These values conflicted with Native American values.

Mays (2021) assessed this conversion to white schooling as a moment of great terror:

> Army officials and missionaries, empowered by the US government, would go into tribal nations and kidnap their children and force them into boarding schools so they would be assimilated into US culture. They wanted to eradicate from the children the meaning of what it meant to be Indigenous so that the US government could fulfill its plan of taking more land.
>
> (p. 58)

According to U.S. Secretary of Interior Alexander H. H. Stuart, there were only two options—civilize or exterminate (Grinde, 2004). The United States' schooling of Native Americans was nothing short of ethnocide, the deliberate destruction of the culture. The National Native American Boarding School Healing Coalition (n.d.) reported that "between 1869 and the 1960s, hundreds of thousands of Native American children were removed from their homes and families and placed in boarding schools," suffering immeasurable physical, sexual, cultural, and spiritual abuse and neglect. Importantly, too, students were punished for speaking their tribal languages and were forced to speak English, resulting in a tremendous loss of language. This restriction was codified when, in 1887, Commissioner of Indian Affairs John DeWitt Clinton Atkins issued an order banning instruction in Native languages in mission and government-operated schools on reservations. His devaluation of Native languages was explicit:

> To teach Indian school children in their native tongue is practically to exclude English, and to prevent them from acquiring it. This language, which is good enough for a white man and a black man, ought to be good enough for the red man. It is also believed that teaching an Indian youth in his own barbarous dialect is a positive detriment to him. The first step to be taken toward civilization, toward teaching the Indians the mischief and folly of continuing in their barbarous practices, is to teach them the English language.
>
> (Atkins, 1887)

The National Day of Remembrance for U.S. Indian Boarding Schools is observed on September 30 to call attention to the atrocities experienced by Native children. Leigh-Osroosh and Hutchinson (2019, p. 2) labeled the violence enacted in these schools as cultural identity silencing, defined as "the active denial of the present living existence of a culture and/or cultural identity as expressed through language, behaviors, norms, values, history, and assets." Contemporary schooling practices still fail Native American students. In a landmark ruling in 2018, a New Mexico court decided that the State of New Mexico had failed its constitutional obligation to provide a sufficient education to Native American students.[2]

Higher education was initially accessible to Native Americans through the Choctaw Academy (Kentucky) in 1818, but this accessibility only lasted a short time due to a lack of funding. Decades later, higher education was made available to Native American students when the federally funded Carlisle Indian School (Pennsylvania) was founded in 1879, and access expanded to the Hampton Institute (Virginia) in 1884. The Carlisle School was described as the "ultimate Americanizer," requiring European assimilation by forcing students to cut their hair, change their names, speak English, wear Eurocentric clothes, and practice Christianity (Hultgren, 1989).

Black (African American) Students: The Nation's Forced Immigrants

Enslaved Black Americans were victimized by anti-literacy laws that forbade them from learning to read and write, and anyone from teaching them. An excerpt from the South Carolina Act of 1740 is illustrative of this forbiddance:

> Be it enacted, that all and every person and persons whatsoever, who shall hereafter teach or cause any slave or slaves to be taught to write, or shall use or employ any slave as a scribe, in any manner of writing whatsoever, hereafter taught to write, every such person or persons shall, for every such offense, forfeit the sum of one hundred pounds, current money.

Black Americans refused to simply comply with this unjust law. I'm deeply inspired by justice worker John Berry Meachum, who found an ingenious way to provide education for Black children in Missouri. In 1825, Meachum partnered with a white missionary to create a Black church where free and enslaved Black children could learn to read and write. Later, Missouri banned education for all "Negroes and mulattoes" on February 16, 1847. Unrelenting, Meachum turned a steamboat into a school—the Floating Freedom School—and anchored it on the Mississippi River, outside the state's jurisdiction, to continue to provide education to free and enslaved Black children in the St. Louis area. Jarvis Givens (2021) called these covert acts of resistance against anti-literacy laws *fugitive pedagogy*.

Consequently, widespread formal education was denied to Black children until the Freedmen's Bureau, formed in 1865, established schools for freed

African Americans during Reconstruction. Because of the equal protection clause of the 14th Amendment (1868), states were forced to provide public education for Black children. The education of Black children has always been a threat to the existing social hierarchy. Ortiz (2018) quoted a Mississippi plantation owner as saying, "I will be glad when free schools are abolished. Our tenants don't need them and we can get along without them" (p. 119). He saw Black people as a permanent part of an uneducated working class, not an educated people with opportunities for upward mobility. For many Black children in the rural South at the turn of the century, schooling competed with working. (I have experience with this phenomenon within my immediate family, as my maternal grandmother, born in Alabama in 1927, was forced to leave school in fourth grade to work.) Forced pullouts were common, as sharecropping parents relied on the children's labor to plant and harvest enough crops (Brooker, 2024).

Early Black schools were segregated and underfunded, leading to a dual but unequal system of education that lasted de jure (by law) for almost a hundred years, before the Supreme Court outlawed school segregation in *Brown v. Board of Education* (1954). There was tremendous resistance to school desegregation by whites, with many schools throughout the South remaining segregated until the 1970s. Senator Harry Byrd of Virginia created a coalition of politicians that agreed to resist following the order of *Brown*. This agreement was called the "Southern Manifesto." Egregiously, some school districts, like Prince Edward County, Virginia, closed its entire public school system rather than have its white students attend schools with Black students. When public schools were finally forced to desegregate, segregation academies, private schools, sprang up throughout the South for white families fleeing public schools.

Woodson described the Eurocentric curricula of early Black schools: "Negroes are taught to admire the Hebrew, the Greek, the Latin and the Teuton and to despise the African" (1933, p. 1). He reported that out of the hundreds of "Negro" high schools, only 18 offered a course in Negro history. In colleges where the Negro is included in curricula, the race is "studied only as a problem or dismissed as of little consequence" (p. 1). (In my own undergraduate experience at a historically Black college, I had to take courses in Western civilization and humanities as part of the core curriculum but not a single course that centered African or African American culture.) Woodson believed that the goal of this education for Negroes was to make them "successfully imitate whites" (p. 7). Although segregated Black schools experienced material lack designed to create an inferior education, many scholars—myself included—have written about the cultural and familial traditions that enriched these schools, features that were lamented in desegregated, white schools that were Eurocentric in every manner of academic expression.

The Civil Rights Act of 1964 greatly expanded access to higher education for African Americans because it provided legal protection from discrimination in admission to public universities. It was later bolstered by the Higher Education Act of 1965, which provided financial assistance and support services for low-income students. Higher education enrollment increased after the affirmative action decision in *Regents of University of California v. Bakke* (1978), which allowed race-based admissions. It's important to point out, however, that many Black Americans attained higher education beginning in the mid-1800s when Black colleges and universities were formed during the Reconstruction Era.

Hispanic/Latino(x) Students: The Nation's "Illegal" Immigrants

Because of the complicated cultural, historical, and geographic significance of Mexico to the United States, the experiences of Mexican American students will be centered as a reflection of the experiences of Hispanic students broadly. Mexican American students were forbidden from attending schools with white children, but not in the same way as Black students were. In an article exploring Latino(x)'s struggle for educational equity, the National Parks Service offered this comparison:

> Unlike the strict de jure segregated schooling for African Americans in the South based upon race, Mexican American children in Southwestern and Midwestern states such as Iowa and Kansas, were placed in "Mexican" classrooms or schools as a result of "color of the law" or "custom" beginning in the early 1900s.
>
> (para. 11)

Like Black schools, Mexican schools were underresourced and focused mainly on vocational education instead of offering academic curricula. Redlining aided with keeping schools segregated. Segregation from white students was mostly based upon supposed language deficits and perceptions of uncleanliness. Taken together, these accusations rendered them undeserving of attending schools with white children. One of the earliest litigations involving desegregation for Mexican Americans was *Roberto Alvarez v. the Board of Trustees of the Lemon Grove (CA) School*

District (1931). Alvarez was successful, with the judge ruling that there was no reason to segregate Mexican children. Later successful cases include *Mendez v. Westminster School District* (1946) and *Delgado v. Bastrop* (1948). After Mexican students were allowed in white schools, they were punished for their languaging practices (speaking Spanish) and indicted for their immigration status, the latter leading to the Supreme Court case *Plyler v. Doe* (1982), which forbids states from denying a free and public education to undocumented students. Similar to the white supremacist aims of Native American education, the education of Mexican American students during these early years was Americanization through assimilation. Interestingly, some middle-class Mexicans bought into the need for Mexicans to be Americanized. With the support of the League of United Latin American Citizens (LULAC), the Little School of the 400 (LS400) was established with assimilationist aims (Vázquez Rios, 2013). Vázquez Rios (2013, p. 5) concluded that "the Little School of the 400 came about because Mexican Americans in Texas, faced with rampant discrimination, decided to adapt and 'Americanize' and this included language instruction in English" (p. 5). It was "an Americanization project designed to incorporate Mexicans into Texas society" (p. 4). Regarding higher education, Mexican Americans were not legally prohibited from attending college but were discouraged from doing so.

Asian Americans: The Nation's "Problem-then-Model" Immigrants

Asian Americans have experienced shifting societal sentiments. Although they are now widely (and problematically) known as the "model minority," they were not always regarded as such (DiAlto, 2012) In fact, they were once viewed as the "Oriental problem" (Tsu, 2013). Treated much like Latinos(x), they experienced discrimination based on languaging practices and immigration status. During the mid-1800s, Chinese students were prohibited from attending public schools with white students in San Francisco and were forced to attend the "Chinese School," later known as the Oriental Public School, which served Korean and Japanese students in addition to Chinese students. The California Supreme Court declared this exclusion based on ancestry unlawful in the 1885 case *Tape v. Hurley*. To counter the forced assimilation Chinese students faced in white public schools, Chinese families created Chinese heritage language schools to preserve their culture—the first established in San Francisco in 1886. The establishment of these schools gave white Americans a reason to see Chinese people as "foreign," leading to othering that has endured until the present day.

The segregation experienced by Chinese students was reflective of the hostility they faced in greater society as the U.S. government passed the Chinese Exclusion Act (1882), placing a 10-year ban on Chinese laborers immigrating to the United States. Similarly, rooted in nationalism, the Asiatic Exclusion League was formed in 1905 to end Asian immigration that was causing white schools to become more diverse with the forced admission of Chinese, Japanese, and Korean students. Decades after the segregation of Asian American students was lifted, they were still fighting for equitable treatment in schools, namely language equity. In *Lau v. Nichols* (1974), the U.S. Supreme Court ruled that schools must provide language support for students who use a home language other than English. Asian Americans were never prevented by law from higher education. Historical knowledge of their early higher education experiences is limited.

In summary, when racially minoritized groups were allowed to attend schools, their schooling experiences were rooted in white supremacy. As is evident from the brief examination above, historically, the education of racially minoritized students has been characterized by the following manifestations of white supremacist schooling, by policy, practice, or both:

- denial of access
- exclusion from rigorous coursework
- tracking
- curricula restrictions
- educator bias
- physical and psychological violence
- othering
- exploitation
- ostracization
- usurpation of authority from communities of color
- curricula marginality
- segregation
- physical and psychological abuse
- cultural repression
- racialized cultural violence
- language loss

- deficit thinking
- inadequate resources
- forced assimilation

The Disruption

Marginalized communities sought to disrupt whiteness, or European cultural imperialism, in PK–12 schools and institutions of higher education and to make schooling more diverse, equitable, and inclusive for students, families, and communities of color. As a result of their grassroots efforts, two impactful areas of academic study emerged: ethnic studies and multicultural education. In addition to these areas of academic study, a remarkable body of research emerged around cultural differences. In this work, I refer to this body of learning theories as cultural difference studies. The aims of this work in ethnic studies, multicultural education, and cultural difference studies are similar: visibility, voice, respect, and representation. It is their work to resist white supremacy in teaching and learning, performed over the last 70 years, that has been facing fervent counter-resistance since 2020. To be clear, this work has always faced challenges, but recent opposition has been more widespread.

Ethnic Studies (Late 1960s)

In the aftermath of the civil rights movement, ethnic studies in higher education arose and gradually made its way into PK–12 education. Ethnic studies is an interdisciplinary field that aims to develop an understanding of racial/ethnic groups' histories, cultures, and experiences. It also aims to develop critical consciousness about systemic inequities. Tintiangco-Cubales and colleagues (2014) recapped the origin of ethnic studies:

> Historically, Ethnic Studies emerged from social movements in the 1960s as students, educators, and scholars of color pressed schools, school districts, and textbook companies to produce and offer curricula that reflect the diversity and complexity of the United States population.
>
> (p. 3)

More specifically, the push for ethnic studies can be attributed to a student movement at UC-Berkeley, the Third World Liberation Front (UCLA Center X, 2016):

> Experiencing political exclusion, economic exploitation, and deculturalization in schools, Black, Chicana/o, and Filipina/o activists formed the Third World Liberation Front in 1968, which became the grassroots vehicle in the struggle to institutionalize Ethnic Studies courses at the high school and college levels throughout California.
>
> (para. 1)

According to Delgado-Bernal (Banks, 2019), ethnic studies, specifically Chicano studies, began at California State University, Los Angeles, in 1968 as an outgrowth of the Chicano movement. The birth of ethnic studies was in response to the "Americanization" of the curriculum that sought to assimilate Mexican students by enforcing American ideals. Similarly, Black studies was first offered at San Francisco State University, also in 1968. Now named Africana studies, their department website (San Francisco State University, n.d.) summarized the conception of the program:

> The birth of Black Studies at San Francisco State in 1968 was inspired by student-led opposition to the then Western intellectual hegemony and racist scholarship that characterized the limitations found in traditional approaches to college education.

The first Asian American studies courses were established at the University of California, Berkeley; San Francisco State University; and the University of California, Los Angeles, in 1969. Morris affirmed that "the emergence of Native American/Native or Indian studies began in the late 1960's" with "the first department of American Indian, First Nations, and Indigenous Studies being founded at the University of Minnesota in 1969." *Diverse* cultural groups—long marginalized and dismissed in academic studies—were finally being included. Professional associations were formed to support this work (Espinoza-Kulick, n.d.):

- The Association for Ethnic Studies was formed in 1972.
- The National Association for Chicano Studies was established in 1972 and renamed the National Association for Chicano and Chicana Studies in 1995.
- The National Council for Black Studies began in 1975.
- The Association for Asian American Studies was formed in 1979.
- The American Indian Studies Association was later formed in 1999.

Through establishing ethnic studies programs, institutions of higher education were creating curricula offerings that better represented the diverse ethnic landscape of the United States, but these course offerings were only available because of the demand of marginalized communities.

Although the origin of ethnic studies in high schools is more nebulous, what is clear is that Mexican American studies courses were offered by the Tucson Unified School District in Tucson, Arizona, in 1998 for elementary, middle, and high school students (Gomez & Jimenez-Silva, 2012). El Rancho United School District is thought to be the first school district in California to include ethnic studies as a high school graduation requirement (Alvarez, 2015), and Berkeley High School claims to be one of the first high schools to mandate ethnic studies for high school graduation in 1990 (Markovich, 2021).

Multicultural Education (1960s)

Multicultural education emerged around the same time as the civil rights movement. It was the academic resistance to racial exclusion and white dominance. Banks, in 1974, believed that multicultural education is a broad concept that is concerned with all cultural groups within a society, not just racial/ethnic groups. Gorski (1999) traced the origin of multicultural education to "separate actions of various groups who were dissatisfied with the inequities of the education system, along with the resulting action of educational institutions during the late 1960s and 1970s." Though conceptualizations of multicultural education vary, Gorski (2010) put forth this definition:

> Multicultural education is a progressive approach for transforming education that holistically critiques and responds to discriminatory policies and practices in education. It is grounded in ideals of social justice, education equity, critical pedagogy, and a dedication to providing educational experiences in which all students reach their full potentials as learners and as socially aware and active beings, locally, nationally, and globally. Multicultural education acknowledges that schools are essential to laying the foundation for the transformation of society and the elimination of injustice.

Significant to note in Gorski's definition is that multicultural education involves critiques, is grounded in social justice, and endeavors to provide education that cultivates the potential of all students. The National Association of Multicultural Education (NAME), founded in 1990, encapsulates why multicultural education matters:

NAME believes that multicultural education promotes equity for all regardless of culture, ethnicity, race, language, age, gender, sexual orientation, belief system or exceptionality. NAME believes that multicultural education enables the individual to believe in one's own intrinsic worth and culture, to transcend monoculturalism and, ultimately, to become multicultural.

James Banks (2014), known as the father of multicultural education, described multicultural education as having several characteristics:

1. Multicultural education maintains that all students should have equal opportunities to learn regardless of the racial, ethnic, social-class, or gender group to which they belong.
2. Multicultural education is an educational reform movement that tries to reform schools in ways that will give all students an equal opportunity to learn.
3. Multicultural education describes teaching strategies that empower all students and give them voice.

Cultural Difference Studies (1970s–Present)

James Banks (2013, p. 75), a Black scholar and pioneer in the development of multicultural education in the 1970s, observed that educators in ethnic studies found that ethnic studies was "not sufficient to actualize educational equality and to improve the academic achievement of students from diverse groups." Consequently, educational equity reformers began focusing on other factors that affect student success, such as school policy and politics, school culture and hidden curricula, the languages and dialects of the school, instructional materials, teaching styles and strategies, and attitudes, perceptions, beliefs, and actions. These examinations led to cultural difference theory, based on the following beliefs:

> Groups such as African Americans, Mexican Americans, and American Indians have strong, rich, and diverse cultures. These cultures… consist of languages, values, behavioral styles, and perspectives that can enrich the lives of all students. Schools frequently fail to help ethnic minority and low income students achieve because they ignore or try to alienate these students from their home and community cultures and languages.
>
> (Banks, 2013, p. 76)

Mexican American scholars Cárdenas and Cárdenas (1977) proposed a similar theory—the theory of incompatibilities, espousing that the cultures of racially and linguistically minoritized children were incompatible with "typical instructional programs." They identified five areas of incompatibility: poverty, culture, language, mobility, and societal perceptions. Moreover, Moll and colleagues (1992, p. 134) learned that students' homes and communities held funds of knowledge upon which teachers should draw in their instruction.

> Our analysis of funds of knowledge represents a positive (and, we argue, realistic) view of households as containing ample cultural and cognitive resources with great, potential utility for classroom instruction (see Moll & Greenberg, 1990; Moll et al., 1990). This view of households, we should mention, contrasts sharply with prevailing and accepted perceptions of working-class families as somehow disorganized socially and deficient intellectually; perceptions that are well accepted and rarely challenged in the field of education and elsewhere.

Several educational approaches would be theorized as functions of cultural learning, what Kishimoto (2022) calls "diversity and equity pedagogies." These approaches are all undergirded by a central idea—that schools must respect and reflect the rich cultural strengths of students and align their teaching with students' cultural characteristics (Banks, 2013). This work has been conceptualized in nuanced ways and given several names, all of which express value for students' and families' cultures in teaching and learning. Together, this robust body of theorizing can be considered cultural difference studies, or culturally centered education (Education First/Ed Reports, 2021). A historical chronology of these terms is listed below:

1970s:
- **Culturally responsive education** (Cazden & Leggett, 1976)—Education that considers cognitive and affective aspects of how different children learn so that appropriate teaching styles and learning environments can be provided that will maximize their educational achievement. Education that is responsive to cultural differences. This term was introduced in 1976 but further conceptualized in the 1990s.

1980s:

- **Culturally appropriate pedagogy** (Au & Jordan, 1981)—Instruction in which teachers integrate aspects of students' cultural background into their reading instruction.
- **Culturally congruent instruction** (Mohatt & Erickson, 1981)—Instruction in which teachers' language interaction patterns resembled students' home cultural patterns.
- **Culturally compatible education** (Vogt, Jordan, & Tharp, 1987)—Instructional practice, classroom organization, and motivation management that are compatible with students' culture and lead to academic achievement. Instruction that is specific to the culture.

1990s:

- **Culturally sensitive instruction** (Franklin, 1992)—Culturally sensitive instruction rests on six assumptions: (1) quality instruction should incorporate resources from the learner's environments outside the school parameters; (2) special education should not be the primary solution for African American learners whose cognitive and behavioral patterns are incompatible with schools' monocultural instructional methods; (3) African American learners' differences should not be perceived as genetic deficiencies but, rather, as sources of strength; (4) culturally sensitive teachers will identify and build on the learner's strengths and interests; (5) language and dialectical differences are important cultural influences that affect communication and the intersection between the teacher and learner; (6) culturally sensitive instruction should be integrated with activities that provide learners with opportunities to learn and practice new skills.
- **Culturally responsive pedagogy** (Jordan Irvine, 1990, 1992)—Teaching that, among other things, demonstrates an understanding and appreciation of students' personal cultural knowledge and uses students' prior knowledge and culture in teaching. It helps students of color become multicultural and multilingual.
- **Culturally relevant pedagogy** (Ladson-Billings, 1995)—Pedagogical practice that helps students become academically successful, cultivates cultural competence (helps students accept and affirm their cultural identities), and develops critical consciousness.

2000s:
- **Culturally mediated instruction** (Serverian-Wilmeth, 2002)—Instruction is culturally mediated when it incorporates and integrates diverse ways of knowing, understanding, and representing information.
- **Culturally based education** (Lipka et al., 2005)—Connections to students' experiences and prior knowledge that originate and often reside outside of the traditional school curriculum are brought into dialogue with the academic content knowledge taught in school.
- **Culturally responsive teaching** (Gay, 2002)—Culturally responsive teaching is defined as using the cultural characteristics, experiences, and perspectives of ethnically diverse students as conduits for teaching them more effectively. It is based on the assumption that when academic knowledge and skills are situated within the lived experiences and frames of reference of students, they are more personally meaningful, have higher interest appeal, and are learned more easily and thoroughly.
- **Culturally conscientious classroom** (Ukpokodu, 2006)—Culturally conscientious classrooms are defined by six principles of pedagogy:
    - Principle 1: Provide substantive work within a learning community.
    - Principle 2: Build on students' cultural and linguistic capital.
    - Principle 3: Make students' lives the starting point for learning.
    - Principle 4: Advocate on students' behalf.
    - Principle 5: Teach social activism and self-efficacy.
    - Principle 6: Work with families and communities to contextualize teaching and learning.

2010s:
- **Culturally and linguistically responsive teaching** (Hollie, 2011)—Culturally and linguistically responsive pedagogy is the validation and affirmation of the home (Indigenous) culture and home language for building and bridging the student to success in the culture of academia and mainstream society.
- **Culturally sustaining pedagogy** (Paris, 2012)—Pedagogy that maintains heritage, values, and cultural and linguistic pluralism. It has the explicit goal of sustaining and supporting bi/multilingualism and multiculturalism.

- **Culturally affirming education** (Allen et al., 2013)—Culturally affirming education extends the discussion of cultural relevancy because it does not simply implicate accommodation but rather affirmation. Affirming education means that one's background, culture, and experiences are viewed with high regard and esteem.
- **Critical culturally sustaining and revitalizing pedagogy** (McCarty & Lee, 2014)—An approach designed to address the sociohistorical and contemporary contexts of Native American schooling. It has three components: (1) it attends to the asymmetrical power relations and the goal of transforming legacies of colonization, (2) it recognizes the need to reclaim and revitalize what has been disrupted and displaced by colonization, and (3) it recognizes the need for community-based accountability.
- **Culturally proactive teaching** (Garcia & O'Donnell-Allen, 2015)—Teaching that anticipates students' needs in the context of 21st-century demands and adjusts teaching practice both preemptively and in the daily process of working with students in the classroom. It is teaching that requires ongoing vigilance, a sense of intentionality and urgency, and an awareness that this work must be initiated rather than prompted by others.
- **Culturally restorative teaching** (Re'vell, 2019)—A pedagogical approach that combines culturally responsive teaching, which centers students' cultural backgrounds as assets for learning, with restorative practices, which build community and address harm by fostering dialogue, accountability, and positive relationships.

2020s:
- **Culturally and historically responsive education** (Muhammad, 2020)—Culturally and historically responsive education is both a theory and a model to respond to students' histories, identities, literacies, and liberation in pedagogy. Youth voices are at the center.
- **Culturally inclusive pedagogy** (Thompson & Cuseo, 2020)—Inclusive pedagogy may be defined as a student-centered teaching process that motivates and engages students from all cultural backgrounds, allowing their voices to be heard and giving them opportunities for intercultural interaction.
- **Culturally connected instruction** (Powell, 2021)—Practices and instructional/policy decisions that intentionally (1) acknowledge

cultural realities and (2) work to create meaningful linkages between cultural perspectives and curricular content.
- **Culturally situated instruction** (Viner & Murphy, 2021)—The teacher constructs authentic, student-appropriate learning activities that will impart the objectives of the lessons to her students who have brought the sum of their internalized experiences to the event and can connect authentically to the totality of the unique learning milieu.
- **Culturally relevant and sustaining education** (Cole-Malott & Samuels, 2022)—Supports resisting and dismantling institutionalized racism, whiteness as an ideological stance, and the examination of critical race theory across diverse groups, situations, and identities, while also supporting the languages and cultures of children and communities.

Though a close, in-depth analysis of these terms is beyond the purview of this current work, a synthesis is useful in conveying the overarching tenets of the pedagogical theories. Theorists encourage educators to do the following when teaching racialized students:

1. Integrate home cultures, languages, communities, and broader societal contexts intentionally into the classroom.
2. Acknowledge, appreciate, and affirm students' cultures and languages.
3. View cultural knowledge, experiences, realities, and histories as conduits, vehicles, and foundations for learning.
4. Incorporate sociopolitical issues, recognize systemic barriers, and collaborate to dismantle inequities.
5. Preserve and/or restore the cultures and languages of marginalized communities.

Paris (2012) described them as "resource pedagogies" because they center students' culture, race, language, and other identities as resources to be drawn upon, not deficiencies to be overcome. This is education that seeks to reshape education that is rooted in whiteness. Scholars, educators, and advocates in the 21st century are still working to make multicultural education a reality in today's schools. In a 2022 report by the National Education Association, the organization's president emphasized the importance of these pedagogies:

> An established body of research affirms what educators have long known: a culturally responsive and racially inclusive education benefits all

students—and is the most effective pedagogical approach. These studies show that students who participate in ethnic studies and a curriculum that is culturally responsive and racially inclusive are more academically engaged, perform better academically, and graduate at higher rates. This pedagogical approach also facilitates many of the core goals of public education.

(paras. 1–2)

Through grassroots activism, whiteness as the default position in schools was challenged during the 1960s and 1970s. As a result of the efforts by justice workers to advance ethnic studies, multicultural education, and cultural difference studies, schools are more diverse, equitable, and inclusive than they were before the civil rights movement.

Still, outcomes for racially minoritized students lag behind the outcomes of white students. As Payne (2022, p. 14) stated in his insightful examination of school reform in Chicago, "We can point to some improvements yet come up well short of suggesting fundamental change." Love (2019, p. 90) described this work as "tugging at the system of injustice," while Duncan-Andrade (2022, p. 3) asserted that "a century of 'tinkering' has not fundamentally impacted outcomes for all children because it has been just that—tinkering." Love (2019, p. 90) offered a similar appraisal: "For centuries, we have tried to tweak, adjust, and reform systems of injustice. Ma (2026, p. 13) directed, "We cannot fix the machine, nor can we replace it with a better machine. We have to tear down the machine." These courageous efforts, righteous and just in their causes, are examples of the pursuit of freedom." She urged educators to replace the gimmicks and quick fixes with examinations of root causes. Villegas's (1988, pp. 262–263) estimation of cultural difference theories encapsulates my strong beliefs: "Culturally sensitive remedies to educational problems of oppressed minority students that ignore the political aspect of schooling are doomed to failure." To this end, her view of culturally responsive teaching includes teachers' sociocultural competence, which entails being aware of societal inequities and the roles that schools play in perpetuating and challenging those inequities (Villegas & Lucas, 2002). The work of educational justice is necessarily and unequivocally the work of getting to the root, which mandates disrupting white supremacy in schools, and, in fact, all societal institutions. Because we failed to purify the soil of white supremacy before planting, the trees of advancement are fragile.

I'm reminded of an interview Dr. Martin Luther King Jr. gave in 1967 when appraising the status of the civil rights movement. He acknowledged progress but lamented a lack of commitment to genuine equality.

It's much easier to integrate a lunch counter than it is to guarantee an annual income, for instance, to get rid of poverty for Negroes and all poor people. It's much easier to integrate a bus than it is to make genuine integration a reality, quality education a reality in our schools. It's much easier to integrate even a public park than it is to get rid of slums. I think we are in a new era, a new phase of the struggle where we have moved from a struggle for decency, which characterized our struggle for 10 or 12 years, to a struggle for genuine equality. And this is where we're getting the resistance, because there was never any intention to go this far.

(as cited in Hunsaker, 2021)

The white resistance to equality was strong, and the fight was never won. In other words, the United States never truly achieved genuine equality, or sameness in opportunities, resources, and access, in schooling. I appreciate the honesty and directness of Duncan-Andrade's (2022) judgment: "To be frank, it is absolutely absurd to talk about an equal education system in a nation that has spent nearly the entirety of its existence committed to ensuring inequality among its inhabitants" (p. 18). He argues that today's struggle must be for equity, which means ensuring what is fair and right instead of what is equal. It is the pursuit of equity—a tool for achieving justice by addressing disparities—that is meeting resistance today. This is the focus of Part II, the blighting of the fruit.

Questions to Ponder

1. In what ways do you think schooling for students of color is different than it was at its inception? The same?
2. How would you summarize the fruit bearing examined in this chapter?
3. Does culture always impact learning? Why or why not?
4. What facts and perspectives are missing from this historiography? What is the impact of this missing information?

Notes

1 Plyler v. Doe, 457 U.S. 202 (1982), No. 80-1538.
2 Yazzie/Martinez v. State of New Mexico, No. D-101-CV-2014-00793/No. D-101-CV-2014-02224.

Part II

The Blighting of the Fruit

Central questions answered: How and why is the fruit being blighted? Said differently, how and why are advancements toward educational justice being threatened? Who are the targets of these attacks?

4

Leading Up to the Blighting

The United States, in 2025, is experiencing a deliberate, strategic, violent attack on educational justice, one that is spearheaded by conservative elected officials, conservative think tanks, conservative organizations, conservative news outlets, conservative communities, and conservative families. MAGA. This powerful opposition aims to dismantle the hard-won gains by marginalized communities detailed in Chapters 2 and 3. Simply put, these regressive policies aim to keep white supremacy a forever part of the country's infrastructure—to keep white supremacy in the soil of the nation. And the conservative machine is succeeding. Like lava furiously building pressure underground, waiting to be violently expelled through the mouth of a volcano, today's onslaught of conservative legislation has been latently brewing for several years. The eruption is happening now. Or, to better align with the metaphor framing this book, the *blighting of the fruit* has been in operation underground for several years. This metaphor is taken from the foreword to Zora Neale Hurston's (1937/2018) *Their Eyes Were Watching God*, where Sherley Anne Williams wrote:

> And when we (to use Alice Walker's lovely phrase) go in search of our mother's gardens, it's not really to learn who trampled on them or how or even why—we usually know that already. Rather, it's to learn what our mothers planted there, what they thought as they sowed, and how they survived the blighting of so many fruits.

This section of the book focuses on the blighting, or the violent destruction, of so many fruits.

Patterson, Santiago, and Silverman (2021) wrote that civil rights advancements of the 1960s, while representing a watershed moment in history, were accompanied by backlash from opponents to racial justice.

It can be surmised, then, that whenever there is bearing of fruit, there is blighting of fruit. In 2009, the United States made history by electing its first Black president. Not only was he Black, but he had an Arabic name, Barack Hussein Obama. President Obama served for eight years (2009–2017), and during that time, he appointed the first Latina Supreme Court justice, Sonia Sotomayor, in 2009 and a white woman, Elena Kagan, in 2010. A Black man represented the executive branch of the federal government, and two women were added to the judicial branch, disrupting a long tradition of white men presidents and justices. Consequently, it is conceivable that a political party that opposes efforts to increase race and gender diversity was likely embittered by having to share power with people of color and women. Hundreds of years of white dominance had been disrupted, at least temporarily, leading some to suggest that the United States was becoming a postracial society, a society in which race has no significance. The rhetoric of racial transcendence raised questions about whether Obama's presidency had elevated the nation beyond race (Wise, 2010). Any beliefs about racial transcendence would soon be dispelled.

Widespread Commitment to Racial Justice or Something Else?

I was on the academic job market in 2020–2021, seeking a faculty position in teacher education. (Teacher education is a program that prepares students to work in PK–12 schools as classroom teachers. It is also a field of study that encompasses teaching, learning, curriculum, classroom management, and more.) The demand for scholars in teacher education who focus on racial justice was tremendous! Many of the postings, far more than usual, reflected an unusual interest in candidates with "a commitment to social justice," who viewed education through a "critical lens," or whose research centered "race and racism," namely, "anti-Black racism." They all required a diversity statement, an essay that describes applicants' experience with and approaches to working with diverse student populations. I submitted more application packages than I care to remember, was interviewed more than a dozen times, had several campus visits (virtually, because of Covid-19 restrictions), and received job offers for tenure-track faculty positions from each institution I visited, except one. Although it was an exhausting experience, I was encouraged by the interest in my work, specifically, but more so by the general commitment to educational justice that the academic job market suggested was there. Allow me to shed light on the sociopolitical context that might explain this sudden interest in social justice in teacher education. Keep in mind the interconnectedness between schools and society, explained in Part I. Systemic failures in the criminal justice system over the previous decade had led to institutions shining a spotlight on anti-Black racism.

Black Lives Matter (BLM)

In February 2012, Black teenager Trayvon Martin was killed by a member of a neighborhood watch association while visiting his father, leading to the formation of the Black Lives Matter movement. Eric Garner was killed by police officers in Staten Island in July 2014, and 12-year-old Tamir Rice was killed while playing at a neighborhood park in Cleveland later in the same year. Sandra Bland and Freddie Gray died while in police custody in 2015. Alton Sterling was killed by police in 2016. Bothan Jean was killed when an off-duty police officer entered his apartment and shot him. Elijah McClain was killed by police in August 2019. Atatiana Jefferson was killed by police in October 2019. Ahmaud Arbery was killed by white vigilantes in February 2020. Breonna Taylor was killed in her home by police in March 2020. All of these victims were Black. And, with the exceptions of Trayvon Martin and Ahmaud Arbery, they were all victims of state-sanctioned violence, or violence carried out by agents of the government.

These atrocities led to a spotlight being shined on a long-standing issue—unfair policing in the Black community. However, it was George Floyd's horrific murder on May 25, 2020, that catapulted anti-Black racism to the forefront of national and international consciousness. When Floyd was killed, people around the world were on lockdown because of the pandemic. Nonessential businesses and entertainment venues were closed, leisure travel was halted, and many employees were working from home. These conditions created a rare opportunity for the world to witness Floyd's murder. The rest of the world was coming to learn what the Black community already knew—that Black people have always been victims of state-sanctioned violence and dispensable to white supremacy. After Floyd's death, there were protests in cities and towns throughout the country, as many Americans expressed outrage at Derek Chauvin's brutality against Floyd. The Black Lives Matter movement, which began in 2013, intensified and spurred movements across the globe, with Black people leading racial justice protests in the United Kingdom, New Zealand, France, and other countries. (Remember that white supremacy is global.) *Forbes* reported that "more than 1,100 organizations committed a total of $200 billion to racial justice initiatives between June 2020 and May 2021" (Harper, 2022). Elected officials denounced police violence against the Black community, businesses offered proclamations, organizations adopted DEI statements, school systems established racial equity offices, and colleges/universities started recruiting faculty in varied fields who do racial justice work. This period became known as a "racial reckoning." Myths about being postracial were dispelled, emphatically.

Four additional tragedies against marginalized communities during this same period are worth noting: (1) The Charleston, South Carolina, church shooting in 2015 that left nine Black worshippers dead. (2) The Orlando, Florida, nightclub shooting in 2016, a violent attack on the LGBTQIA+ community, that resulted in 49 deaths. (3) The Pittsburgh, Pennsylvania, synagogue shooting in 2018 that took the lives of 11 members of a Jewish community. (4) The El Paso, Texas, Walmart shooting in 2019 that targeted Hispanic/Latino(x) individuals and left 23 dead. Undoubtedly, these hate crimes also contributed to the awakening to the violence experienced by racial, religious, sex, and gender minorities.

The Black Lives Matter movement, viewed by some as the modern-day civil rights movement, expanded from being focused mainly on criminal justice to educational justice with the formation of Black Lives Matter in Schools in 2017, an organization working toward the liberation of Black students. The Black Lives Matter in Schools (2025) movement put forth four demands: (1) end zero tolerance and implement restorative justice; (2) hire and retain Black teachers; (3) mandate Black history and ethnic studies; and (4) hire counselors, not cops. Taking its cue from the BLM movement that preceded it, BLM in Schools emphasized the importance of eliminating disparities in discipline for Black students and shifting from punitive to restorative responses to misbehavior. Society and schools shared a common foe—racial injustice that took the form of anti-Black racism.

BLM and the Covid-19 Pandemic

As stated earlier, around the same time that the nation elevated its focus on criminal justice, the Covid-19 pandemic began impacting the United States, demanding that light be shed on inequities in health care. The pandemic revealed widespread racial disparities in access and outcomes. African Americans were dying from Covid-19 at rates higher than any other ethnic group. Important, too, students of color were being negatively impacted by Covid-related school closures due to the digital divide, defined as a lack of access to technology and other resources needed for school success experienced by students of color compared to white students. In an article published in *The Washington Post*, UC-Berkeley professor Osagie K. Obasogie (2020) claimed, "Police killing Black people is a pandemic, too." A *New York Times* article echoed Obasogie's appraisal, describing the times as a "pandemic within a pandemic" (Stolberg, 2021). This overlap revealed a dire need to address systemic racism in society and in schools.

Race/Ethnicity-Centered Curricula

Curricular and pedagogical advances were occurring in PK–12 around this time as well. In August 2019, *The New York Times Magazine* published Nikole Hannah-Jones's *The 1619 Project*, commemorating the 400th anniversary of the arrival of the first enslaved Africans, which historians argue is not factually accurate. The central argument of Jones's project, however, is that the United States' founding was rooted in slavery and not in independence from Great Britain and that the American Revolution stemmed from a desire to protect the institution of slavery. This controversial publication was followed by a podcast, a book anthology, a children's picture book, and a documentary. Most significantly, *The New York Times Magazine* released curricula and resources to accompany the project so that schools can help students develop a different perspective (a counternarrative) on the nation's founding.

Moreover, access to ethnic studies, long viewed as a way to create more inclusive curricula (see Chapter 3), was expanding across the United States. For example, in 2020, Washington State passed SB 6066, calling for the development of a framework to support the teaching of ethnic studies to students in grades kindergarten through 12. Similarly, in 2020, Texas approved an elective high school course in African American studies, becoming the fifth state to do so. (The Texas State Board of Education had approved Mexican American studies two years prior.) North Dakota passed a bill in 2021 requiring the curriculum to include Native American studies. Connecticut passed a similar bill. Virginia formed the Culturally Relevant and Inclusive Education Practices Advisory Committee to strengthen culturally relevant education practices in 2020. This legislation and others were a continuation of the tree planting highlighted in the 1960s (Chapter 3). Those of us working to strengthen education for marginalized students nervously appreciated the progress and potential ushered in during this time of racial reckoning. Still, we feared the backlash. Benjamin (2022, p. 267) noted the following:

> One symbolic step forward, two violent steps backward—so is the history of white backlash in the United States. So long as competition and scarcity are the governing logics of our social order, what seems like advancement for subordinate groups will always be met with hostility from dominant ones.

She confirmed my belief that true progress demands the absolute destruction of white supremacy.

The Backlash

It was against this backdrop that the 21st-century culture wars in education escalated. The recent advancements in racial equity were built on the backs of Black suffering, and the fierce backlash came because of fear that the nation was moving too close to establishing justice for all. Historian Carol Anderson described the emotions that lead to a white, conservative backlash:

> The trigger for white rage, inevitably, is black advancement. It is not the mere presence of black people that is the problem; rather, it is blackness with ambition, with drive, with purpose, with aspirations, and with demands for full and equal citizenship. It is blackness that refuses to accept subjugation, to give up. A formidable array of policy assaults and

legal contortions has consistently punished black resilience, black resolve (Anderson, 2017, p. 3).

It can be concluded, then, that Black advancement and resilience—in social, political, and economic spheres—gave birth to white rage that fueled the culture wars.

Though the culture wars themselves weren't new, the attacks that began in 2020 and continue in 2025 are particularly threatening and disheartening. These regressive conservative attacks that have occurred since 2020 mainly have several targets: critical race theory (CRT), or more accurately, what was perceived as CRT, and social and emotional learning (SEL). These attacks have implications for all students but especially students of color, LGBTQIA+ students, immigrant students, emergent bilinguals, and religious minorities.

The continued onslaught against educational justice was outlined in Project 2025, a federal policy agenda published by the Heritage Foundation, a conservative think tank, in 2023. Despite Trump's campaign claims to have never read or seen the 900-page document, he is, unequivocally, following its guidance. He praised the foundation during his campaign and admitted to their influence, saying, "This is a great group and they're going to lay the groundwork and detail plans for exactly what our movement will do" (Hillyard & Marquez, 2024). By July 31, 2025, Trump had signed 176 executive orders (from EO 14147 through EO 14322) since taking office for his second term (*Federal Register*, 2025). A *Los Angeles Times* article drew attention to these alignments:

> [J]ust as *Project 2025* envisioned, Trump as president has pursued aggressive immigration enforcement, ordered a dramatic downsizing of the federal workforce in favor of loyalists, started dismantling the Department of Education, ordered new restrictions on voting, attempted to seize the power of the federal purse from Congress, set out to defund public media institutions and targeted transgender people with an array of threats, regulations and restrictions.
>
> One prominent community tracking project says Trump has already implemented more than 40% of *Project 2025*'s recommendations. To help usher in those changes, he has appointed a cadre of *Project 2025* contributors to powerful positions in his administration.
>
> (Rector, 2025)

Even though executive orders alone have little actual power, they can influence public perceptions and often serve as models for state policies. The next two chapters delve into the blighting of the fruit. These white supremacist attacks have led to racism, sexism, heterosexism, and gender binarism in schools.

Questions to Ponder

1. What other factors might have led to the MAGA blighting that will be examined in the next two chapters?
2. This chapter refers to Trump conservatives' actions as blighting. How might someone with a different perspective see these actions?

5

Blighting the Fruit: Opposition to CRT and DEI

At the outset of this examination into the opposition to critical race theory (CRT) and diversity, equity, and inclusion (DEI), I want to revisit my early years as a middle school English teacher. When I started teaching in 1998, there was little to no national discussion on how to improve outcomes for marginalized students. Then, in 2001, President George W. Bush (Republican) introduced the landmark No Child Left Behind Act,[1] legislation that sought to overhaul schooling. With its focus on teacher quality, standardized tests, accountability, and school choice, NCLB was met with strong criticism. Significantly, however, NCLB required schools and school districts to disaggregate student assessment data by racial/ethnic groups, economically disadvantaged students, students with disabilities, and limited English proficient (LEP) students. The goal was to shed light on "subgroups" that had been historically underserved and consequently experienced achievement gaps, defined as persistent, significant disparities between groups. Schools were compelled to use disaggregated data to create interventions, supports, curricula changes, and resources that would ensure that all students had a fair chance at academic success. These efforts to reduce the achievement gap, initiated by a conservative president, were attempts at equity. Instead of ignoring or denying that different considerations should be made for marginalized students who had a history of structural disadvantages, educators were encouraged to mitigate the effects of these disadvantages through equitable teaching practices. It is this attention to long-standing differences in access, resources, and opportunities that is being targeted through Trump conservatives' opposition to "CRT" and DEI.

In discussions about the conservative opposition to educational justice, CRT and DEI are sometimes conflated, as both are viewed as "woke" ideology, a term used disparagingly by Trump conservatives to describe efforts to make society just. "Woke" actually means to be aware of the ways society restricts the freedom of marginalized individuals and to be committed to liberation for all. (Read more about my conception of woke pedagogy in "Woke Pedagogy: A Framework for Teaching and Learning"). This chapter analyzes both CRT and DEI and the impact they've had on both PK–12 and higher education since 2020.

Critical Race Theory (CRT)

CRT was conceived in the mid-1970s by Derrick Bell at Harvard University School of Law but made its way to the field of education in 1995 by Gloria Ladson-Billings and William F. Tate in their landmark article, "Toward a Critical Race Theory in Education." Ladson-Billings stated the following in a 2022 interview: "Critical race theory is a theoretical tool that began in legal studies, in law schools, in an attempt to explain racial inequity. It serves the same function in education" (quoted in Anderson, 2022). To explain further, when used in education, CRT is a set of beliefs—an ideology—that helps researchers in education explain the existence of long-standing disparities in outcomes between students of color and white students and differential treatment experienced by students of color. CRT is theory that has been supported by decades of scholarship, but still, not all scholars in education accept this theory, and not all scholars who study race draw upon it in their research and scholarship.

Consequently, CRT is just one theory among many theories used by researchers to help them interpret data and explain phenomena. Other race-related critical theories include Black critical theory/Black crit, Native American critical theory/Tribal crit, Latina/o critical theory/Latcrit, and Asian American critical theory/Asiancrit. Because CRT is a theoretical approach used by researchers, most people don't study critical race theory until graduate school when conducting academic research. I was a teacher for many years and had never encountered the term before my doctoral studies. During my first research study as a first-year doctoral student and emerging researcher, I examined how desegregation in the Fort Worth Independent School District (Texas) impacted a local community, which was at that time an all-Black community (Caldera, 2023). My findings— from data collected through interviews with community members affected by the closing of the Black high school, examination of artifacts, and analysis of newspaper articles—were illuminated by critical race theory, among other theories.

CRT is used by researchers in a variety of fields, not just education, and not all education scholars are critical race theorists. CRT theory is not taught in public schools. To be fair, however, some education policies and practices might be shaped by research that is informed by CRT. For example, a central, shared belief of critical race theorists in education is that institutional racism impacts the experiences and outcomes of students of color. As a result, critical race theorists examining school discipline would likely see racism as a central reason for discipline disparities between white students, and students of color and might propose policies that mitigate the impact of racism. Similarly, critical race theorists in education might purport that schools reflect white supremacy and might have come to this conclusion by examining school funding schemes that create underresourced schools attended by mostly Black and Latino(x) students. Understanding and revealing how white supremacy and white privilege show up in schools is a key function of CRT. For these reasons "CRT" became a perfect label to summarize the key beliefs Trump conservatives reject—that race matters, white privilege exists, and white supremacy dominates institutions. The next section examines how the attacks on "CRT" originated and the negative implications of these attacks.

Attacks on CRT

In response to what has been called the nation's "racial reckoning," a plan to inhibit the surge of justice work that had just begun was on the horizon. The conservative response to efforts to make Black lives matter should be viewed as exactly what it is—backlash and retaliation. This powerful propaganda was set into place, in part, by Christopher Rufo, a conservative activist who described himself as a "brawler" (Wallace-Wells, 2021). It started in July 2020 when an employee in Seattle undergoing antibias training sent the training documents to Rufo, who wrote an article about the training for a conservative newspaper (Wallace-Wells, 2021). This article garnered widespread attention, and employees from all over the country began sending Rufo copies of their companies' antibias and antiracism training (Wallace-Wells, 2021). By studying the references and footnotes in these materials, Rufo found that "the anti-racism seminars did not just represent a progressive view on race but that they were expressions of a distinct ideology—critical race theory" (Wallace-Wells, 2021). Instead of seeing antibias training as attempts to better ensure that workplaces are more diverse, equitable, and inclusive, Rufo began criticizing the work, often sharing his commentaries about what he called "CRT" on Tucker Carlson and other conservative talk shows (Wallace-Wells, 2021). (I enclose CRT in quotations when referring to the intentional conservative misuse of the term.)

In one of his appearances on Tucker Carlson, Rufo said that he was "declaring a one-man war against critical race theory in the federal government" (Stelter, 2020). He went on to say, "I'm not going to stop these investigations until we can abolish it within our public institutions" (Stelter, 2020). He tweeted on August 20, 2020, "My goal is simple: to persuade the President of the United States to issue an executive order abolishing critical race theory in the federal government" (Stelter, 2020). Shortly thereafter, Rufo assisted in drafting Executive Order 13950 that was issued on September 22, 2020, by then-President Trump, limiting how federal contractors providing federal diversity seminars could talk about race. President Biden reversed this order in January 2021. Trump's ban was short-lived, but the damage had already been done.

Rufo described "CRT" as "the perfect villain" (Wallace-Wells, 2021). He went on, "Its connotations are all negative to most middle-class Americans, including racial minorities, who see the world as 'creative' rather than 'critical,' 'individual' rather than 'racial,' 'practical' rather than 'theoretical.' Strung together, the phrase 'critical race theory' connotes hostile, academic, divisive, race-obsessed, poisonous, elitist, anti-American" (Wallace-Wells, 2021). So, in the words of Rufo himself, "This entire movement [against CRT] came from nothing" (Wallace-Wells, 2021).

Over the next two years, the "anti-CRT movement" turned into highly effective, deeply harmful right-wing propaganda designed to unite conservatives who were already discontent about a myriad of issues that had led to resistance movements—from the Black Lives Matter movement (Defund the Police[2]) to immigration on the southern border (Abolish ICE[3]) to Native Americans' demand for visibility and land repossession (the Land Back movement[4]). Moreover, the anti-"CRT" campaign ignited some white people who already held fears about being displaced and replaced by people of color, who are already the global majority and will soon become the majority in the United States. This fear, which has been called *white anxiety*, has been capitalized on by conservative politicians who incite their base with concerns about a loss of national identity and antiwhite discrimination. Attacking "CRT" was a way to rally those who'd rather ignore the historical and present-day realities of racism because their whiteness shields them from having to acknowledge and confront racism, unlike people of color who are forced to reckon with it as a part of our everyday lives. These conservative Americans want to move into a race-blind future without first acknowledging and accounting for the lasting effects of hundreds of years of systemic racial oppression and the present-day racism experienced by people of color. They readily jumped on the "anti-CRT" bandwagon, though most of them held very little knowledge of the term. As I wrote in a 2021 editorial, "Although many of those who denounce CRT don't understand its tenets or purpose, they do recognize that it requires a critical examination of race and racism," work that they find insignificant, though its relevance lies in their insistence that it be avoided. Conservative think tank Texas Public Policy Foundation (2021) included the following concepts as "CRT" buzzwords to help parents recognize CRT in schools:

- equity
- social justice
- systemic racism
- antiracism
- white privilege
- colonialism

This list reveals that the true opposition is to any efforts to bring about racial justice in schools. In essence, the term "CRT" was an easy way for conservatives to oppose (what one would think are) the fundamental principles of our democracy without actually naming this opposition. In a July 2021 article in the *Fairfax County Times*, ironically a school district where I've conducted antiracism workshops, the author's title declared to readers, "Yes, Virginia—there is Critical Race Theory in our schools" (Schultz, 2021). The reality is that it's highly unlikely that CRT is being taught in any PK–12 school. It's important to know that anti-CRT legislation was based on an intentional, strategic misnomer.

Anti-CRT Legislation

With Rufo's assistance, by the fall of 2020, state legislators, using language that was nearly identical to that found in Trump's executive ban, had begun drafting model "anti-CRT" legislation that sought to restrict race-related curricula and limit diversity training for educators. In 2020–2021, more than a dozen states introduced such laws, and a handful were passed. Texas, where I was living at the time, was one of the first states to pass anti-CRT legislation. As an education policy fellow for the Intercultural Development Research Organization (IDRA), an education policy and advocacy organization based in San Antonio, Texas, I worked alongside other advocates to stop this harmful legislation, but after a highly contentious and dubious path to the governor's desk, Governor Greg Abbott signed the bill, SB 3, into law on September 17, 2021. Though these laws didn't ban "critical race theory" outright, they prohibited the following:

- teaching about anything that makes students feel discomfort, guilt, anguish, or any other form of psychological distress
- books that promote certain ideas about race
- requiring students to engage in or observe a discussion of public policy
- promoting or including particular ideas about sex or race superiority
- discussing controversial issues or divisive concepts
- presenting any version of American history other than established truths
- portraying the country's founders in a negative light

This state's laws against "CRT" impacted local school districts immediately. I witnessed this impact firsthand in my Texas county. Two examples come to mind. The first incident happened in Colleyville, Texas, an affluent suburb of Fort Worth with a white population near 80%. The principal of Colleyville High School, Dr. James Whitfield, became a victim of the "anti-CRT" attacks. *The Texas Tribune* reported that during the summer of racial reckoning in 2020 following the murder of George Floyd, Mr. Whitfield wrote a letter to families of his students acknowledging the impact of racism in the United States (Lopez, 2021). He's quoted as saying, "Education is the key to stomping out ignorance, hate, and systemic racism," and "It's a necessary conduit to get 'liberty and justice for all.'" His letter went largely unnoticed until the Texas legislature, in late 2020 and early 2021, ushered in arguments about whether schools were teaching students that the United States is a racist country. In July 2021, a former school board candidate accused Mr. Whitfield of advancing "critical race theory." The school board placed Mr. Whitfield on leave, accusing him of causing division in the district. He later resigned.

Similarly, in the school district adjacent to Colleyville, Carroll Independent School District, district administration responded to repeated racist behavior from students by forming a diversity council that spent two years designing a plan to help the district become more respectful of cultural diversity. In 2021, NBC News reported

> The result of the effort—a 34-page document known as the Cultural Competence Action Plan—was made public in July. It called for mandatory cultural sensitivity training for all Carroll students and teachers, a formal process for reporting and tracking incidents of racist bullying, and changes to the code of conduct to hold students accountable for acts of discrimination. The plan also proposed creating a new position at Carroll, director of equity and inclusion, to oversee the district's efforts.
>
> (Hixenbaugh, 2021)

When the plan was presented to the board in the fall of 2020, the Texas state legislature was embroiled in fervent arguments over its "anti-CRT" bill, and these arguments ignited conservatives in Carroll ISD. A powerful, wealthy parent group, characterizing it as critical race theory, contested the plan, resulting in its being halted by a judge. I criticized the district's failure to protect students of color by following through with the plan in an editorial published in a local newspaper. I wrote, "It comes as no surprise that the mostly white, affluent parents oppose initiatives aimed at racial parity. Whiteness always tries to protect its position at the top of the racial hierarchy, and the primary tool of protection is avoidance" (Caldera, 2021b).

In "The Race to Ban Race," Miller, Fernandez, and Hutchens (2023, p. 64) commented on the spread of "anti-CRT" legislation to higher education: Most of the current legislative bans on "CRT" primarily focus on curriculum in elementary and secondary education, such as limiting course content and course materials. However, lawmakers in nearly thirty states have also introduced bills targeting "CRT" or other "divisive concepts" in higher education. Lantz and Carter (2024) expressed several concerns that these bans, among other things, ignore the fact that racism and sexism are produced and replicated beyond interpersonal acts of discrimination and will fail to prepare students for work where understanding causes, consequences, and potential solutions to complex social problems is fundamental.

Anti-CRT bans have the potential to impact teacher preparation in higher education. If preservice teachers are forbidden from learning the truth about racism as part of their teacher training, they will not develop racial literacy, which I define as having the willingness to acknowledge the impact of race, the ability to recognize the existence of historical and present-day racism, and the skills for examining the effects of race and racisms on individuals and groups. The truth is that opponents hate actual critical race theory, but they love "CRT" because "CRT" (the language) has been an effective weapon against educational justice.

After tracking legislation through December 31, 2024, CRT Forward, an initiative of the Critical Race Studies Program at UCLA School of Law, reported the following:

> Since September 2020, a total of 249 local, state, and federal government entities across the United States have introduced 870 anti-Critical Race Theory bills, resolutions, executive orders, opinion letters, statements, and other measures.

A graphic from CRT Forward (Figure 5.1) illustrates the increase since 2020 (used with permission).

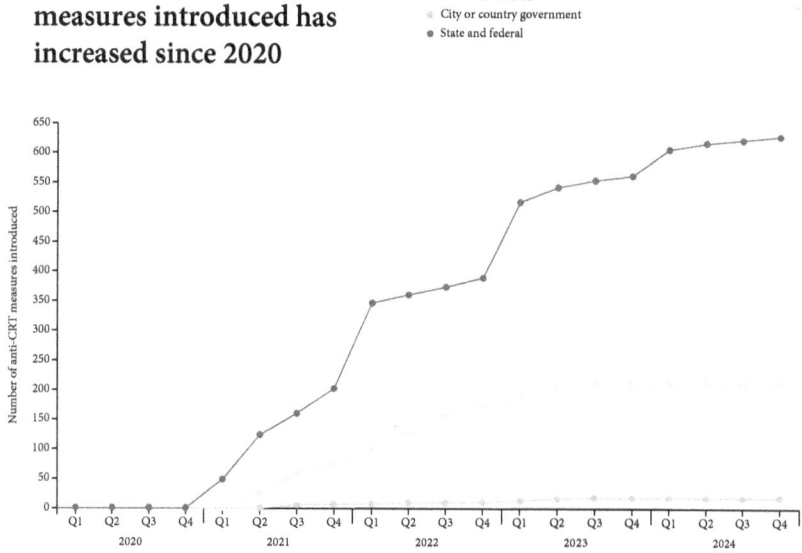

Figure 5.1 Increase in Anti-CRT Legislation Since 2020.

Anti-CRT laws have been passed in the following states:

1. Alabama (public schools and higher education)
2. Arkansas
3. Arizona
4. Florida (public schools and higher education)
5. Georgia
6. Iowa (public schools and higher education)
7. Idaho (public schools and higher education)
8. Indiana
9. Kentucky
10. Maine
11. Missouri
12. Mississippi (public schools and higher education)
13. North Carolina
14. North Dakota (public schools and higher education)
15. New Hampshire (public schools and higher education)
16. Ohio
17. Oklahoma (public schools and higher education)
18. South Carolina
19. South Dakota (public schools and higher education)
20. Tennessee (public schools and higher education)
21. Texas
22. Utah
23. Virginia

Shortly after taking office in January 2025, Trump issued Executive Order 13985, "Ending Radical Indoctrination in K–12 Schooling," bolstering existing anti-CRT legislation and possibly inspiring future policies.

CRT and Social & Emotional Learning (SEL)

Alongside CRT resistance is opposition to social and emotional learning. I wasn't shocked by the attacks on CRT, but I must admit that I was taken aback by states' attempts to pass anti-SEL legislation. I couldn't understand why conservatives would want to resist schools' efforts to meet students' social and emotional needs, in addition to their academic needs. Besides, many scholars questioned the merits of SEL for racially marginalized students, seeing it as lacking cultural responsiveness and criticality (Attaya & Hilliard, 2023; Camangian & Cariaga, S., 2021; McCall et al., 2022). Their observation is understandable, considering that the definition of SEL from the Collaborative for Academic, Social, and Emotional Learning (CASEL), the leading organizational proponent for social-emotional learning, doesn't acknowledge the impact of culture in SEL in its definition:

> SEL is the process through which all young people and adults acquire and apply the knowledge, skills, and attitudes to develop healthy identities, manage emotions and achieve personal and collective goals, feel and show empathy for others, establish and maintain supportive relationships, and make responsible and caring decisions.

However, CASEL has made an explicit commitment to equity and excellence through social and emotional learning and lists *transformative social and emotional learning*, defined as focusing on "skills needed to ensure democratic, fair, and inclusive communities," as a form of SEL that schools may consider. Transformative SEL has the potential "to mitigate the educational, social, and economic inequities that derive from the interrelated legacies of racialized cultural oppression in the United States" (McGee et al., 2021). Ostensibly, then, this is likely where the conservative problem lies: SEL has been linked to equity.

Additionally, embedded in CASEL's SEL competencies is learning that Trump conservatives adamantly oppose, whether explicitly or implicitly: cultural diversity, justice, cultural competency, and standing up for the rights of others. Important, too, is the possibility that the principles of SEL will foster solidarity among the oppressed and between the oppressed and the privileged, and the far right finds solidarity threatening. When students are able to see from the perspective of someone who is positioned differently on the social hierarchy, understand feelings held by diverse others, and collaborate effectively with diverse communities, they can begin to work together to dismantle an unjust system.

Attacks on SEL and Anti-SEL Legislation

The title of a 2023 article published by the American Psychological Association sounded an alarm—teaching social-emotional learning is under attack (Abrams, 2023). It can be deduced that Trump conservatives attacked SEL because of (1) its potential to advance educational equity, (2) its emphasis on understanding social and political contexts, and (3) the possibility of developing inter- and intragroup solidarity. They have been successful at equating SEL to CRT, and unfortunately this false claim has gained traction. Teaching socio-emotional learning is part of the "woke agenda," they accuse. Still, most anti-SEL attacks have played out in the state agency and at the local level. Fortunately, very few states have introduced or passed legislation. In 2022, the following states introduced legislation to restrict SEL implementation:

- Arizona SB 1211 (failed)
- Indiana HB 1134 (failed)
- Kansas HB 2662 (failed)
- Missouri HB 2189 (failed), SB 810 (failed), SB 645 (failed)
- Oklahoma SB 1442 (failed)
- Virginia HB 781 (failed)
- West Virginia HB 4016 (failed)
- Wisconsin SB 411 (failed)

Between 2023 and 2025, eight states (Montana, North Dakota, Iowa, Oklahoma, Maine, Indiana, Alabama, and Kentucky) have introduced legislation specifically restricting or banning social-emotional learning. Most anti-SEL bills have been introduced in Oklahoma and Iowa (Committee for Children, personal communication, July 30, 2025).

Significantly, no explicit bills to ban SEL have passed at the state level. Two have passed that introduce restrictions or remove mandates (Indiana passed HB 1002 this year, which removes certain requirements to teach social-emotional competencies in the classroom). These anti-SEL bills have been introduced and then soundly defeated thanks to strong advocacy and community support.

The propaganda that we've witnessed over the last several years has succeeded largely because of an unexamined use and misapplication of the term *critical race theory*, which has led to purposeful mischaracterization of racial equity work in schools. Unfortunately, Rufo's agenda has been successful in conflating racial equity and antiracist work with critical race theory. Their achievement cannot be discounted. Anti-CRT sentiments flowed naturally into anti-DEI ideology.

Diversity, Equity, and Inclusion (DEI)

When I think of *diversity*, I envision, of course, a forest with a plethora of trees—oak, pine, pecan, cedar, magnolia, and more. When related to humans, diversity means the existence of identity differences, including but not limited to gender, race, ethnicity, language, ability, sexuality, religion, socioeconomic status, age, national origin, and geographic religion. As a value, diversity is an appreciation for many perspectives, voices, experiences, and cultural backgrounds. Those who embrace this ideology believe that environments are stronger, more powerful, more rewarding, and more complex when they are composed of diverse individuals and groups; consequently, they intentionally strive to bring together people who hold a multitude of identities. To clarify, an individual cannot be diverse, but an individual can contribute to the diversity of a group. Through laws and policies that prevent discrimination and promote access, schools, organizations, businesses, and other institutions can become more diverse.

Equity is needed because diverse societies have failed to treat individuals and groups fairly. In that case, equity, then, is fairness. Proponents of equity insist on the recognition of differences and demand that responses to individual and community needs are rooted in an awareness of the ways systems have created disparities in access and opportunities. Different forms of equity are needed for educational justice—racial equity, gender equity, language equity, and more. *Equity* is distinguished from *equality* in its emphasis on difference. Whereas *equality* is the state of sameness, or upholding the same rights for everyone, *equity* is about doing what is fair as a response to long-standing systemic biases , or the legacy of white supremacy.

If diversity is the *what*, inclusion is the *now what?* Now that diversity exists in a given space, what can be done to make sure that all identities are represented? Said differently, inclusion asks, "What can be done to make sure that each individual's and group's perspectives, voices, experiences, and cultural backgrounds are embraced?" Its premise is based on the recognition that individuals who hold certain social identities have not been meaningfully included in the institutions that comprise society. Inclusion, then, is an expression of respect for historically marginalized groups that is shown through purposeful validation and integration. To be included is to have the full rights of citizenship. What the far right finds threatening about DEI is that DEI is more than an ideology; it is a framework from which to see who is afforded the full rights of citizenship and who is not.

Diversity, Equity, and Inclusion: Origins

Diversity, equity, and inclusion as professional practice has a pointed origin—the civil rights movement with its corresponding legislation and judicial decisions, outlined in Chapter 2 (Kratz, 2024). DEI is perhaps most closely associated with the affirmative action decision in *Regents of the University of California v. Bakke* (1978) and, among others, the following federal legislation:

> Equal Pay Act of 1963
> Title VII of the Civil Rights Act of 1964
> Age Discrimination in Employment Act of 1967
> Equal Employment Opportunity (EEO) Act of 1972

To illustrate, the EEO Act forbade employers from discrimination in hiring, resulting in workplaces becoming more diverse. As the EEO Act brought about workplace diversity, a need for dedicated professionals to lead diversity initiatives and tailor them to an organization's needs emerged in the 1990s (Kratz, 2024). This led to new roles like chief diversity officers and vice presidents of diversity, with diversity training following in the 2000s (Kratz, 2024). Affirmative action caused colleges and universities to become more diverse. In many cases, these offices have been lifelines for the marginalized.

Moreover, diversity, equity, and inclusion has historically situated itself in institutions of higher education. In "Where Did DEI Come From?" Charles (2023) wrote,

> DEI was formed and reshaped by political crises. What we know as DEI today emerged from the smoke, fire, and ash of hundreds of urban uprisings following the assassination of the Rev. Martin Luther King Jr. in 1968. The killing of the country's most visible civil-rights leader forced higher education to reckon with both the demands of minorities, in that case Black Americans, and its own legacy of racism.

The rise of DEI offices post–Dr. King's assassination and post–George Floyd's murder suggests that commitment to DEI work is often a response to crises rather than a way to prevent them. I cautioned readers about this reactionary, often temporary, positioning in DEI work in higher education in a 2021 article I wrote for a special issue journal on anti-blackness in education.

> It is important to remember that this work must not devolve into a fad or trending topic. It must not be rhetorical grandstanding or performative gestures. To the contrary, when institutions' statements and resolutions against anti-Black racism have begun to collect dust, we must hold true to our commitment to the liberation of Black students, many of whom are multiply marginalized. We must do this work until there is a real racial reckoning birthed from authentic accountability and radical responsibility.
> (Caldera, 2021a, p. 3)

The same is true for DEI work. It must be ongoing, authentic, and always fervent. Out of necessity, it has become a tool for establishing justice locked up in legislative acts and court rulings. Though DEI is still evolving, both ideologically and pragmatically, the dismantling of white supremacy must always be its goal. The precarity of the state of the work and the impermanence of its achievements exist mainly because of concerted conservative opposition.

Attacks on DEI

Since 2023, the attacks in higher education have been similar to the previous ones on CRT and led by the same conservative perpetrators. Though the language had changed from "CRT" to "DEI," the most recent attacks are against what they have always been against—educational justice. The opposition finally got the courage to name their enemy—diversity, equity, and inclusion. Attacks against DEI, specifically in higher education, have been spurred by Trump conservatives advancing the following myths, which are analyzed and refuted with research by Harper et al. (2024):

1. DEI initiatives are divisive.
2. Too much money is spent on DEI initiatives.
3. DEI initiatives are universally low quality.
4. All DEI initiatives place people into two categories: privileged and oppressed.

5 DEI initiatives are all the same.
6 DEI and critical race theory are synonymous.
7 DEI programs poison campus environments.
8 Too-woke DEI professionals have taken over campuses.

These myths created a narrative that propelled a deluge of anti-DEI legislation.

Anti-DEI Legislation

I saw the impact of this legislation firsthand when an employee who's part of a community college consortium in West Texas reached out to me about conducting professional development workshops in late May 2023. She had read one of my *Education Week* editorials and wanted me to design a workshop that would help faculty and staff better meet the needs of their growing population of students of color. She was careful in the framing of her request because there were, at the time, several anti-DEI bills being considered in the 88th Texas legislature. Two weeks after I received her email, on June 14, 2023, SB 17/HB 5127 was signed into law by Governor Greg Abbott. The section of the bill related to diversity, equity, and inclusion spells out the prohibition: "An institution of higher education may not establish or maintain a diversity, equity, and inclusion office or hire or assign an employee of the institution, or contract with a third party, to perform the duties of the diversity, equity, and inclusion office." Although the bill goes on to say that "guest speakers or performers who may be invited to perform at an institution of higher education for short-term engagements" are not included in the DEI restriction, the Texas legislature had put fear into employees at public institutions of higher education, who were uncertain about what they could and could not do under the new law. The institution did not contract with me to do any work.

Though I no longer lived in Texas when I received the request, I was very familiar with Texas education politics. During the 87th legislative session in 2020–2021, I worked as an education policy fellow for the Intercultural Development Research Association (IDRA). As a policy fellow, I advocated for equitable education policy for racially marginalized postsecondary students in Texas. In my work, I identified and advocated for opportunities to expand access to and ensure success in postsecondary education institutions, particularly for students of color. I believed then, as I do now, that to ensure the success of students of color in higher education, faculty demographics should better reflect the diversity of the student body. Students of color deserve to be taught by faculty who share their cultural backgrounds, so institutions of higher education should be mandated to make faculty diversity a priority. I drafted a faculty diversification bill that was filed by Senators Menendez and Blanco, SB 1709,[5] but, unsurprisingly, did not make it out of committee hearings. In 2023 during the 88th legislative session, Senator Menendez et al. refiled the faculty diversity bill I had written two years prior. SB 2194[6] included the following mandates:

> Each institution of higher education shall develop a five-year, research-based plan to increase racial diversity among faculty members at the institution. The plan must include… strategies for increasing racial diversity among faculty members to the extent necessary to reflect the racial diversity of the institution's student population.

Again, it was left pending in committee. In fact, in the 2023 Texas legislative session, multiple anti-DEI bills were filed, including one prohibiting the consideration of race as a factor in hiring at state universities (SB 5140[7]).

In 2021, the "anti-DEI machine" had been at work against highly acclaimed journalist Nikole Hannah-Jones, who had been offered an endowed chair position with tenure at the University of North Carolina, but the university's board of trustees took the highly unusual step of failing to approve the journalism department's recommendation (Wamsley, 2021). Then the university offered Hannah-Jones a five-year appointment without tenure. She declined. This debacle happened because of criticism of her Pulitzer Prize–winning work, *The 1619 Project*, a book that explores the legacy of slavery (Wamsley, 2021). Similarly, in the summer of 2023, Kathleen O. McElroy, a respected journalist with a long career, accepted the position to run the new program and teach as a tenured professor, pending approval from the Texas A&M University System Board of Regents (McGee, 2023). Shortly thereafter, the "anti-DEI machine" began its take-down by those concerned with her work on race and diversity. McElroy went from being offered a tenured position on A&M's faculty to a one-year contract in which she would be subject to dismissal at will. She declined the offer (McGee, 2023).

For many academics in higher education, this opposition reached a critical juncture in January 2024 when Dr. Claudine Gay, who made history in 2023 when she was appointed the first Black president at

Harvard University, was forced to resign after unfounded accusations of anti-Semitism (Alfonseca, 2024). Her appointment alone angered some who saw her as a diversity hire, during a time when Harvard was already under a spotlight for its affirmative action policy (Alfonseca, 2024). Dr. Gay, whose scholarship focuses, in part, on race, was dethroned by the same "machine" and the same man, Christopher Rufo, who initiated the anti-CRT movement. Politico, who published an interview with Rufo, began the article, "Christopher Rufo has done it again" (Ward, 2024). The article seems to praise Rufo's unscrupulous tactics. "None of that happened by accident…. Gay's resignation was the result of a coordinated and highly organized conservative campaign" (Ward, 2024).

The messaging of "the machine" is powerful enough to change allies into adversaries, despite its inaccuracy and lack of clarity. As an example, *The Salt Lake Tribune* reported that in January 2021, Utah's Governor Spencer Cox signed the Utah Compact on Racial Equity, Diversity and Inclusion and encouraged staff to do the same (Pierce, 2024). After three years of conservative rhetoric, in January 2024 he completely reversed his stance by signing HB 261, Utah's anti-DEI bill. Governor Cox, in three short years, devolved from endorsing a statement that encouraged institutions of higher education to "acknowledge that racism exists, and our actions make a difference. We call out racism wherever we see it and take purposeful steps to stop it," (Richardson, 2020) to forcing public colleges and universities to remove "diversity, equity, and inclusion" from their program names (Pierce, 2024).

Anti-DEI legislation gained momentum in 2025 under the second Trump administration. In Executive Order 14173, "Ending Illegal Discrimination and Restoring Merit-Based Opportunity," Trump opened the order with what sounds like a commitment to civil rights:

> "Longstanding Federal civil-rights laws protect individual Americans from discrimination based on race, color, religion, sex, or national origin. These civil-rights protections serve as a bedrock supporting equality of opportunity for all Americans. As President, I have a solemn duty to ensure that these laws are enforced for the benefit of all Americans."

Yet his true intention shows up in the next paragraph as he claimed that race- and sex-based preferences are immoral, leading to his denouncement of diversity, equity, and inclusion (DEI) and diversity, equity, inclusion, and accessibility (DEIA). He went on to claim that merit (hard work, excellence, and individual achievement) are undermined by an identity-based system. In other words, Trump believes that race and sex don't matter, only merit, so efforts to make institutions diverse, equitable, and inclusive must end. This order ends DEI practices in the federal government promoting diversity and practicing affirmative action, impacting federal employers, agencies, contractors, and subcontractors.

One of the most discussed 2025 cases involving DEI restrictions in higher education involves one of the country's Ivy League institutions—Harvard University. Harvard had recently suffered a blow to DEI when the Supreme Court ruled in *SFFA v. Harvard* (2023) against race-conscious admissions in higher education, causing colleges and universities to rethink their approach to DEI. The Trump administration has pressured Harvard by freezing billions of dollars in federal grants to the university until demands are met for the university to make significant changes to its governance, hiring practices, admissions, and DEI programs. These demands also required Harvard to address its "failure to condemn anti-Semitism and protect Jewish students on campus" (Quinn & Rosen, 2025, para. 5). Though it initially resisted the DEI ban and sued the Trump administration, Harvard has since made the following changes, among others:

1 Diversity statements in hiring were canceled.
2 Harvard's chief diversity officer is now retitled as the university's chief community and campus life officer.
3 The Office of Equity, Diversity, Inclusion, and Belonging has been changed to Community and Campus Life. (Josephy & Yu, 2025)

In a similar manner, Columbia University, accused by the federal government of anti-Semitism leading to workplace harassment, settled with the Trump administration for $200 million. Though the university did not admit to any wrongdoing in its handling of the pro-Palestinian protests, the university president vowed to combat all forms of hatred and discrimination (Columbia Office of the President, nd). Under federal pressure to cancel its DEI initiatives, Columbia agreed to not use "race, color, sex, or national origin in hiring decisions," to not "unlawfully preference applicants based on race, color, or national origin in admission," and to not "maintain programs that promote unlawful efforts to achieve race-based outcomes, quotas, diversity targets, or similar efforts" (quoted in Nadworny & Owens, 2025). In return, the Trump administration will release $1.3 billion in federal funding (Nadworny & Owens, 2025).

Brown University is also among the Ivy League universities succumbing to federal DEI bans after accusations that it permitted anti-Semitism, allegations suggesting that to be pro-Palestinian is to be anti-Semitist (Office of the President, 2025). In response to the Brown agreement, Secretary of Education Linda McMahon declared:

> The Trump Administration is successfully reversing the decades-long woke-capture of our nation's higher education institutions. Because of the Trump Administration's resolution agreement with Brown University, aspiring students will be judged solely on their merits, not their race or sex.
> (in Nitzberg, 2025)

This forcing of the hand is severe government overreach in institutions of higher education, furthering long-standing inequities. Moreover, some believe that in the name of combating anti-Semitism, Trump is actually targeting and punishing left-wing institutions that he considers to be enemies (*The Washington Post*, 2025).

These anti-DEI sentiments are expressed in state education policies as well. Whereas past legislation forbade "CRT," the most recent state policies attack DEI. As examples, Texas (SB 12), South Carolina (H 3927), and Georgia (SB 36) eliminated DEI in public schools, meaning that they prohibit schools from performing any "DEI duties," compelled DEI statements, or race-/gender-based hiring. North Carolina and Kentucky aim to pass similar legislation. Stated plainly, these anti-DEI policies uprooted trees planted during the civil rights movement that sought to protect students from racism and sexism, increase access and opportunities, and provide resources for historically disadvantaged groups.

Best Colleges published an anti-DEI tracker, updated on May 6, 2025, that illustrates the pervasiveness of anti-DEI legislation across the United States. The map shows a sobering reality, one that has been brewing for several years in academia. Nearly half of the states in the United States have proposed or could be in the process of proposing anti-DEI legislation, which looks similar in most states. According to *Best Colleges* (Bryant & Appleby, 2025), the following states have signed anti-DEI legislation into law:

1. Florida
2. North Dakota
3. South Dakota
4. Tennessee

5. Texas
6. Utah
7. Alabama
8. Idaho
9. West Virginia
10. North Carolina
11. Iowa
12. Wyoming
13. Arkansas
14. Ohio
15. Indiana (by executive order, signed into law)
16. Kansas (allowed to become law without the governor's signature)
17. Kentucky (allowed to become law without the governor's signature)

State legislation since 2023 either has done or threatens to do some or all of the following:

- Close DEI offices at public colleges/universities.
- Prohibit requiring students and/or employees to undergo DEI training.
- Forbid DEI consideration in hiring decisions.
- Disallow funding, sponsoring, supporting, or maintaining DEI programs.
- Put a stop to offering general education courses based on theories of racism, sexism, etc.
- Eliminate race- and sex-based scholarships.
- Remove statements of ideology, such as DEI statements, from employment and enrollment applications.
- Forbid mandatory teaching about divisive concepts.

Anti-DEI Judicial Decision

Moreover, the Supreme Court has been complicit in this assault as well, through the repeal of affirmative action. In the 1978 Supreme Court case *Regents of the University of California v. Bakke*, the Court decided that affirmative action programs can take race into account, as a component of holistic consideration, in the college admissions process.[8] Affirmative action in higher education was doubly beneficial:

1 Through affirmative action, marginalized groups would be afforded the access and opportunities in education that they rightfully deserve (equity).
2 Resultantly, institutions of higher education would be enriched by the cultural diversity of the student population.

The Education Trust describes how affirmative action has been a way to balance the scales in college admissions (2023, para 1):

> Affirmative action has historically been an instrument that colleges can use to ensure that students of color receive fair consideration for admissions given the systemic barriers, underinvestment in schools that students of color attend, inequities in access to advanced coursework, and non-academic factors that overwhelmingly advantage White and wealthier applicants.

Though affirmative action is an imperfect attempt at race and gender equity, the extent to which it has impacted communities of color is immeasurable. As an example of this impact, the NAACP (n.d.) reported,

> In 1970, white students made up 91% of college enrollment. In 2021, that number decreased to about 50%, with Black students accounting for 12.6% of college enrollees, Hispanic students 21.4%, and Asian students 7.1%. Undergraduate representation is more proportional to the US population today.
>
> The percentage of Black, Hispanic, and Asian 18 to 24-year-olds enrolled in college has steadily increased since the Bakke decision in 1978, with all three groups seeing an increase between 14 and 18 percentage points.

In a book that has been one of the most impactful in understanding race relations in the United States, Cornel West (1993) wrote,

> The prevailing discriminatory practices during the sixties, whose targets were working people, women, and people of color, were atrocious. Thus, an enforceable race-based—and later gender based—affirmative action policy was the best possible compromise and concession.... Given the history of this country, it is a virtual certainty that without affirmative action, racial and sexual discrimination would return with a vengeance.
>
> (p. 189)

Conclusion

On a basic, albeit reductionist, level, it can be concluded that people who resist DEI efforts hold values that are not aligned with diversity, equity, and inclusion. As the word "opposition" implies, their values represent the "opposite" of diversity, equity, and inclusion, those being homogeneity, inequity, and exclusion. The latter group of words describes schooling in the United States at its inception and for many years afterward. We are witnessing a dangerous regression in schooling. Through their anti-CRT and anti-DEI campaigns, they've been effective at the following:

1. intimidating educators who want to center racial equity in their work;
2. creating fear in teachers and administrators who want to create learning environments that cultivate success for racially and ethnically diverse students;
3. making educators doubt whether diversity, equity, and inclusion should be prioritized in their work;
4. convincing the general public that race doesn't matter; and
5. confusing educators and parents about what acceptable and unacceptable educative practices are.

One can surmise from this probe into the motivation behind anti-CRT and anti-DEI legislation that Trump conservatives see several threats posed by education guided by justice aims. They are threatened by:

- education that liberates;
- educators who believe in teaching historical truths;
- an inglorious portrayal of whiteness;
- a diverse, educated citizenry that understands their history and culture;
- racialized communities that hold positive racial identities; and
- critical education, which is the biggest threat and is the subject of Chapter 11.

This is the state of PK–12 and higher education today, and it is a travesty. Prohibitions, bans, limitations, restrictions, and attacks—all designed to impede the function of justice workers in education. If justice workers relent in our efforts, we run the risk of the 2020s being known as the "injustice decades." Frederick Douglass, in his 1857 speech titled "If There

Is No Struggle, There Is No Progress," cautioned justice workers about the need for struggle:

> This struggle may be a moral one, or it may be a physical one, and it may be both moral and physical, but it must be a struggle. Power concedes nothing without a demand. It never did and it never will.
>
> (cited in Black Past, 2007)

Justice workers must keep making a demand. Our foreparents planted trees of justice, and just as the trees started to experience a couple of cycles (generations) of fruit bearing, we are witnessing nothing short of tree demolition and blighting of the fruit.

Questions to Ponder

1. What similarities and differences do you see between the anti-CRT and anti-DEI attacks?
2. What impact have you experienced personally as a result of the anti-CRT and anti-DEI legislation, if any?
3. How have these attacks impacted the work of your school, district, institution, or organization?
4. Who benefits from these policy changes? How?

Notes

1. https://www.congress.gov/bill/107th-congress/house-bill/1
2. A slogan that calls for reallocating funds from policing to community services.
3. A movement to reimagine immigration enforcement to be more humane and just.
4. An initiative for Indigenous people to regain ancestral lands.
5. https://capitol.texas.gov/tlodocs/87R/billtext/pdf/SB01709I.pdf#navpanes=0
6. https://capitol.texas.gov/tlodocs/88R/billtext/html/SB02194I.htm
7. https://capitol.texas.gov/tlodocs/88R/billtext/html/HB05140I.htm
8. https://www.federalregister.gov/executive-order/10925

6

Blighting the Fruit: Attacks Against Other Minoritized Students

The bans against "CRT" and DEI directly impact students of color, limiting access, opportunities, and support that were secured during the civil rights movements. It's important, however, to address the ways other historically marginalized communities have been harmed by conservative-led executive orders and policies. The term "historically marginalized" is commonly used when describing victims of white supremacy, to the point that there is a risk of it becoming empty of meaning. It's worth emphasizing that, as shown in Part I, there is a documented history of discrimination against these populations. There are no new targets in these current attacks, just a resurfacing of longstanding marginalization. The blighting of fruit has impacted the following populations:

1. LGBTQIA+ students
2. Students who are religious minorities
3. Immigrant and emergent bilingual students

LGBTQIA+ Students

Laws criminalizing homosexuality have existed since before the nation's independence. Grounded in religious mores of the Abrahamic religions, colonial settlers passed laws making gay sex punishable by death (Death Penalty Information Center, 2025). In fact, it wasn't until 2003 that the U.S. Supreme Court[1] ruled that states could not punish adults for consensual sexual acts. More than a decade later, gay marriage was legalized in the United States.[2] Given this history of discrimination, it's unsurprising that sexuality and gender identity came under assault during the culture wars of 2020s. According to the Trevor Project (2024), an organization that provides support for LGBTQIA+ young people,

> As of July 2024, seven states have laws censoring discussions of LGBTQ+ people or issues throughout all school curricula, six states require schools to provide advance notice to parents when LGBTQ+ issues will be discussed and offer parents the opportunity to opt their children out of these lessons, and four states have laws that restrict how "homosexuality" is discussed in certain settings.

Specifically, anti-LGBTQIA+ education laws do the following (ACLU, 2024):

- ban or restrict access to books that include LGBTQIA+ people, themes, or topics;
- prevent or censor discussions of LGBTQIA+ people and topics in school;
- force school staff to out LGBTQIA+ students;
- allow teachers and staff to refuse to call transgender students by the pronouns they use;
- prevent transgender and nonbinary students from using bathrooms and locker rooms that align with their gender identity;
- prevent transgender students from participating in school sports; and
- restrict or prevent transgender young people from getting gender-affirming care and punishing supportive parents.

Perhaps the issues that most impact classroom instruction are banning books featuring LGBTQIA+ characters and forbidding dialogue about LGBTQIA+ topics. When I lived in the Dallas/Fort Worth metroplex in 2018, a gay teacher in my area (two-time teacher of the year) was placed on administrative leave for promoting "a homosexual agenda" simply because she showed her class a photo of her and her now-wife (Platoff, 2018). I was teaching a graduate-level diversity course at a university serving in-service teachers in school districts not far from this one. When I tried to use this discriminatory experience as a "teaching moment," most of my students thought the district had made the right decision. They contended that elementary school students should learn about sexuality from their parents, not teachers. I did my best to help them to see that the teacher was not teaching about sexuality; she only shared a photo of her own family and taught students that all families don't look the same. The teacher's lesson was not about sexuality. It was about respect for differences. Preventing the teacher from talking about her family—which is something heterosexual teachers do all the time—was not fair. Further, restrictions of this nature constitute family structurism, communicating to students that certain families are good (evidenced by their being allowed in classroom discussions) and others are bad (evidenced by their being disallowed from classroom discussions).

Unfortunately, restrictions on classroom discussions involving LGBTQIA+ topics have only intensified since this 2018 injustice. Perhaps the most well known of this legislation is Florida's "Parents Rights in Education" law, HB 1557, passed in May 2022. Also known as the "Don't Say Gay" law, it prohibits teachers from discussing sexual orientation or gender identity before the fourth grade. This prohibition restricts students from learning about diverse sexualities and gender identities. The Associated Press (Demillo, 2023) reported, "At least 30 proposals similar to Florida's law have been filed in 16 states." Teachers are also restricted in their use of instructional materials because of states' banning of books that feature LGBTQIA+ characters. Frequently labeled "pornographic" or "indecent," 26% of banned books in the first half of the 2022–2023 school year feature LGBTQIA+ characters or content (PEN America, 2023). Our society is made up of diverse individuals, families, and communities who deserve equal representation in schools. In this contentious debate, librarians have been threatened with prison and have been called "sexual predators" and "the arm of Satan" for simply making available to students books that feature LGBTQIA+ characters (Fleishman, 2023). To be clear, the central issue is exclusion, despite the opposition's claim to be protecting students from sexually explicit content or materials. Their goal is to exclude materials that depict gender and sexuality diversity, furthering a hidden curriculum that is heteronormative (presenting heterosexual relationships as normal). At the time of this writing, the ACLU (2025) is tracking 598 anti-LGBTQIA+ bills, with 268 of those being bills that restrict educators' and students' rights.

Transgender students have suffered horrific discrimination. In 2016, North Carolina became the first state to bar transgender individuals from using the public restroom, including in public schools, that is consistent with their gender identity (Prichep, 2024). Other states were soon to follow this public restroom ban and other trans restrictions like school sports and the definition of *sex*. I learned about the outrageous number

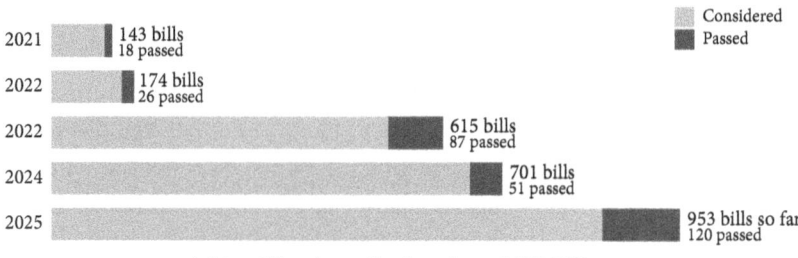

Anti-trans bills under consideration and passed, 2021-2025

Figure 6.1 Data from Trans Legislation Tracker Showing the Rise in Anti-Trans Bills.

of proposed restrictions in a spring 2023 class during which I mentioned that nearly a dozen states had introduced anti-trans legislation. A trans student corrected me: "Dr. Caldera, there are hundreds of anti-trans laws being considered." The Trans Legislative Tracker (2025), which tracks the rise of anti-trans bills specifically, shows that in 2025, 49 states have introduced 953 anti-trans bills and 120 anti-trans bills have passed. Figure 6.1 illustrates how the number of anti-trans bills has increased over the last four years. When disaggregated by bill type, of the 953 anti-trans bills that have been introduced, 262 are directly related to education.

The 2025 Trump administration ushered in a new round of attacks on LGBTQIA+ students. Project 2025 (The Heritage Foundation, 2023) directed,

> The next conservative President must make the institutions of American civil society hard targets for woke culture warriors. This starts with deleting the terms sexual orientation and gender identity ("SOGI") diversity, equity, and inclusion ("DEI"), gender, gender equality, gender equity, gender awareness, gender sensitive… out of every federal rule, agency regulation, contract, grant, regulations, and piece of legislation that exists.
>
> The noxious tenets of "critical race theory" and "gender ideology" should be excised from curricula in every public school in the country. These theories poison our children, who are being taught on the one hand to affirm that the color of their skin fundamentally determines their identity and even their moral status while on the other they are taught to deny the very creatureliness that inheres in being human and consists in accepting the givenness of our nature as men or women. Allowing parents or physicians to "reassign" the sex of a minor is child abuse and must end. For public institutions to use taxpayer dollars to declare the

superiority or inferiority of certain races, sexes, and religions is a violation of the Constitution and civil rights law and cannot be tolerated by any government anywhere in the country.

(p. 4–5)

Following Project 2025's lead, Trump issued Executive Order 14168, "Defending Women From Gender Ideology Extremism and Restoring Biological Truth to the Federal Government." Section 2 of the order states, "It is the policy of the United States to recognize two sexes, male and female. These sexes are not changeable and are grounded in fundamental and incontrovertible reality." This order immediately trickled down to The states. Iowa was the first state that removed "gender identity" as a protected class and restricts teaching "gender theory" from PK–sixth grade (Bestor Townsend & Zagger, 2025). Utah, West Virginia, and Wyoming enacted similar laws recognizing only two sexes (Greco Danaher et al., 2025). Similarly, Trump's Executive Order 14201, "Keeping Men Out of Women's Sports," is anti-trans legislation designed to prohibit trans women from playing on women's sport teams. The executive order proclaims,

> Many sport-specific governing bodies have no official position or requirements regarding trans-identifying athletes. Others allow men to compete in women's categories if these men reduce the testosterone in their bodies below certain levels or provide documentation of "sincerely held" gender identity. These policies are unfair to female athletes and do not protect female safety.

Students deserve to join sports teams that align with their gender identities. Gender Justice (2025) clarified that debates over trans inclusion are not about a genuine concern for fairness and safety. They expressed that trans athletes have been participating in sports for decades and that organizations "have used science-based guidelines, developed with medical experts to ensure fairness and opportunity."

Last, in June 2025, the Supreme Court ruled in favor of parents who would like to opt children out of reading LGBTQIA+-themed books, Justice Samuel Alito writing that refusing to allow parents to opt out "poses a very real threat to undermining their religious beliefs and practices" (Deliso & Dwyer, 2025). Reading books about LGBTQIA+ is not a religious matter, just like reading books about non-LGBTQIA+ families is not. Educators should have a diverse classroom library that reflects the lived experiences of all families and communities.

The attacks against LGBTQIA+ students are egregious. By mandating that students use facilities and participate in sports based on their sex at birth, this legislation attempts to force transgender students into a socially constructed gender binary (male/female) based on biological sex. A policy in Virginia is distinctly appalling. The state policy, from *Model Policies on Ensuring Privacy, Dignity, and Respect for All Students and Parents in Virginia's Public Schools*, requires local school districts to prevent teachers from calling a transgender student by their preferred name or pronouns unless they receive parental permission and gives parents control over what pronouns and names students will use at school. In testimony against the policy, a parent warned the board, "The result of this policy will be homeless and dead children" (Englander, 2023). This parent is right. Creating a policy aimed at giving power to parents of LGBTQIA+ students contradicts what research finds is important in supporting this vulnerable population. As a result of their extensive review of research on the experiences of LGBTQIA+ students, Abreu et al. (2022) recommended that policymakers trust the experiences and listen to the voices of LGBTQIA+ students when crafting policy.

Many scholars have found that schools are unsafe places for LGBTQIA+ students. As a former middle school teacher and as a teacher educator who has worked with hundreds of preservice teachers, this is not surprising to me. I have heard the stories. In their study of the experiences of LGBTQIA+ youth, Earnshaw et al. (2020) found that "transgender students reported bullying related to their gender identity, including verbal, physical, and sexual harassment, deadnaming (referred to by their birth name), and misgendering (called an incorrect pronoun). Russell et al. (2021) summarized, "LGBTQIA students often experience negative school environments, where they are subject to victimization based on sexual orientation, gender identity, and gender expression." Recent laws will exacerbate this hostility for young people whose mere existence makes them a threat (Levengood & Hadland, 2023).

According to the Trevor Project (2024), "28% of LGBTQIA youth reported experiencing homelessness or housing instability at some point in their lives—and those who did have two to four times the odds of reporting depression, anxiety, self-harm, considering suicide, and attempting suicide compared to those with stable housing." They also concluded in their 2023 U.S. National Survey on the Mental Health of LGBTQIA Young People, "For the fifth consecutive year, these data underscore that anti-LGBTQIA+ victimization contributes to the higher rates of suicide risk reported by LGBTQIA+ young people and that most who want mental health care are unable to get it" (The Trevor Project, 2023). Drawing upon two peer-reviewed reports, the Trevor Project also reported that "LGBTQIA young people are more than four times as likely to attempt suicide than their peers." In light of recent legislation, I shudder at the thought of revisiting these numbers in the coming years if justice workers don't disrupt this blighting of fruit.

Students Who Are Religious Minorities

Several years ago, I attended a conference session about discrimination against Southeast Asians in the Coppell Independent School District (CISD), located in a suburban city in the Dallas/Fort Worth metropolitan area. According to the Change.org petition, nearly 50% of the student population are Southeast Asians who are Hindus, Jains, Buddhists, or Sikhs, the majority of whom observe Diwali, a five-day, family-oriented holiday that celebrates the victory of light over darkness and good over evil (Celebrators of Diwali, n.d.). Students in CISD who observe Diwali are forced to choose between school and religion. In order to avoid this dilemma, they petitioned the school board to make Diwali an official school holiday or professional development day. To illustrate how religious equality would be fostered through making Diwali a school holiday, the petitioners explained how the school district designates Good Friday (a Christian holiday that observes the crucifixion of Jesus Christ) a weather or professional development day to allow Christian students to observe Good Friday without being forced into a quandary of choosing school or religion. This example illustrates one way religious bias shows up in schools, with Christian students receiving preferential treatment.

Still, Trump conservatives claim that Christians in the United States are experiencing anti-Christian bias, leading Trump to issue Executive Order 14202, "Eradicating Anti-Christian Bias," stating the following:

> In this atmosphere of anti-Christian government, hostility and vandalism against Christian churches and places of worship surged, with the number of such identified acts in 2023 exceeding by more than eight times the number

from 2018. Catholic churches and institutions have been aggressively targeted with hundreds of acts of hostility, violence, and vandalism.

My Administration will not tolerate anti-Christian weaponization of government or unlawful conduct targeting Christians. The law protects the freedom of Americans and groups of Americans to practice their faith in peace, and my Administration will enforce the law and protect these freedoms. My Administration will ensure that any unlawful and improper conduct, policies, or practices that target Christians are identified, terminated, and rectified.

It is evident that while Trump conservatives claim to advocate for religious freedom, they really want Christian hegemony. In other words, they want the power to infuse the Christian faith in government institutions, like schools. States like Louisiana, Texas, Arkansas, and Alabama have introduced bills and/or passed laws requiring teachers to display the Ten Commandments from the Christian Bible/Jewish Torah[3]. Oklahoma's state superintendent of education and the state school board passed new standards that "would require public schools to teach about the Bible and American patriotism" (Martinez Keel, 2025). Proponents argue for inclusion of the Ten Commandments and the Bible for historical and cultural significance. However, Seidel (2019, p. 4) sees policies such as these as attempts to "press religion into every crevice of the government." To make Seidel's quote more accurate, these pro-Christian policies as attempts to press *Christianity* into every crevice of the government. These recent policies threaten the separation of church and state, outlined in the First Amendment, that the framers of the U.S. Constitution intended. It is important to see pro-Christian education policies for what they are—attempts to keep white supremacy in the soil of the nation. Fortunately, these bills have faced successful legal challenges (Ryan, 2025).

Students of Color, Students with Disabilities, and LGBTQIA+ Students

A federal entity, the U.S. Department of Education was established in 1980, shortly after the justice decades concluded. Their website (U.S. Department of Education, 2025b) summarizes this context and focus:

The anti-poverty and civil rights laws of the 1960s and 1970s brought about a dramatic emergence of the Department's equal access mission. The passage of laws such as Title VI of the Civil Rights Act of 1964, Title IX of the Education Amendments of 1972, and Section 504 of the Rehabilitation Act of 1973 which prohibited discrimination based on race, sex, and disability, respectively made civil rights enforcement a fundamental and long-lasting focus of the Department of Education.

Entities within the department work to support this focus. As an example, a subagency of the Department of Education, the Office of Civil Rights, is the primary protector and enforcer of civil rights in schools. In other words, this office is responsible for ensuring that all students experience schooling in accordance with federal law. Their website states this purpose: "The mission of the Office for Civil Rights is to ensure equal access to education and to promote educational excellence throughout the nation through vigorous enforcement of civil rights" (U.S. Department of Education, 2025a). Additionally, since 2002, through the Institute for Education Sciences, another subagency of the U.S. Department of Education, the federal government has offered research-based guidance and support around education policies and practices. They promote educational policies and practices that improve outcomes for all students, including "special populations such as English Learners and students with disabilities" (Institute for Education Sciences, 2025).

On March 20, 2025, President Trump issued an executive order, "Improving Education Outcomes by Empowering Parents, States, and Communities." Section 2 of this order calls for

"Closing the Department of Education and Returning Authority to the States. (a) The Secretary of Education shall, to the maximum extent appropriate and permitted by law, take all necessary steps to facilitate the closure of the Department of Education and return authority over education to the States and local communities while ensuring the effective and uninterrupted delivery of services, programs, and benefits on which Americans rely."

As with other executive orders, Project 2025 was Trump's guide: "This department is an example of federal intrusion into a traditionally state and local realm. For the sake of American children, Congress should shutter it and return control of education to the states (The Heritage Foundation, 2023, p. 285)."

The destruction of the Office for Civil Rights (OCR) means that, even though policies were not perfect before, students no longer have protections from the federal government. School districts that were under desegregation orders suddenly aren't anymore, and families with complaints about such things as extreme racial and gender bullying have been shut down. The OCR dismissed 3,424 complaints between March 11 and June 27, 2025 (Quilantan et al., 2025). Gender identity and LGBTQIA+ challenges against book bans are no longer considered among discrimination claims, leaving these students without federal protection (Quilantan et al., 2025). Moreover, the National Education Association warns that dismantling the Department of Education will make it more difficult for the 7.5 million special education students in the U.S. to receive the services they need (Walker, 2025).

Immigrant and Emergent Bilingual Students

Immigrant communities have had to fight for access to an appropriate education for their students for many decades, leading to the the bearing of fruit, for example, passing of the Bilingual Education Act (BEA) in 1968. Moreover, in *Lau v. Nichols* (1974), the Supreme Court affirmed that the San Francisco school system's failure to provide English language instruction to Chinese students who didn't speak English violated their rights under Title VI of the Civil Rights Act. Justice workers fought to ensure that states would be obligated to ensure that emergent bilinguals (also English language learners—ELLs) would have equal access to education. This fruit is in jeopardy of being blighted with Trump's issuance of Executive Order 14224, which establishes English as the official language of the United States of America. Consistent with the executive order, the Department of Justice will lead a coordinated effort across federal agencies to minimize nonessential multilingual services, redirect resources toward English language education and assimilation, and ensure legal compliance with the executive order through targeted measures where necessary (U.S. Department of Justice Office of Public Affairs, 2025b). Although the executive order does not regulate state policies, its symbolic significance cannot be disregarded. Trump's new order "revokes Executive Order 13166, a quarter-century-old order requiring federal agencies to take several steps to improve access to their programs for the nation's nearly 28 million limited English proficient (LEP) individuals" (Hofstetter, 2025). Consequently, federal education programs are no longer compelled to make their materials language accessible.

According to the Pew Research Center, immigrants are 14.3% of the U.S. population, composed as follows:

- 49% naturalized citizens
- 24% lawful permanent residents
- 23% unauthorized immigrants (or 3.3% of the total U.S. population) (Passel & Krogstad, 2024)

Additionally, about 4.4 million U.S.-born children under 18 live with an authorized immigrant parent (Passel & Krogstad, 2024). In Executive Order 14159, "Protecting the American People Against Invasion," Trump continued his mischaracterization of immigrants, accusing them of participating in espionage and terror-related activities and committing vile and heinous acts. Research (Light & Miller, 2017) shows, however, that "undocumented immigration does not increase violence." The order states,

> It is the policy of the United States to faithfully execute the immigration laws against all inadmissible and removable aliens, particularly those aliens who threaten the safety or security of the American people. Further, it is the policy of the United States to achieve the total and efficient enforcement of those laws, including through lawful incentives and detention capabilities.

Since this order, Immigration and Customs Enforcement (ICE) has unleashed mayhem in immigrant communities, mainly on immigrants of color. Trump's mass immigrant deportation orders are deeply impacting these students and their families. In some cases, ICE has deported teenagers and children through raids on their homes, schools, churches, or workplaces. In an article examining how deportations have impacted the state of Maryland, Gauntt (2025) reported that "while Trump has said the deportations will target criminals, 40% of those who have been detained by ICE had no criminal record. About 45% detained had been convicted of a crime, while another 15% had criminal charges pending, according to ICE." Deportations have led to family separations, a surge in school absenteeism, and increased anxiety among children of immigrant families, and have traumatized students of immigrant families (Spector, 2025). The National Immigration Law Center (Pak et al., 2022) reported that "student attendance drastically falls off where there is a greater law enforcement presence. In one school, attendance decreased by 60% the day after an immigration raid. When students avoid classes out of fear, they are not able to take advantage of their educational rights." Moreover, many of the nearly three-fourths of a million undocumented immigrant students become entangled in what is being called the "school to deportation pipeline," a discriminatory system that causes undocumented students who face school discipline issues to be deported (Pak et al., 2022). Minor behavioral problems at schools can lead to encounters with school resource officers, acting as police, and eventually land them in ICE custody.

Immigrant students in institutions of higher education are facing challenges in continuing to access postsecondary education. For example, immigrant students in Texas are seeing the repeal of the DREAM Act. Since 2001, Texas's undocumented students have qualified for in-state tuition at the state's public colleges and universities under the DREAM Act. According to *The Texas Tribune*, Texas was one of 24 states to offer in-state tuition to undocumented students (Klibanoff & Priest, 2025). The repeal of the DREAM Act presents another barrier to already marginalized students, furthering white supremacy in schools.

In another executive order (14188), "Additional Measures to Combat Anti-Semitism," Trump targeted immigrant college students participating in pro-Palestinian protests. The executive order states, "It shall be the policy of the United States to combat anti-Semitism vigorously, using all available and appropriate legal tools, to prosecute, remove, or otherwise hold to account the perpetrators of unlawful anti-Semitic harassment and violence." Al Jazeera (2025) reported that more than 1,000 students have had their visas revoked; others have been detained. It is clear that this administration is committed to stifling opposition to Israel, not

Table 6.1 Discriminatory 2025 Executive Orders That Impact Schooling

Executive Order[4]	Date	Targets
Additional Measures to Combat Anti-Semitism, 14188	January 29, 2025	Immigrant students and Muslim students
Designating English as the Official Language of the United States, 14224	March 1, 2025	English language learners
Protecting the American People Against Invasion, 14159	January 20, 2025	Immigrant students and students of immigrant families
Improving Education Outcomes by Empowering Parents, States, and Communities, 14242	March 20, 2025	Students of color and LGBTQIA+ students

Eradicating Anti-Christian Bias, 14202	February 6, 2025	Non-Christian students
Defending Women from Gender Ideology Extremism and Restoring Biological Truth to the Federal Government, 14168	January 20, 2025	Trans students
Keeping Men Out of Women's Sports, 14201	February 11, 2025	Trans students
Ending Radical Indoctrination in K–12 Schooling, 13985	January 29, 2025	Students of color/ LGBTQIA+ students
Ending Illegal Discrimination and Restoring Merit-Based Opportunity, 14173	January 21, 2025	Students of color/girls

protecting Jews from discrimination. Because identity and oppression are intersectional, some students are distinctly and profoundly harmed by these attacks.

Table 6.1 lists Trump's 2025 executive orders highlighted in this and the last chapter. Pointing out the targets of the conservative onslaught is necessary to reveal the ways white supremacy is impacting schools:
Justice workers during the justice decades planted trees that were beginning to bear fruit. In plain speak, society was becoming more just for many conditional citizens, with laws forbidding linguicism, racism, ableism, sexism, heterosexism, gender binarism, and religious discrimination. Then came the blighting of the fruit elucidated in this chapter—a destruction of rights that inhibits progress toward a liberatory education. In the next chapter, I examine why trees planted decades ago are being destroyed in this way.

Questions to Ponder

1. What emotions are you experiencing after reading this chapter?
2. What impact have you experienced personally as a result of these attacks against minoritized students?
3. How do these attacks further white supremacy?
4. What assumptions is the author making? Are they sufficiently supported with evidence?

Notes

1. Lawrence v. Texas, 539 U.S. 558 (2003), No. 02-102.
2. Obergefell v. Hodges, 576 U.S. 644 (2015), No. 14-556.
3. https://alison.legislature.state.al.us/files/pdf/SearchableInstruments/2025RS/5VU8763-1.pdf
4. Executive orders can be found on the *Federal Register* webpage: https://www.federalregister.gov/presidential-documents/executive-orders

7

Harmful Lies and Ideologies

As the previous chapter illustrates, the attacks on justice have mainly come in education. The answer to why can be found in *Teaching to Transgress* by bell hooks: "the classroom remains the most radical space of possibility" (1994, p. 12). The culture wars, at their root, are about who controls this "radical space of possibility." Whoever has the most influence on schooling controls society and, consequently, moves the country further toward or away from realizing its promise of a democratic society that is governed by ideals such as fairness, freedom, and fundamental rights. Make no mistake about it: the challenges examined in the previous two chapters are not just opposition to DEI or CRT: they are attacks on educational justice in public schools and postsecondary institutions. Because PK–16 schools are fundamental to upholding democracy, these attacks hold monumental significance for the country.

Think back to the exclusive schools that existed in the colonial period (described in Chapter 3). Students were white, English-speaking boys; curricula focused almost exclusively on the history and culture of European civilizations; instructional materials likely featured gender-conforming, heterosexual characters. The primary goal of schools was Christian indoctrination; discriminatory practices against individuals with disabilities were pervasive; and girls were restricted to gender-confining roles. Considering the panoply of anti-DEI and anti-CRT laws that have been recently enacted, it is not far-reaching to ask ourselves and each other if this is the kind of schools Trump conservatives want to reinstate. The impetus for their attacks is clear—they want schools throughout the PK–16 spectrum that are rooted in uniformity, conformity, and ostensibly "normality." Or, said plainly, they want schools to be as they once were, ruled entirely by imperialist white supremacist capitalist cisheteropatriarchy. Their regressive actions are unleashing many of the forms of oppression listed in Chapter 1: linguicism, racism, sexism, heterosexism, xenophobia, and others.

In creating schools that demand blind patriotism, eliminate examinations of oppression, and enforce biblical rules, conservative lawmakers—backed by think tanks like the Heritage Foundation and advocacy groups like Moms for Liberty—are able to control how students think and behave, which is a necessity for maintaining white supremacy. Benjamin (2024, p. 37) pointed out the impact of a white supremacist curriculum: "The whiteness of the curriculum in many schools continues to perpetuate, albeit more subtly and usually without the threat of physical harm, an ongoing campaign of erasure that arrests the creativity and ingenuity of young people." When creativity and ingenuity are quelled, whiteness in schools continues to be the status quo.

Lies They Tell Others

Their desire to maintain white dominance in a country steadily heading toward a white minority population is so strong that they have stealthily and successfully created what Harper (2024, p. 41) called "one very big reprehensible, destructive, and politically poisonous lie." This lie convinced the voting populace to enact the widespread curricular restrictions in place across the country. The big lie: Educators in PK–12 and higher education are

1. indoctrinating students with racist falsehoods about America;
2. teaching homoerotic and otherwise inappropriately pornographic content in classrooms;
3. exposing third graders to CRT, erasing the founding fathers and long-celebrated white American heroes from the curriculum;
4. discarding Shakespeare and other classics in exchange for racially inflammatory texts;
5. forcing kids to pick genders than misalign with who they feel they really are at the time;
6. telling white students they are all racist oppressors;
7. convincing students of color they are all inferior to white applicants for everything;
8. wasting enormous sums of taxpayers' money on divisive programming, supporting hateful CDOs (chief diversity officers)

who aim to embarrass white people and fracture campus communities along racial lines; and
9 grooming young people to hate America because it is so racist (Harper, 2024).

If these accusations were true, there would certainly be reason for outrage, by conservatives and anyone who loves children. Harper (2024) made it clear however, that there is no evidence or proof to support the veracity of any of these statements. Taken together, each element of the big lie communicates to the public that educators are too "woke." It was created to instill fear among conservative whites and advance an agenda that would further ingrain white supremacy in schooling. Benjamin (2024, p. 105) called our educational system "a propaganda machine for producing a whitewashed version of history." In resistance to this one big lie and propaganda machine, justice workers launched a Teach Truth[1] campaign, including a Teach the Truth Day of Action, and a Freedom to Learn[2] campaign. Still, there is much more to do to reimagine educational justice, this time from a proactive rather than a reactive standpoint. We who stand for justice, we who are "woke," must continue to insist on transparency and truth—data, not dogma—even when they are disregarded by those on the right. Otherwise, education continues to be a propaganda machine.

Lies They Tell Themselves

Perhaps the most harmful lies are the ones Trump conservatives tell themselves to maintain an illusion of supremacy. These lies are birthed from conservative political ideologies about how society is structured and how individuals and groups operate within this structure. In the next section, I reveal five ideologies behind the opposition to efforts by justice workers to bring about educational justice. Justice workers must see and understand the lies Trump conservatives tell themselves. Saad (2020, p. 38) reminded us why: "You cannot dismantle what you cannot see. You cannot challenge what you do not understand." These five ideologies—racial colorblindness, meritocracy, Eurocentrism, Black inferiority, and nationalism/white nationalism/Christian nationalism—are evident in all the attacks examined in Chapters 5 and 6. Though I analyze them separately, these belief systems, which range from mildly implicit to wildly explicit, are enmeshed and lean into each other to form a strong stance against educational equity.

Ideology I. Racial Colorblindness: Blind to Race, Blind to Racism

> **The (Explicit) Lie:** An individual's race/ethnicity has no bearing on his/her/their lived experiences. Consequently, societal institutions and systems do not, advertently or inadvertently, (1) impose racial barriers, (2) restrict access based on race, (3) cause race-related violence, (4) create disparities among races, or (5) limit opportunities for racialized individuals/communities.

The first set of beliefs underlying conservative opposition to DEI is racial colorblindness. Colorblindness is not only a failure to see racial differences but also the corresponding "refusal to acknowledge the costs and benefits associated with one's racial and cultural identity" (Caldera, 2018). Said differently, it describes the way some people avoid recognizing how race impacts, whether positively or negatively, one's lived experiences. Racial colorblindness is easily adopted by white people whose whiteness is rendered invisible and valueless. As a result, justice workers must make visible the ways whiteness grants power and privileges to those who own this property. Racial colorblindness, including white invisibility, is evident through much of the opposition to DEI.

Anti-DEI state judicial rulings and legislation have imposed restrictions on college admissions, diversity in hiring, and support for diverse students and employees by diversity offices. As mentioned in Chapter 2, in 1978 the Supreme Court ruled in favor of affirmative action. It ruled that a state may constitutionally consider race, alongside other factors, in determining merit in its university admissions to promote educational diversity, but only if considered alongside other factors and on a case-by-case basis. Because of affirmative action, the landscape of college enrollment became much more racially/culturally diverse. A reversal of this decision came 45 years after this initial ruling. The ACLU (Hinger, 2023) summarized the Court's 2023 decision:

> At the end of its term, the Supreme Court upended established equal protection law with its decision in *SFFA v. Harvard* and *SFFA v. UNC*, effectively eliminating the use of affirmative action in college admissions. The court's decision disregards prior precedent, as well as the societal realities of race discrimination and inequality.

Cornel West (1993, p. 190) warned us about the potential consequences of losing affirmative action protections: "Given the history of this country, it is a virtual certainty that without affirmative action, racial and sexual discrimination would return with a vengeance." And here we are.

Chief Justice Roberts explained the Court's 2023 decision that applicants should be "treated based on his or her experiences as an individual—not on the basis of race."[3] In her dissent, Justice Sotomayor explained that the Court's decision was based on a harmful colorblind ideology that leads adherents to claim that race no longer matters in a society built on racial stratification. She wrote that the Court "ignores the reality of race" and "imposes a superficial rule of race blindness on the Nation."[4]

Similarly, other 2023 legislation reflects the conservative goal of dismantling DEI in higher education based on a racially colorblind ideology. In some cases, states are disallowed from funding, sponsoring, supporting, or maintaining DEI programs that are often the sole source of support for students of color on university campuses. Students from historically racially marginalized backgrounds need the access and opportunities DEI offices provide, such as mentoring, culturally responsive programming, and access to resources. Important, too, DEI offices often facilitate meaningful connections among students of color. I have often heard elected officials quote Dr. Martin Luther King Jr.'s "I Have a Dream" speech in defense of their colorblind stance. When Dr. King said, "I have a dream that my four little children will one day live in a nation where they will not be judged by the color of their skin, but by the content of their character," his hopes were for his children to be free of racial bias and to be treated fairly. It should be interpreted as meaning that he envisions a society in which race no longer matters and not interpreted as suggesting that race does not—in the present—matter. We are yet to realize King's hope, though conservatives eagerly purport a postracial society that is predicated on "race-burying" and "political muteness" (Maxwell & Shields, 2019).

I can see why they choose racial colorblind beliefs. In a white-dominated society, whiteness is rendered invisible. White, for the most part, is not a racialized identity, so white people can remain ignorant of the ways they are precluded from racial bias. Moreover, white people, for the most part, live lives separated from Black, Latino(x), and Indigenous folks. Residential neighborhoods are segregated, which means public schools are segregated. So, too, are places of worship. It is only in our jobs, where conversations about race and racism are taboo, that many white people interact with people of color regularly. Consequently, they are unaware of the ways race shows up in the lives of people of color. University classrooms can offer some enlightenment. In one of my graduate classes, I have my students write a racial autobiography in which they describe their experiences around race. Without fail, every single one of my students of color has a story to tell of a racialized experience. My white students, on the other hand, write that race was a mute factor in their lives. It is only through hearing stories from my students of color that my white students become aware of how their whiteness has shielded them from the realities of racism. As a result of these experiences, I have seen white students shift from colorblind beliefs.

Trump conservatives must tell themselves the lie that society is colorblind, that race is an insignificant factor in schools and in the greater society in order to maintain white supremacy.

Ideology II. Meritocracy

> **The (Explicit) Lie:** Upward social and economic mobility is attributed solely to hard work, discipline, drive, and other forms of merit. Consequently, only merit—not social identity—should be the basis for access, opportunity, promotion, and other forms of advancement.

Closely related to racial colorblindness is another belief system: meritocracy. With the root word *merit*, the term refers to the idea that individuals rise or fall solely based on their merit (character or behavioral traits). Belief in meritocracy leads legislators to enact policies that eliminate race and gender as considerations in hiring, college admissions, scholarship opportunities, and more. I realize now that early in life I had bought into this deeply flawed ideal, which I now know is the myth of meritocracy. Because I had failed to examine the world through a critical lens (more on this in Chapter 11), I held little knowledge of the ways that bias, discrimination, and prejudice restricted opportunities and limited access to resources that lead to success. It is indeed a myth that anyone, regardless of their race or ethnicity, can succeed if they work hard enough. It is an American ideal that is deeply embedded in capitalism, an economic system that has historically led to exploitation of people of color, immigrants, and women, inevitably positioning these groups at the bottom of the socioeconomic hierarchy. Meritocracy drives immigrants' hope in the American Dream that they can be anything they want to be if they can get to the United States. I wrote in an article published in 2020:

> This myth of meritocracy—hard work equals upward mobility—completely negates the impact of longstanding, inequitable systemic policies and practices that present impenetrable barriers to upward mobility for minoritized populations, regardless of how hard we work.
>
> (Caldera, 2020, p. 712)

Trump conservatives embrace meritocracy because it allows them to ignore the ways in which a myriad of -isms negate the efforts of many marginalized populations, and it relieves them of any responsibility for working toward systemic change. It is easier to blame the individual instead of recognizing the role that systemic oppression plays in preventing upward mobility. (Conversely, it is easier for Trump conservatives to attribute their own success to hard work instead of to structural advantages.) With recent legislation restricting institutions of higher education from awarding race-, class-, and gender-based scholarships that attempt to mitigate the harm that racism, classism, and sexism cause in certain students' lives, minoritized students will have to compete for merit-based scholarships that create further inequities in education. Indisputably, individual attributes matter. Tenacity, creativity, adaptability, and discipline are important to an individual's success. However, these attributes (and others) are insufficient when stifled by discriminatory structures that limit the possibilities and aspirations of far too many marginalized individuals and groups. Just schools not only cultivate positive qualities in their students, but they also work to dismantle white supremacist structures. Educators don't have to choose one or the other.

Trump conservatives must tell themselves the lie that society operates on meritocracy in order to maintain white supremacy.

Ideology III. Eurocentrism

> **The (Implicit) Lie:** European/Western culture (shared standards, norms, practices, and values that are passed down through generations) and history represent the epitome of civilization. Consequently, institutions and systems should (1) center European standards in establishing policies and practices, (2) focus on European culture and history, (3) minimize the cultures and contributions of non-Europeans, and (4) judge non-European cultures according to European standards and norms.

Eurocentrism means to center European (white) culture and history. This necessarily includes race, but also includes language, religion, and gender/sexuality. Schools and classrooms that are Eurocentric imply that European cultural values which have come to represent traditional conservative values, should be the basis for policies and practices. Black educator Booker T. Washington (1901) captured Eurocentrism with one sentence in his autobiography, *Up from Slavery*: "No white American ever thinks that any other race is wholly civilized until he wears the white man's clothes, eats the white man's food, speaks the white man's language, and professes the white man's religion" (p. 98). A Eurocentric belief system has influenced education since the first schools were established in the 1600s. It is worthwhile to reflect on this history before pinpointing Eurocentrism in present-day legislation.

Nowhere was Eurocentrism more evident than in Native American boarding schools, or reservation schools. Existing from the mid-1600s to the 1900s, these schools had but one purpose—to "civilize" Native Americans. Of course, "civilize" was synonymous with "Europeanize." As a result of this forced assimilation, Native American tribal nations were robbed of their cultures, languages, and religions. Forced assimilation in schools would later be evident with California's English-only movement, a movement that began in the late 1990s to legislate against bilingual programs. Proposition 227 sought to make English-only instruction the default program throughout the state, and in 1998, it passed. Other states were soon to follow (Beykont, 2002).

The common school movement of the early 1800s made public education widely available for white students. It was at this time that most girls (white) attended public schools. The purpose of the common schools was twofold: to inculcate Christian moral values and to educate citizens to participate in a democracy. Educated citizens who shared the same moral values were needed to develop a budding country that was less than a hundred years old. A country with the promise and possibility of democracy was unfolding, but both were limited by schools that were far from egalitarian—schools governed by white dominance.

Though Trump conservatives would likely never overtly admit to a desire for Eurocentric schooling, recent conservative policies reflect their Eurocentric beliefs:

- restrictions on access to rigorous ethnic studies courses
- discouraging teaching that respects the cultures of students of color
- inadequate funding for bilingual education
- bans on books written by Black authors

Eurocentrism, in belief and practice, antagonizes the spirit of multiculturalism that is the essence of a democracy, which is characterized by shared governance and egalitarianism. Anti-CRT and anti-DEI legislators can be described in the words of justice worker Bettina Love (2023, p. 40), "Though they might profess a love of democracy, their actions directly contradict its basic principles" (p. 40).

Ideology IV. Black Inferiority

> **The (Implicit) Lie:** Black people are inferior to white people in every regard. Consequently, (1) to be white is to be human, and to be Black is to be nonhuman; (2) whiteness is normal, while blackness is deviant/deficit; (3) Black people do not deserve the rights of citizenship; and (4) Black history/culture should be relegated to the margins.

In 1954, Mississippi Judge Tom P. Brady gave a speech saturated with ideas of Black inferiority and white superiority. He draws upon pseudoscience in his portrayal of Black people: "We don't know what happens to the brain of man, but we do know that he negro's brain pan seals and hardens quicker than the white man's. We do know that the negro has, in certain instances, elliptical blood cells, which cause disease. We do know that his skull is one-eighth thicker…"

As I wrote in a 2020 article that explained how to eradicate anti-blackness in schools, society's racial hierarchy depends upon white superiority and Black inferiority. White humanity necessitates Black inhumanity. Beliefs about Black (also African) inferiority can be traced back to at least the 1500s when the first Europeans (the Portuguese) traveled to Africa spreading Christianity and immediately afterward institutionalizing the trans-Atlantic slave trade. By these explorers/colonizers, Africans were viewed as immature, savage, barbarian, and inhuman—a direct contrast to themselves, whom they saw as civilized, intelligent, and the epitome of human. By deeming Africans (and their descendants) subhuman, European slaveholders rationalized holding their fellow humans in bondage. It was easier on their conscience to sell and own property than to sell fellow humans. Later in the 18th and 19th centuries, scientific (or biological) racism sustained beliefs about white supremacy and Black inferiority due to misinformation about the brains and intellectual capacity of people of African descent.

It is important to point out, however, that while Black people are not inherently inferior to whites (or any other racial group), society has positioned Black people at the bottom of the racial hierarchy. Historically, this devaluing showed up in a myriad of ways that are distinctly anti-Black. Evidence to support this belief that Black students are inferior and therefore undeserving can be traced to the segregated, underfunded, and underresourced schools attended by Black students during Reconstruction. In *Brown v. Board of Education* (1954), Chief Justice Warren wrote that segregation "generates a feeling of inferiority as to their status in the community that may affect their hearts and minds in a way unlikely to be undone." This belief in Black inferiority is also evident in the ways schools are intent on controlling Black students' bodies. Black students are disproportionately disciplined for cultural hairstyles. Although Texas passed the CROWN Act in 2021 to protect students from natural hair discrimination, a Black Texas high school student with dreadlocks has been excluded from his peers through in-school suspension and being assigned to an alternative school. The school claims that his hair is in violation of the dress code because his hair extends past his shoulders. *The Texas Tribune* shared the student's perspective: "I am being harassed by school officials and treated like a dog," George said. "I am being subjected to cruel treatment and a lot of unkind words from many adults within the school including teachers, principals and administrators." Unfortunately, George's experience is not an anomaly. Many Black students report experiencing "hair harassment" from schools that weaponize Black hair. Biased school policies involving Black students' hair is one of many ways recent laws and policies support beliefs about Black inferiority. State legislators have introduced and passed laws that do the following:

- Create discriminatory school policies that lead to the over-suspension and incarceration of Black students.
- Ban children's and young adult books by Black authors and that center Black characters.
- Oppose the Black Lives Matter movement through anti-protest bills.
- Deny teachers the right to teach the truth about slavery.
- Restrict how and when African American studies is offered.

Historian Carter G. Woodson emphasized the impact of schooling that teaches Black inferiority:

> If you can control a man's thinking you do not have to worry about his action. When you determine what a man shall think you do not have to concern yourself about what he will do. If you make a man feel that he is

inferior, you do not have to compel him to accept an inferior status, for he will seek it himself. If you make a man think that he is justly an outcast, you do not have to order him to the back door. He will go without being told; and if there is no back door, his very nature will demand one (1933, p. 21).

Trump conservatives must tell themselves the lie that Black citizens are inferior to continue the legacy of white supremacy.

Ideology V. Nationalism/White Nationalism/Christian Nationalism

> **The (Explicit) Lie:** The United States of America is exceptional to other countries, and this exceptionalism can be attributed to the hard work of white founding fathers and democratic ideals set forth in the founding documents. Consequently, (1) citizens must be loyal and devoted; (2) the country is above critique; (3) national pride is equated to obedience, not dissent; and (4) there is a singular national identity that individuals must embrace at the expense of their own cultures.

> **The (Explicit) Lie:** The United States of America is a Christian country founded on Judeo-Christian principles by Christians. Consequently, (1) select Christian values should underpin societal institutions and systems, (2) the government is best led by Christian elected officials, (3) respect for other religions/faiths results in Christian persecution, and (4) to be American is to be Christian.

Nationalism can be defined as deep devotion to a nation combined with a strong sense of a national identity. While these attributes seem innocuous, nationalism can be (and is often) violent when it leads to forced assimilation, othering, and exclusivity (McCorkle & Rodriguez, 2023). Harmful, too, is the belief in the nation's superiority, a belief that can lead to xenophobia and international conflicts. Closely connected to Eurocentrism is white nationalism, as adherents of both ideologies believe in the superiority of the white race. For white nationalists, white superiority also means white purity, which led to laws to protect whiteness and determine who gets to be white. As an example, the desire for white racial purity led to segregation laws, anti-miscegenation laws, and anti-immigration laws to prevent the "mongrelization," or mixing, of the white race. Moreover, white people constructed de jure (legally enforced) and de facto (existing in practice) rules around racial categories that were not based in science:

1. **Forced sterilization:** policies and practices that coerced women of color to get sterilized to reduce the African American, Latino(x), and Native American populations.
2. **Blood quantum laws:** laws to determine how much Native American ancestry a person has that were used by the federal government to limit tribal membership and access to resources. Blood quantum laws have been used by some tribes to determine tribal enrollment.
3. **One-drop rule:** a principle that defined individuals with any Black ancestry as Black to withhold white privilege from those with mixed Black and white ancestry.
4. *Partus sequitur ventrem*: doctrine that ensured children born to slave mothers (even if their fathers were white) were considered Black and, therefore, enslaved.

These laws led to nonwhite racial categories, such as mulatto (one Black and one white parent) and mestiza/o (mixed Indigenous and European). By creating these categories, whiteness remained the property of those who were "pure" whites. White purity yields white privilege, white power, and the preservation of white supremacy.

White nationalists in the United States work to sustain a white majority that holds power over other racial/ethnic groups (white racial hegemony) and to maintain a national identity that is defined by whiteness. Broadly speaking, however, this national identity is reserved for those who were born in the United States, speak English, and are Christian, heterosexual, and, most importantly, white. White nationalists' actions are inspired by the great replacement theory, which they believe is spearheaded by powerful Jews. The Southern Poverty Law Center sheds light on this theory: "The 'great replacement' theory is inherently white supremacist. It depends on stoking fears that a non-white population, which the theory's proponents characterize as 'inferior,' will displace a white majority" (Wilson & Flanagan, 2022). This fear of white extinction leads radicals to inflict violence upon nonwhite people. The National Immigration Forum (2021) outlines recent consequences of the great replacement theory:

> On Aug. 11, 2017, hundreds of individuals representing antisemitic and white supremacist groups including the Ku Klux Klan gathered for the

"Unite the Right" rally in Charlottesville, Virginia, a two-day event that sparked extreme violence and led to the death of a counterprotester. The extremists kicked off the rally by referencing the "great replacement" theory, chanting "You will not replace us" and "Jews will not replace us."

On Oct. 27, 2018, 11 congregants in a Pittsburgh synagogue were killed in one of the deadliest attacks against the Jewish community in the U.S. The shooter's belief in the "great replacement" theory precipitated the attack, as he believed that HIAS, a Jewish American nonprofit organization that provides aid and assistance to refugees, was working to "bring invaders in that kill our people."

On March 15, 2019, 51 people were killed in consecutive terrorist attacks on mosques in Christchurch, New Zealand. The shooter's manifesto repeatedly and directly referenced replacement theory. Its title was The Great Replacement.

On Aug. 3, 2019, 23 people were killed in a mass shooting at a Walmart in El Paso, Texas. The terrorist targeted Latino shoppers, and his manifesto referenced the "great replacement" theory and fears of a "Hispanic invasion of Texas." The manifesto also listed the Christchurch shooter as an inspiration.

White nationalists want a societal landscape that is monochromatic, when in reality, the national landscape is kaleidoscopic. Instead of respecting the diverse cultures that comprise a country like the United States, white nationalism insists on white dominance and therefore frowns upon cultural pluralism and democratic multiculturalism. These beliefs, prompted by fear of a nonwhite majority, lead to discriminatory immigration policies and stereotypical views of nonwhite immigrants. The president of the United States has displayed prototypical white nationalist behavior:

1 portrayed immigrants from Mexico and Central America as criminals (ABC News, 2016);
2 denigrated Black countries (Fram & Lemire, 2018);
3 imposed bans on individuals from Muslim countries (Frelick, 2017);
4 promoted dangerous, false claims about Haitian immigrants (Thomas & Wendling, 2024);
5 provided extreme funding for mass deportations of mostly Latino(x)s (American Immigration Council, 2025); and
6 promoted immigration of white individuals to the United States (Nawaz et al., 2025).

Today's nationalistic policies are not new. Since the country's inception, white men have sought to shape a national identity that mirrors whiteness and to control who has access-by-proximity to this identity.

Moreover, the United States has historically used Christianity as a weapon to uphold white supremacy and is still doing so today. Abolitionist Angela Gremke (1863) quoted a friend as describing slavery as a "divine institution." Gremke specified how deeply the South entangled their religion with white supremacy: "the South has incorporated slavery into her religion; that is the most fearful thing in this rebellion. They are fighting, verily believing that they are doing God service." It should not come as a surprise, then, that white Christianity has led to Christian nationalism, which is the deliberate conflating of Christianity with the United States. McCorkle and Rodriguez (2021, p. 5) summarized this conflation:

> For many to be American is to be religious, or even more specifically, Christian, and to be a good person of faith is to be a good American. This may be why the potential conflict between national loyalty and religious values seems so foreign to many Americans.

Instead of acknowledging that one of the country's core values is religious freedom, Christian nationalists insist upon religious intolerance—forcing the country to resemble a theocracy more than a democracy. Instead of keeping religion and government "on either side of an impregnable wall" (Seidel, 2019, p. 5), Christian nationalists forcibly meld them together in hopes of forming an inextricable bond. Seidel emphasized the problems of Christian nationalism:

> First, it seeks to alter our history, values, and national identity. Then it codifies Christian privilege in the law, favoring Christians above all others. Finally, it legally disfavors the nonreligious, non-Christians, and minorities such as the LGBTQIA community, by, for instance, permitting discrimination against them in places of public accommodation or in employment.
>
> (p. 6)

In her book *How to End Christian Nationalism*, Tyler drew upon an analogy similar to the one framing this book. Tyler (2024, p. 3) contended, "Christian nationalism is deeply entrenched in US society… the ideology has grown deep roots, creating an underground system that makes it harder to extricate." Christian nationalism is rooted in white supremacist soil and leads to an intentional bias against non-Christians, people of color, and immigrants who are locked out of the national identity. Tyler shared a poignant statement written by Christians Against Christian Nationalism that distinguishes Christianity from Christian nationalism:

> Christian nationalism seeks to merge Christian and American identities, distorting both the Christian faith and America's constitutional democracy. Christian nationalism demands Christianity be privileged by the State and implies that to be a good American, one must be Christian. It often overlaps with and provides cover for white supremacy and racial subjugation. We reject this damaging ideology.
>
> (p. 14)

In 2025, the Pew Research Center found that 62 percent of U.S. adults describe themselves as Christians (Smith et al., 2025). In her important book, Tyler pleads with these Christians to denounce Christian nationalism.

Because nationalism presumes superiority, the United States, its history, and its founders are beyond criticism, and citizens are encouraged to adopt blind patriotism. Eurocentric history is protected by statues and monuments that center white "heroes" and by whitewashed school curricula and materials. Nationalists hold pride in the nation's white heritage, as seen, for example, in the worship of the Confederate flag and the desire to "make America great again." Nationalism/Christian nationalism is reflected in "English-only" mandates, restrictions on immigration from non-Western countries, and violence inflicted upon Muslims, Jews, and other religious minorities. It is characterized by exclusion, elitism, and ethnocentrism. White nationalists hold firmly to their ideology, "believing that they are doing God service."

Recent legislation also shows evidence of this political ideology:

- attempts to whitewash history, or to present it in a way that glorifies white leaders
- failure to allow for a curriculum that confronts white supremacy and racism, in the past and the present day
- removal of books with LGBTQIA+ characters
- uncritical approaches to social studies and civics
- inclusion of the Ten Commandments in classrooms
- offering incentives to schools that offer a Bible curriculum

Conclusion

Woven together, these five ideologies form present-day conservative ideology, and it is this ideology that imbues opposition to educational justice and fuels unjust education policy. A reflection of nationalism, Governor Ron DeSantis (Florida) spearheaded anti-CRT legislation. He justified his opposition to WOKE ("Wrong to Our Kids and Employees") education by falsely concluding that schools are forcing students to hate the United States: "We won't allow Florida tax dollars to be spent teaching kids to hate our country." This is the fear of nationalists—that students will rebel against the country instead of complying with its nationalistic aims.

> *Questions to Ponder*
> 1. What other lies do Trump conservatives tell others? Tell themselves?
> 2. Why has this campaign to deceive been successful?
> 3. Thinking back to Part I of this book, can you see ways that these ideologies have influenced laws around citizenship and education?
> 4. How might the opposition challenge the ideas put forth in this chapter? What evidence might support their claims?

Notes

1. Learn more here: https://www.zinnedproject.org/campaigns/teach-truth/
2. Learn more here: https://www.nea.org/advocating-for-change/racial-social-justice/tools-justice/freedom-learn
3. Students for Fair Admissions, Inc. v. President and Fellows of Harvard College (2022), No. 20-1199.
4. Full dissent. https://democrats-edworkforce.house.gov/imo/media/doc/justice_sotomayor_dissent_-_students_for_fair_admissions_vharvardunc.pdf

Part III

Healing the Trees

Central questions answered: How can justice workers heal the trees planted by our ancestors? In other words, how can we reimagine the movement for educational justice given current opposition?

8

Healing the Trees Through (Critical) Introspection

In Part I of this book, you learned that imperialist white supremacist capitalist cisheteropatriarchy poisoned the soil of the United States. Consequently, the tree roots were damaged, causing all the trees that were planted by justice workers to be stunted. Still, these trees bore fruit, though limited. The blighting of the fruit by conservative opposition was the focus of Part II. In Part III, I aim to put forth ideas for healing the trees, instead of deracinating, or uprooting, them. The Gullah/Geechee people, descendants of enslaved Africans who reside on the Carolina coast, have a proverb: "Mus tek cyear a de root fa heal de tree" (Must take care of the roots in order to heal de tree) (Gullah/Geechee Nation, 2021). To this end, the chapters in Part III focus on healing the tree roots that were sickened by white supremacist soil.

First, to heal the roots of trees, justice workers must engage in critical introspection. Critical introspection can be defined as a process of self-examination of one's perceptions, beliefs, thoughts, and emotions to uncover latent motives, biases, and patterns. It requires individuals to look deeply and honestly within, make meaning of what is seen, and use the knowledge gained through meaning-making to inform future actions.

Knowledge That Matters

I matriculated through my teacher education program in the mid-1990s, beginning my teaching career in 1998. In one of my courses, the professor enumerated the seven kinds of knowledge that effective teachers must hold. In preparation to write this chapter, I found and reread the oft-cited article from which my professor based her instruction. Shulman (1987) listed these seven knowledge categories:

1. content knowledge;
2. general pedagogical knowledge;
3. curriculum knowledge;
4. pedagogical content knowledge;
5. knowledge of learners and their characteristics;
6. knowledge of educational contexts; and
7. knowledge of educational ends, purposes, and values.

This list reaffirms my appreciation for the artistry of teaching, as these varied knowledges must be woven together to be an effective teacher. (We ask a lot of teachers while deprofessionalizing and undervaluing their work.) As a scholar whose entire body of work makes an argument for the importance of educators responding to students' cultural backgrounds and sociopolitical contexts, I appreciate Shulman's inclusion of categories 5 and 6—knowledge of learners and their characteristics and knowledge of educational contexts. In addition, as a former teacher and current professor, I can attest to the need to have strong pedagogical (teaching) knowledge. Teachers must be good at, well, *teaching*. But there's even more. Missing from Schulman's list is what I have come to believe, through my work with hundreds of preservice and in-service teachers, is the most important kind of knowledge that justice-oriented teachers need—self-knowledge. Teachers are their own best tool in the classroom. For that reason, they should hold deep knowledge of this tool.

Theorists behind the diversity and equity pedagogies defined in Chapter 3 stressed the value of student knowledge (number 5 on Shulman's list). Specifically, they argued that knowledge of students' cultural backgrounds is essential for designing instruction that optimizes student learning. At the same time, many of these scholars came to understand that knowledge of students must be coupled with knowledge of oneself. Palmer (1997) believed that knowledge of students and the subject depends heavily on self-knowledge. Santoro (2009) described this synergy: "What is needed in teacher education are opportunities for knowledge about 'the other' to be developed in conjunction with knowledge of self. These knowledges are mutually constitutive, as each builds upon, and is dependent on, the other to make meaning" (p. 41). Said differently, educators need knowledge of the *ethnic self* and the *ethnic other* (Santoro, 2009). As educators learn about students' cultures, they should also examine themselves as cultured beings in order that they can be aware of how their identities shape their work with their students. One of the pioneers of culturally relevant pedagogy, Gloria Ladson-Billings, explained in a 1998 interview that cultural incongruence between students and their teachers necessitates teacher self-knowledge and understanding.

> The major thing that I think people who are going to teach kids, any kids—not just kids different from themselves, but particularly if they're teaching kids who are different from themselves culturally, racially, ethnically, linguistically—is to understand that they, themselves, are cultural beings. What that understanding will do is help them understand that the kinds of decisions they make, the way they think, the way they see the world, is culturally mediated.
>
> (in Ingram Willis & Lewis, 1998, p. 3)

Santoro's (2009) findings support Ladson-Billings's explanation. In asking what knowledge of self teachers need, she found that "the preservice students had little awareness of their own subject positionings in relation to ethnicity. They understood 'ethnic' as a label for 'others' but not themselves" (p. 40). I recently facilitated a workshop for a class of graduate students studying language and literacy. I asked each student (all white) to describe the aspect of their cultural identity that most impacts their lives. Not a single one named race as a factor affecting their daily lives. I appreciate Altman's (2006) explanation for this phenomenon:

> Consider for a moment the unreflectiveness of many white people about the meaning of their whiteness. If you ask white people what it means to them to be white, many will greet you with a blank stare. For many whites, whiteness is a kind of baseline or standard; it does not refer to a particular ethnic or racial group.
>
> (p. 49)

It's important for all teachers, but especially white teachers whose whiteness often goes unexamined, to realize that their cultures impact every aspect of the classroom—from discipline expectations to the knowledge they value. To see themselves as cultural beings, white educators must engage in critical introspection, which involves "honest self-reflection and critique" of one's actions and thoughts (Howard, 2024, p. 198).

Critical reflection challenges educators to recognize how their positionality impacts their work with students (Howard, 2003). It requires educators to be "willing to look in the mirror and not run from what [we] see." "To look in the mirror" is to examine how one sees themselves and what they bring to justice work. After all, we are not robots—"objective individuals immune to biases and prejudices" (Caldera, 2018). When we begin with the self, we acknowledge our subjectivities and proclivities. Parker (1997) explained:

> Teaching, like any truly human activity, emerges from one's inwardness, for better or worse. As I teach, I project the condition of my soul onto my students, my subject, and our way of being together.... Viewed from this angle, teaching holds a mirror to the soul. If I am willing to look in that mirror, and not run from what I see, I have a chance to gain self-knowledge—and knowing myself is as crucial to good teaching as knowing my students and my subject.
>
> (p. 15)

Starker Glass and Carter Berry (2022) described critical reflection as a constant process of learning and unlearning by which educators acknowledge privilege and biases and work to confront and disrupt them.

The Role of Bias

Howard J. Ross (2014, p. xi), the author of *Everyday Bias*, claims that "human beings are consistently, routinely, and profoundly biased." There are two types of bias: explicit, or conscious, and implicit, or unconscious. Explicit bias refers to the attitudes, prejudices, and beliefs about certain groups that we are fully aware of. Implicit bias, on the other hand, describes unintended, subtle, and subconscious associations learned through past experiences or enculturation. They are harmful because they might lead to discriminatory or unfair treatment of others. Biases are human nature, not necessarily an indictment of your "goodness" as a person or a reflection of your morals. At the same time, you're responsible to reflect and reform these biases. I recently taught an English composition course. The racial composition of the students was approximately 60% white and 40% Black. One day, I realized that I frequently reprimanded the Black boys (who sat in a group) for talking even though I rarely reprimanded the white boys (who sat in a different group), even though they talked just as much, or more. Unconscious associations about Black boys and misbehavior in the classroom had shown up in my teaching. Because of my critical introspection, I recognized my bias and changed my actions. *Learning for Justice*, a leading resource to support educators in pursuit of educational justice, suggests that educators take Harvard's Implicit Association Test[1] to get an indication of their implicit biases. I invite my students to survey themselves using this tool. After taking one of these assessments, one of my students wrote about her shift from using "churches" in her classroom to using "places of worship," realizing her bias toward her Christian faith.

We see the world mainly through our own experiences. In other words, what we believe to be true, what we value, and the perspectives we take are often due to what we've experienced, what we've witnessed, and what we've been taught. The broader and more varied our personal experiences are, the better we can be at seeing multiple points of view and understanding others. Because we live in a society that centers white culture and experiences and relegates the cultures of people of color to the margins, white justice workers, particularly, need to be intentional about learning about the lived experiences of these groups. Having meaningful, authentic experiences with minoritized individuals and groups can help reduce bias.

Doing the Work

Because all justice work, but especially teaching, begins with the self, I've created a framework for critical introspection that addresses the need for teachers to (1) understand themselves as cultured beings; (2) explore their values, beliefs, and assumptions about cultural differences; and (3) deduce how their values, beliefs, and assumptions impact their justice work (see Tables 8.1–8.3). Critical introspection can begin with carefully constructed questions or prompts that serve as guides to uncovering the self. I've provided examples of what these questions and prompts might look like. Critical introspection should not be a curricular add-on or an optional assignment. It should not be the opening or closing minutes to a professional development workshop. Preferably, critical introspection should be a sustained, intentional, and integral aspect of teacher preparation and professional learning. Moreover, educators who commit

Table 8.1 Framework for Critical Introspection, Part I

Part I is designed to reveal who you are and what has shaped you into this person.	
Cultural Identity: Cultural identity encompasses religion, socioeconomic class, sexuality, (dis)abilities, gender, ethnicity, race, geography, and age or generation. What dimensions of your culture impact your identity most/least? In other words, which dimensions most/least define you? Explain with detailed examples.	**Experiences:** How have your experiences shaped how you see the world and your approach to justice work? What experiences have helped to define you? In what ways have your lived experiences limited/expanded your understanding of the world? What is one experience that has changed you, positively or negatively? Why did it impact you the way it did?
Societal Institutions: Social institutions are systems with rules, expectations, and procedures that meet a societal need. Institutions can be families, schools, places of worship, universities, prisons, libraries, media, and more. Which institution has shaped your identity most? Explain how.	**Individuals:** What individuals have helped shape you into the person you are? Who has influenced you the most, positively or negatively? In what ways has this individual helped shape your understanding of the world? Describe the individuals and explain how they've influenced your beliefs, particularly around justice.
Social Positionality: How do your cultural identities position you with power and privilege?	**Congruence/Incongruence:** How can you leverage your cultural congruence with the students and families you serve (or hope to serve)? Or what benefits or challenges might your cultural incongruence create?

to this work should be careful to not judge themselves harshly for past mistakes and allow sufficient time to process, and possibly recover from, revelations. To achieve the three goals stated above, those who engage in critical introspection must do so with honesty, humility, and bravery. Remember, critical introspection involves learning and unlearning. The questions in the tables can be a guide. As you answer these questions, respond with your core truth instead of what you think you should say. This is the only way to uncover truths about yourself. Because we are our most important tool in reimagining the movement for educational

Table 8.2 Framework for Critical Introspection, Part II

Part II uncovers your beliefs, values, and assumptions. Answers to these questions will help you better understand your thinking and actions.

Marriage/Family:
What makes one a good parent? What do you truly believe to be right/true for marriage and families? What kinds of marriage and families do you think are best for children? What marriage and family structures do you believe are acceptable? Unacceptable? How have these beliefs/values shifted over time, if at all?

Religion/Faith:
Do you believe children should be raised within a religious community? What do you truly believe to be right/true in terms of religion/faith? What religions/faiths do you believe add most value to children's lives? What stereotypes do you hold about religious minorities, atheists, and agnostics? How have these beliefs/values shifted over time, if at all?

Gender/Sexuality:
What do you truly believe to be right/true about gender and sexuality? Who (what individuals and/or institutions) do you believe should teach children about gender and sexuality? How have these beliefs/values shifted over time, if at all?

Race/Skin Color:
What do you truly believe about racial and skin color differences? What students do you tend to notice? Not notice? What do you assume about students of color? White students? When are you race neutral? How have these beliefs/values shifted over time, if at all?

Ability/Disability:
What assumptions do you have about students with disabilities? What group—students with disabilities or students without disabilities—do you believe you are best equipped to support? Do you know anyone personally with a disability? Do you notice when a facility is inaccessible? How have these beliefs/values shifted over time, if at all?

Language/Languaging Practices:
What language(s) do you truly believe should be used in schools? What language(s) do you prioritize most? What do you assume about English language learners (ELLs)? How have these beliefs/values shifted over time, if at all?

Citizenship/Nationality:
What do you believe makes a person a citizen? A foreigner? What rights do citizens deserve that noncitizens don't? What assumptions do you make about immigrant students? How have these beliefs/values shifted over time, if at all?

Social Class:
What are some words you associate with each social class? How often do you associate with people outside of your own social class? Describe students of the social class you serve (or hope to serve). Generally speaking, members of which social class do you believe work the hardest? Perform better academically? How have these beliefs/values shifted over time, if at all?

Table 8.3 Framework for Critical Introspection, Part III

Part III will help you better understand how your beliefs, values, and assumptions impact your work as an educator.

Marriage/Family:
How do (or might) your beliefs, values, and assumptions about marriage and family impact your teaching practice? How might your beliefs determine what content and materials you include or exclude? What biases do you hold? How might you have caused harm as a result of these biases? How can you mitigate the impact of these biases?

Religion/Faith:
How do (or might) your beliefs, values, and assumptions about religion and faith impact your teaching practice? How might your beliefs determine what content and materials you include or exclude? How might you have caused harm as a result of these biases? What biases do you hold? How can you mitigate the impact of these biases?

Gender/Sexuality:
How do (or might) your beliefs, values, and assumptions about gender and sexuality impact your teaching practice? How might your beliefs determine what content and materials you include or exclude? How might you have caused harm as a result of these biases? What biases do you hold? How can you mitigate the impact of these biases?

Race/Skin Color:
How do (or might) your beliefs, values, and assumptions about race and skin color impact your teaching practice? How might your beliefs determine what content and materials you include or exclude? What biases do you hold? How might you have caused harm as a result of these biases? How can you mitigate the impact of these biases?

Ability/Disability:
How do (or might) your beliefs, values, and assumptions about ability and disability impact your teaching practice? How might your beliefs determine what content and materials you include or exclude? What biases do you hold? How might you have caused harm as a result of these biases? How can you mitigate the impact of these biases?

Language/Languaging Practices:
How do (or might) your beliefs, values, and assumptions about language and languaging practices impact your teaching practice? How might your beliefs determine what content and materials you include or exclude? What biases do you hold? How might you have caused harm as a result of these biases? How can you mitigate the impact of these biases?

Citizenship/Nationality:
How do (or might) your beliefs, values, and assumptions about citizenship and nationality impact your teaching practice? How might your beliefs determine what content and materials you include or exclude? What biases do you hold? How might you have caused harm as a result of these biases? How can you mitigate the impact of these biases?

Social Class:
How do (or might) your beliefs, values, and assumptions about social class impact your teaching practice? How might your beliefs determine what content and materials you include or exclude? What biases do you hold? How might you have caused harm as a result of these biases? How can you mitigate the impact of these biases?

justice, we must prioritize self-knowledge as much as we do the forms of knowledge outlined by Shulman (1987).

As you perform the work of critical introspection, you may begin to recognize that you've been deeply shaped by white supremacy: We all have.

Me and White Supremacy

In *Me and White Supremacy*, Layla F. Saad (2020, p. 14) conveyed the importance of truth-telling when engaging in critical introspection: "If you are willing to dare to look white supremacy right in the eye and see yourself reflected back, you are going to become better equipped to dismantle it within yourself and within your communities." The ultimate goal in this uncovering of truths through deep excavation is to pinpoint ways we have perpetuated white supremacy in our policies, practices, and procedures. Revisiting the forms of systemic oppression outlined in Chapter 1 will be helpful in this work.

Teacher educators must model this bravery for our students. As a result of the lack of focus on rigorous, critical examinations into the self during my own teacher preparation, it would be many years into my teaching career before I began to engage in this enlightening work. Now I do it routinely. I share with my students an example of my own deep excavation into how I had been complicit in upholding white language supremacy as a teacher and professor (Caldera & Babino-Ruiz, 2020). My sharing as a Black woman demonstrates to my students that women of color, though oppressed ourselves, can become oppressors by internalizing white supremacist values and beliefs. This idea of the oppressed internalizing the oppressor's worldview and replicating the structures of oppression is an important theme in Paulo Freire's *Pedagogy of the Oppressed* (1970/2000), one of the most impactful books I've read.

In an interview, Toni Morrison (Hoby, 2015) recalled a conversation with author James Baldwin in which Baldwin described internalized white supremacy as "a little white man deep inside of all of us." Similar to Baldwin, Black feminist Audre Lorde (1984/2007) taught that "the true focus of revolutionary change is never merely the oppressive situations which we seek to escape, but that piece of the oppressor which is planted deep within each of us" (pp. 112–113). We heal the trees by first purifying our own soil.

Introspection holds value for at least one additional reason that is apropos for teachers who are members of historically marginalized groups and may not fit the white supremacist mold of an ideal teacher—white, English-speaking, middle-class background, heterosexual, Christian. My colleagues and I wrote about the significance of teachers of color unpacking their identities because we believe they should be cognizant of the ways their cultural identities are marginalized in academic spaces (Calderon-Berumen, Babino, & Caldera, 2023). It is important that teachers who hold marginalized identities "embark in a decolonizing identity process to break with westernized ideas of what education should be and what a teacher should look like" (p. 50). These white supremacist ideas impose standards regarding languaging practices, dress, sexuality, race, and more. As an example, in 2016, a fourth-grade teacher in Atlanta who became known as #TeacherBae received criticism for looking "too sexy" at work (Lucas D'Oyley, 2020). This characterization of Ms. Brown is part of a long history of sexualization and objectification of Black women. Similarly, a Kentucky "Teacher of the Year" resigned from his job in 2022 after facing LGBTQIA+ discrimination (Lavietes, 2022). In his testimony before the U.S. House of Representatives, Mr. Carver (2022) admitted, "I've faced hatred, bigotry, and discrimination my whole career as a gay teacher, and I've weathered the storm because my presence saves lives." This is an example of how critical introspection can lead to enlightenment about how one's marginalized identities impacts one's work.

The following questions, adapted from Calderon-Berumen, Babino, and Caldera (2023), can help teachers from historically marginalized groups reconcile their identity with their work.

1. Which aspects of your cultural identity do you feel are welcomed in schools?
2. Which aspects do you feel are excluded, or do you feel you are forced to exclude?
3. What experiences have caused you to feel this way?
4. How have these experiences affected the way you show up in the classroom?
5. How might you reconcile all aspects of your identity at work?

Healing trees damaged by white supremacy can sometimes involve healing ourselves. Teachers who hold historically marginalized identities—for example, those who are LGBTQIA+, who grew up in impoverished homes, who speak English variations such as African American English (AAE), who are religious minorities—must exercise their right to fully and audaciously exist in academic spaces. Just like students need schools that have an atmosphere of inclusivity and belonging, teachers deserve this same kind of work environment. Critical introspection unveils the true self and allows nontraditional educators to reckon with white supremacist values that challenge their presence in schools.

Healing the Trees

Healing the trees starts with examining the roots damaged by white supremacist soil. We should

1. recognize how our beliefs and actions have been shaped by white supremacy;
2. admit to holding biases, identify them, and work to mitigate them;
3. commit to the ongoing work of critical introspection; and
4. be intentional about having authentic experiences with diverse individuals and communities to avoid stereotyping.

Although critical introspection is integral to effective teaching, Benjamin (2022, p. 54) cautioned justice workers to not just do internal work: "If we only concentrate on our internal work while ignoring the fires burning all around us, we'll eventually be consumed." This is the focus of the next chapter, working to change institutions.

> *Questions to Ponder*
>
> 1. Engaging in critical introspection can be unsettling for some educators and downright terrifying for others. How do you feel about engaging in critical introspection?
> 2. Why do you think Shulman omitted "knowledge of self" as a form of knowledge effective teachers should hold?
> 3. Do you think critical introspection is an important aspect of reimagining educational justice? Why/why not?

Note

1. https://implicit.harvard.edu/implicit/takeatest.htmlhttps://implicit.harvard.edu/implicit/takeatest.html

9

Healing the Trees Through Institutionalizing

In order to heal the trees harmed by white supremacy, justice workers must institutionalize just policies, meaning make them a permanent part of an institution's, in this case a school's, structure. I have quoted Madiba's (a name that Mandela was called as an expression of reverence) words, "Education is the most powerful weapon which you can use to change the world," many times in my work as a professor, scholar, and consultant. Like Mandela, I see education as essential to changing the world from how it is to how it ought to be. (In Chapter 11, I describe the kind of education needed for socio-political-economic change, so I won't go into that topic here.) Having witnessed the attacks on public education in recent years, however, I now believe that public education can only be just if policies are just. Perhaps, then, education *policy* is the most powerful weapon that we can use to change the world. Despite the precarious nature of our democracy, we are still a nation governed by laws and policies that dictate how systems operate. Ball (2021, p. 12) stressed the importance of policy in education: "Policy does not simply change what we do, it can and may also change what we are." The idea of policy having the power to change who we are is profound. One way that policy can change who we are is our social identities. For example, a policy change around citizenship can make us "legal" or "illegal," a classification that has major implications for our identities. Ball went on to say that "policy action is almost always about reform, about doing things different, about change and improvement." These were the goals of the legislative milestones examined in Chapter 2—to improve education for students who were not currently being served effectively because of education policy that was sown in white supremacist soil. Instead of seeing policy as a way to *reform* schools, we must see it as a tool to *transform* schooling.

What Is Education Policy?

Education policy can be defined as the body of federal, state, and local laws that govern the functioning of schools. Education is largely a function of state and local governments, so state and local policies have the strongest effects on schooling. Education policy is wide-ranging, impacting broad issues such as districting and funding to specific topics such as dress code and attendance. Policies are created by lawmakers who hold certain beliefs about the following:

- the purpose of schooling,
- teaching and learning strategies,
- what students should learn,
- the role of teachers,
- student safety,
- resources/materials that should be available to students,
- student behavior and punishment,
- the needs of specific student populations,
- and more

It can be concluded that policymakers—grounded in their educational philosophies, influenced by a multitude of societal factors, shaped by biases, and compelled by economic shifts—control every aspect of schooling. This is especially true of state legislatures because they hold the primary responsibility for establishing, funding, and regulating public education. Historically, this power has been hoarded by white men who have created policies that establish and uphold white supremacy (with or without intention). Even as public schools have become more racially/ethnically diverse, white men, functioning as state legislators, have maintained control of public schooling. Findings from a 2021–2022 survey by the National Conference of State Legislators (2025) revealed that 70% of state legislators are white men, while students of color (African American, Asian American, Latino(x)/Hispanic, Native American, and mixed race) comprised more than 50% of the U.S. public school student population in 2022. The percentage of students of color is expected to increase by 2031, and the white student population is expected to decrease (National Center for Education Statistics,

2024). We need policymakers who reflect the interests of an increasingly diverse student population.

Love and Justice

As a justice worker, I'm intrigued by the connection between love and justice. In *All About Love: New Visions*, bell hooks (2000/2018) wrote that love must lead to justice and that every movement for social justice emphasized a love ethic. Likewise, Cornel West's definition of *justice* makes a similar connection: justice is what love looks like in public. In other words, love compels one to act justly toward the beloved. These actions include challenging the oppressive system that leads to marginalization. In her study of Black teachers, Beauboeuf-Lafontant (2005) found that these teachers exhibited "care as activism that challenged the subordinate social position of their students" (p. 442). In other words, Teachers who care about marginalized students demonstrate their care, not just through affection, but also through activism. The argument that justice hinges on love is sometimes challenged by those who believe that just laws are not dependent on love. In a 1964 speech at Oberlin College, Dr. Martin Luther King Jr. conveyed his thoughts on the relationship between love and justice: "It may be true that the law cannot make a man love me, but it can stop him from lynching me, and I think that's pretty important" (King, 1965, para 6). Similarly, civil rights and gay rights activist Bayard Rustin expressed sentiments about the importance of legislation:

> Our job is not to get those people who dislike us to love us. Nor was our aim in the civil rights movement to get prejudiced white people to love us. Our aim was to try to create the kind of America, legislatively, morally, and psychologically, such that even though some whites continued to hate us, they could not openly manifest that hate.
>
> (quoted in Gilmore, 2020)

Still, I've often heard folks lament the lack of love in society, reflecting sentiments of songwriter Burt Bacharach's 1965 lyrics:

> What the world needs now is love, sweet love
> It's the only thing that there's just too little of
> What the world needs now is love, sweet love
> No not just for some oh, but just for everyone

I share this concern for a loveless world, but as King and Rustin expressed, we can't rely on love alone to make the world more just. Unless love leads one to legislate justice, it is not enough. Schools will not become more equitable by wishing for it to happen, talking about making it happen, or praying for it to happen. Justice must be legislated, whether or not it is compelled by love.

My Policy (Dis)Engagement

I remember taking an education policy class as part of my teacher certification program in the mid-1990s. School Law. It was taught by a white man who lectured for three hours about the major policies that had shaped education. I didn't connect with the lessons in any way because they seemed focused on a distant past with little relevance to the work on which I was embarking. The only law I remember from the class was the Individuals with Disabilities in Education Act (IDEA), which requires that students be educated in the least restrictive environment. I think I remember this one because our professor told us that we'd teach special education students "whether we like it or not" and that we could be sued if we didn't follow the law. This scared me because I felt unprepared to meet the needs of students with special needs. As I reflect on this experience, I now see how policies about classroom instruction must be met with aligned teacher preparation.

I don't remember being taught that I can (and should) have an active role in shaping education policy as an educator. And in my early years as a middle school teacher, I was discouraged from being "too political." Untenured teachers were dissuaded from attending board meetings or speaking up in any way. I am ashamed to say that although I have worked in education since my early twenties, I was not knowledgeable of or involved in education policy in any way until my doctoral studies 13 years ago. I voted every four years in presidential elections, but I didn't "do politics."

My political disengagement changed when I enrolled in a course called Public and Political Discourses on Education in 2013. The entire course focused on the impact of neoliberal ideology on education policy. I spent the first half of the semester trying to understand the term *neoliberalism*. Once I did, I saw how neoliberal beliefs about investments and profits, competition in markets, privatization, and deregulation shaped education policies that led to the proliferation of high-stakes standardized testing, charter schools, competition among schools for funding, rigid accountability, and appointed (as opposed to elected) leadership. The theoretical knowledge developed in class was concretized when I observed policymaking on a local level. As a research apprentice of my professor, I witnessed firsthand how Chicago educators resisted these neoliberal reforms by working to change policies that negatively impacted neighborhood schools and the students and families they serve. These educators, organized as the Chicago Teachers Union and a subgroup, Teachers for Social Justice,[1] marched, occupied Chicago City Hall, testified before Congress, hosted conferences, and went on strike. (My professor, Dr. M. Francyne Huckaby, wrote a book on this topic, *Researching Resistance: Public Education After Neoliberalism*.) They knew that they could change the infrastructure, or the basic framework of the system, of Chicago Public Schools only by changing its policies. For the first time in my life, I witnessed teachers actively shaping education policy. I left this class, and its corresponding practicum, with a deeper knowledge of how local policies shape practices. Schools are the way they are, in large part, because policies caused them to be this way.

Several years later, I had the chance to deepen my knowledge of state education policy by participating in a fellowship sponsored by the Intercultural Research Development Association (IDRA). IDRA is a nonprofit organization based in San Antonio, Texas, that, among other things, works to make education policy in Texas equitable. Morgan Craven, IDRA's national director of policy, advocacy, and community engagement, conceived the idea for the fellowship, recognizing that

> education policy decisions are largely made and influenced by people who do not reflect the population of Texas' and Georgia's K–12 schools or institutions of higher education, the majority of whom are students of color. The state-level advocacy community has not adequately provided space to advocates with experience with communities of color and is missing their important expertise.
>
> (IDRA, 2024)

I was one of four inaugural fellows who advocated for state policies that would improve access and opportunities for underrepresented students in Texas. The experience was life changing. As a fellow, I was given a seat not only at the decision-making table but also at the idea-creation table. Over the 10-month fellowship, I listened to the voices of marginalized communities, joined coalitions, wrote bills, persuaded lawmakers to file them, provided testimony, conducted research to inform legislation, performed analysis of bill language, and more. A snapshot of my work can be found here: https://www.idra.org/idra-education-policy-fellows/.

Perhaps the most important realization that came from this experience is that anyone can impact state education policy. Whereas I had formerly seen education policy as something imposed upon educators, students, families, and communities, I now saw policy as something that can be created and influenced by educators, students, families, and communities. It is our responsibility to promote educational justice by ensuring that policies reflect the needs, aspirations, and hopes of historically underserved students. This was the work of justice workers before us, and it is our work today.

Policymaking

Having general knowledge about policymaking can be constructive for justice workers. Gillborn (2005) recommended the following questions to those involved in policymaking, as these questions reveal the material consequences of policy:

> First, the question of priorities: who or what is driving education policy? Second, the question of beneficiaries: who wins and who loses as a result of education policy priorities? And finally, the question of outcomes: what are the effects of policy?

Moreover, Starker Glass and Carter Berry (2022, p. 29) cited Dr. Jewell Cooper's more equity-focused questions that should guide educational policymaking:

1. Who is marginalized or reduced? How are they seen, valued, and encouraged?
2. Who benefits?
3. Who made the policy?
4. Who created the standard?
5. Who is impacted?
6. How are people with social advantages seen, valued, and encouraged?
7. How are people who have been marginalized seen, valued, and encouraged?

Guided by answers to questions like these, justice workers are positioned to create and advocate for just educational policies. Policies are not static. They are dynamic. Ball (2021, p. 12) emphasized the point that "policies are made and remade." "Policy cannot be treated simply as an object, a product or an outcome but rather *it is a process, something on-going, interactional and unstable*" (p. 12). Sadly, this supposedly democratic process often excludes the individuals who are best positioned to influence policy—educators (Watkins, 2022). From her review of literature on the role of teachers in educational policymaking, Watkins concluded, "Creating policies without input from educators often results in ill-conceived and nearly impossible to implement policies. Offering teachers more direct input into the policy process could improve innovative, sustainable educational policy" (p. 18). Politicians, then, should find innovative ways to involve teachers in their work.

Educators can't afford to take an apolitical stance on schooling. To the contrary, educators concerned about educational justice must seek opportunities to take on leadership roles in shaping (and implementing) policy. Educators should realize the importance of having a political voice, which means "recognizing that one's perspective and ideas have power" (Watkins, 2022, p. 1). They can exercise their political voice through organizations like TeachPlus,[2] which helps teachers become equity-focused leaders who are policy advocates. Educators for Excellence[3] also works to ensure that teachers have a leading voice in policies that impact them and their students. Similarly, Teachers for Social Justice organizes educators to advocate for educational equity. But education policy is not just the work of educators but of justice workers who occupy a multitude of roles. Admittedly, policy work can be time consuming, confusing, and laborious. I believe it is designed to be this way to ensure that decision making is left to only a few. We must not be dismayed. I recommend that justice workers join coalitions and organizations working to advance educational justice. These coalitions and organizations produce legislative agendas containing policy priorities and tool kits for those wanting to take action around issues that matter to them. As examples, in addition to IDRA, I support the work of the Georgia NAACP and the Georgia Coalition for Education Justice. Nationally, I support the American Civil Liberties Union (ACLU) and the Southern Poverty Law Center (SPLC). Find out what education and education-adjacent organizations are leading this work in your state and join them. This work cannot be done alone.

Last, and maybe obviously, education policies are shaped by the people—the voting populace, whose opinions are influenced by narratives about schools and society. The importance of helping to shape these narratives cannot be overstated. Policymaking, in making cases, comes down to who is able to tell the most compelling story and is able to get the story to the largest audience. Consequently, media—in all its forms—must be utilized effectively to institutionalize just educational policies. Civil rights leader Malcolm X is quoted as having said the following about the power of media:

> The media's the most powerful entity on Earth. They have the power to make the innocent guilty and to make the guilty innocent, and that's power. Because they control the minds of the masses. The press is so powerful in its image-making role, it can make the criminal look like he's the victim and make the victim look like he's the criminal. If you aren't careful, the newspapers will have you hating the people who are being oppressed and loving the people who are doing the oppressing.
> (quoted in *Austin Daily Herald*, 2021)

The truths of marginalized folks must saturate the media in order to influence policy, making journalism essential to policymaking. Considering the enormity of education policy, it should be obvious that a just education can only be realized when rights are codified by policy, in other words, when they are institutionalized. When rights are institutionalized, they become part of the structure and practice of an institution or society. In the United States, institutionalization happens through policymaking.

Healing the Trees

Healing the trees starts with examining the roots damaged by white supremacist soil. We should

1. recognize that schooling is a political act,
2. vote in every election for officials who are boldly committed to justice,
3. form/join coalitions to advance our concerns,
4. get involved in policymaking to help ensure that laws are just for all, and
5. stay committed for the long haul.

In sum, institutional oppression must be dealt with institutionally. We must always be cognizant of Coretta Scott King's words: "Freedom is never really won, you earn it and win it in every generation." The dynamic nature of policymaking is both a blessing and a curse. As is evident by recent attacks on freedoms won decades, even centuries, before, we must be relentless in our pursuit of justice. Education can change the world. It can change societies. It can change communities. It can change individuals. But these possibilities can only be realized if education is shaped by policies that speak to the needs of all students. We heal the trees by instituting just school policies that are informed by the histories, perspectives, experiences, and knowledges of those who have been silenced in policymaking. Most importantly, justice workers who aim to reimagine just education policies must be cognizant of the ways white supremacy continues to restrict the liberties of marginalized students and their families and must eradicate these policies.

Questions to Ponder

1. What role does love play in education policymaking?
2. Can you think of 2–3 educational policies that should be immutable?
3. What has been your involvement in politics?
4. Given your positionality, in what ways can you impact educational policy on local, state, and federal levels?
5. Do you think critical institutionalization is an important aspect of reimagining educational justice? Why/why not?

Notes

1 You can learn more about Teachers for Social Justice on their website: https://t4sj.org/
2 You can learn more about TeachPlus on their website: https://teachplus.org/
3 You can learn more Educators for Excellence on their website: https://e4e.org/

10

Healing the Trees Through Inclusivity and Intersectionality

In order to heal the trees of white supremacy, justice workers must prioritize inclusivity and intersectionality. Simply stated, inclusivity is the deliberate practice of including all types of individuals and communities. The movement for educational justice must be a collective effort to uproot white supremacy. When inclusivity in the movement for educational justice is achieved, all marginalized groups feel valued, respected, and have equal opportunities to participate and thrive. Inclusivity emphasizes the importance of diverse voices and perspectives in the fight for a more equitable society. Relatedly, intersectionality is the idea that individuals have multifaceted identities and, as a result, can be oppressed by the overlapping of multiple forms of oppression. In other words, "There is no such thing as a single-issue struggle because we do not live single-issue lives" (Lorde, 1982).

An Anecdote

As I write this chapter, Trump's mass deportations are happening across the United States, leaving immigrant communities in fear of being arrested by Immigration and Customs Enforcement (ICE). Immigrants and their allies are protesting against these community disruptions and family separations, with Los Angeles becoming the epicenter of anti-ICE demonstrations. *USA Today* explains that Los Angeles is fertile ground for anti-ICE protests because more than one-third, 35%, of the population of Los Angeles was born outside the United States (Trethan, 2025). After months of seeing homes, communities, businesses, and schools terrorized by ICE, I am heartened by the resistance of Los Angeles protestors. At the same time, I'm disheartened, exasperated really, by a question that is stimulating much discussion on social media—*Should Black Americans care about deportations and support the anti-ICE protests?* The only humane answer is yes, but unfortunately, some of us still see each community's struggle for justice as distinct from the other and don't see that deportations affect Black communities, too. We remain separated by the belief that we have our own battles to fight. In the next section, I share my own journey to illustrate how I came to an ardent belief in inclusivity.

My Journey to Viewing Justice Through the Lens of Inclusivity

I must admit that it wasn't long ago that I was guilty of similar thinkinga bout "our issues." During the Covid-19 pandemic, anti-Asian hate led to violence against Asian Americans, antagonism that was fueled by Trump's misnomer for Covid-19, "the Chinese virus" (Riechmann & Tang, 2020). Though my heart ached for Asian Americans, and I spoke out against the attacks, especially the ones inflicted by Black Americans, I realized that I didn't object as powerfully as I should have, not because I didn't care, but because I felt like Asian Americans didn't support Black resistance, so I didn't feel compelled to (strongly) support theirs. I had not yet come to realize that the fight against anti-Asian racism and xenophobia and the fight against anti-Black racism should have been a single battle against the one true enemy—white supremacy. This realization had been a long time coming.

When I began doctoral studies in 2012, I was intent on learning how to improve academic outcomes for students of color, especially Black students. I'm sure that this commitment was rooted in my own experiences as a Black woman who cares deeply about her community. Though I professed an interest in learning about educational equity broadly, I came to realize that my focus was really racial equity in education. I had learned that Black and Latino(x) students experienced harsher discipline than white students; received instruction rooted in Eurocentric curricula;

attended poorly funded, still-segregated schools with the least experienced teachers; had dismal graduation rates; performed lower than average on standardized assessments; and were more likely than white students to be overidentified for special education based on perceived behavior problems. I wanted to better understand why "our" students were being miseducated and undereducated in public schools. I cared about all students, but I felt students of color deserved attention in my teaching, scholarship, and advocacy. In my opinion, my interest in racial equity in schools, especially the liberation of Black students, was rightly placed.

In my first semester, my major professor and advisor, the late Dr. Sherrie Reynolds, cautioned me about what she saw as a "narrow focus" on racism. I remember the consternation I felt when she cautioned, "Don't make race everything." I thought that she, a white woman, was speaking from a place of privilege and, to be completely honest, a place of ignorance. Her whiteness had protected her from experiencing the weight of racial discrimination, and she simply didn't know the importance of race in the lives of people of color. I felt similar frustration when a classmate, an immigrant from Mexico, insisted that we in the United States put too much emphasis on race. "Race is just a social construction, Altheria," she asserted. I acknowledged that race was a flawed categorization created and maintained by society (humans) instead of being a scientifically based system of classification. I had learned from the PBS series *Race: The Power of an Illusion* that attempts to categorize humans based on perceived physical or biological differences are deeply flawed. At the same time, race, in my opinion, was the most powerful determinant of life outcomes, as it had been used as a tool of oppression for centuries. Racializing human beings led to stigmatism, discrimination, exclusion, subjugation, violence, and genocide. Despite the impossibility of racial classification based on physical differences, Cornel West (1993) had taught me that "race matters," unequivocally. The many race-dependent laws and court decisions throughout the nation's existence helped prove this point (see Part I).

In my Qualitative Inquiry II class the next semester, we were assigned to study theoretical approaches to the study of education. This was my introduction to research theories and ideological approaches, so everything was new to me. Because of my interest in race and racism, I was naturally drawn to learning about a theory that centers race. There was one on the list—critical race theory—but another classmate selected it before I did. I asked if there was another approach that illuminated race and racism, and instead of answering my question, Dr. Reynolds, remembering that I was also interested in the education of students from economically disadvantaged homes, suggested, "Why don't you examine Marxist approaches to education?" I did as recommended and learned about socioeconomic inequities, and how schools perpetuate existing inequities by producing workers for certain classed occupations. This is social reproduction theory. I concluded that students from economically disadvantaged backgrounds experienced unjust treatment in schools, and because of the ways race and social class are linked, many students of color were also impoverished. This class taught me that class, too, matters.

As I met with Dr. Reynolds to plan my next semester of classes, she advised me to take Feminism in Education. Although I wasn't interested in feminism and saw it as a movement for white women, I trusted her guidance again. This course signaled a pivotal point in my doctoral studies, for it was the first time that I thought deeply about identity, including but beyond race, and discrimination, including but beyond racism and classism. If I had to study feminism in education, I'd study it from the perspective of Black women, which led me to Black feminist theory.

Encountering Black Feminist Theory

It was through studying Black feminist theory that I began to understand the importance of seeing oppression across many dimensions of identity. Black feminist theory taught me that Black women's lived experiences were shaped by race (racism), class (classism), and sex (sexism), an idea that had never occurred to me. Because there are multiple dimensions to cultural identity, there are multiple dimensions to oppression. For example, I had always seen *The Color Purple* by Alice Walker as a story about anti-Black racism in the U.S. South after Reconstruction. I remember reading the novel with new eyes after having encountered Black feminist theory. Instead of regarding it as a story solely about race, I could now see that the novel was about race, sex, and class oppression. I was so intrigued by my newfound knowledge that it became the focus of my dissertation. I'd later learn that sexuality was a fourth identity that led to victimization, as

Black lesbian women faced discrimination in society but also in the Black feminist movement. Instead of using a cumulative approach to the study of the ways Black women experience oppression, Kimberlé Crenshaw (1991) theorized that, like identity, forms of oppression intersect and overlap, creating distinct categories of privilege and oppression. She called this theory *intersectionality*. This point had been made earlier by Black feminists who recognized that racism is also a feminist issue because feminism is a struggle to free all women, including women of color who were marginalized in the feminist movement (Smith, 1982).

When I read "A Black Feminist Statement," written by the Combahee River Collective in 1977, I unpacked and repacked the ideas, amazed by the truths that lie within them.

> We realize that the liberation of all oppressed peoples necessitates the destruction of the political-economic systems of capitalism and imperialism as well as patriarchy.
>
> If Black women were free, it would mean that everyone else would have to be free since our freedom would necessitate the destruction of all the systems of oppression.

In this statement, the Combahee River Collective identified three systems of oppression—capitalism, imperialism, and patriarchy—and concluded that if these systems were destroyed, everyone, not just Black women, would be free.[1] It was Black feminist bell hooks, however, who implanted the idea that there is only a single system instead of multiple systems. As stated in Chapter 1, she called this overlapping, interlocking system of oppression imperialist white supremacist capitalist cisheteropatriarchy. This system, through its policies, practices, and customs, legitimizes the ways of being of those who hold whiteness, imposes limitations upon those who are outside dominant identities, and forces to the margins those whose values are incongruent with white dominant culture. It bears repeating that white supremacy does not just inflict racial oppression. Instead, white supremacy imposes a plethora of Eurocentric cultural values and beliefs upon all colonized peoples, as if there is one way of being in the world. These "white" values have created dominant social identities that are embedded in a single system that leads to discrimination against those who do not hold those identities.

Although it would take several years for these ideas about identity complexity to become concretized in my work, the seeds had been planted by reading the Black feminist scholarship that I encountered in this class. It was through reading the world, however, that I began to notice—outside of schooling—the commonality among the forms of bigotry experienced by marginalized peoples. The 2015 Charleston church shooting was motivated by anti-Black racism, the 2018 Pittsburgh synagogue shooting was motivated by anti-Semitism, and the mosque shooting in 2019 in Christchurch, New Zealand, was fueled by Islamophobia. The animus behind them all is religious intolerance upheld by white supremacy. The current opposition to educational justice discussed in Chapters 5 and 6—the banning of books related to race and LGBTQIA+ topics, curricular restrictions erroneously known as anti-CRT, forcing the Ten Commandments to be posted in classrooms, canceling ethnic studies, the closing of DEI offices on university campuses, and more—is all driven by one interlocking system, imperialist white supremacist capitalist cisheteropatriarchy.

Justice for All Students

Those involved in the struggle for educational justice must be committed to the liberation of all students who experience discrimination stemming from white supremacy. If we eradicate racism, students of color would be free of racism. However, because of their intersectional identities, Black Muslim students will still be victimized by Islamophobia. Black students who are poor will still be victimized by classism. Furthermore, eradicating racism does nothing to free white students from ableism or queer students from heterosexism. When we purify the soil of white supremacy, we free all students from discrimination. Tyrone C. Howard (quoted in Law & Hollins-Alexander, n.d.) pointed out:

> We cannot create equitable schools without being ever mindful of how we ensure that all students have access to opportunities that they might otherwise be excluded from, such as students who come from low socioeconomic backgrounds, students of color, students who are linguistically gifted (multilingual learners), students who are gender nonconforming, and LGBTQIA+ students, as well as students with physical or intellectual disabilities and members of other minority groups.

The fourth column in Table 10.1 illustrates who is included in "all students."

Table 10.1 Student Identities Privileged and Victimized by White Supremacy

Identity categories[2]	Privileged Identity	Discrimination stemming from white supremacy	Student identities victimized by white supremacy
Race	White	Racism Negrophobia	Students of color (Native American, African American, Latino[x], and Asian American)
Religion	Christian	Islamophobia Anti-Semitism Anti-atheism	Muslim Jewish Atheists Agnostics Other religious minorities
Citizenship/ nationality	Native-born whites	Ethnocentrism Nativism Xenophobia Nationalism/White nationalism White Christian Nationalism	Immigrants/foreign-born Indigenous/Native Americans Asian Americans Latino(x) Americans Africans
Physical ability	Able-bodied	Ableism Fatphobia	Students with physical disabilities and/or physical limitations Students who are overweight
Mental capacity	Mentally sound Sane Neurotypical	Sanism Neuroablism Paternalism Neuronormativity	Students with mental disabilities/disorders Students who are neurodivergent
Age	Youthfulness	Ageism Childism	N/A
Socioeconomic status	Middle-class + affluent Wealthy	Classism/casteism Elitism Aporophobia	Students from impoverished or economically disadvantaged homes and communities

Gender/sex	Male	Sexism Misogyny misogynoir Cisgenderism Gender binarism genderism Transphobia	Girls (Black girls) Nonbinary students Transgender students Two-spirit students
Sexuality	Heterosexual	Heterosexism/ heteronormativity Homophobia	LGBTQIA+ students
Skin color and hair texture	Light skin Straight hair	Colorism Texturism	Dark-skinned students Students with curly or kinky hair
Language	Standard American English	Linguicism	Students whose first or preferred language/language variation isn't Standard American English
Family structure	Nuclear, middle-class family, heterosexual parents	Family structurism	Students from single-parent, economically disadvantaged, and LGBTQIA+ families

About Antiracism

Helping educators to see that all forms of identity-based oppression can be traced to the same source can be a challenge. That's why I found it necessary to unpack white supremacy in Chapter 1. In the past, I've failed to do this successfully. Here's an apt example. A graduate student who had taken several classes with me as part of a graduate certificate program in antiracist education lived in the city where a close friend of mine who identifies as gay was moving. My friend didn't know anyone in the city, so I asked her if she wanted to meet my former student. She did. I connected them. My well-meaning student immediately invited her to church, and my friend asked if the church was LGBTQIA+ affirming. My student told her that her church welcomes everyone but believes the Bible's definition of marriage is the only one acceptable to God. My friend was hurt by what my former student said and never talked to her again. Just like this student, I once failed to see the connection between discrimination based on race and bias against those who are LGBTQIA+. As a doctoral student, Dr. Koritha Mitchell, professor of American literature, delivered a lecture at my university titled "Lynching and Anti-LGBT Violence." From her lecture, I learned that she had paired racism with heterosexism to underscore the workings of white supremacy.

I had been naive in thinking that I didn't need to tell my student that my friend is gay. I didn't think it would matter to a passionate and committed student who had completed a graduate certificate in antiracist education and had taken several classes with me. I assumed she knew that heterosexism, like racism, stemmed from white supremacist values and beliefs. I assumed she believed that LGBTQIA+ individuals, like individuals of color, deserve full citizenship and all the rights that accompany it. I had failed, and I vowed to do better. Brown (2017, p. 156) admonished justice workers of the dangers of limiting our work to one form of oppression:

> The [other] tragedy of this quick narrowing is that people get left out, not just in a slightly hurtful way, but left out of how we construct every aspect of society, infrastructure and culture. We come up with incredible plans that don't account for crucial segments of our communities—I've witnessed this as well, unity that entails leaving behind people with disabilities; or trans, Indigenous, immigrant communities, and others.

We reimagine the movement for educational justice by ensuring that it is inclusive of all students, families, and communities that are victimized by white supremacy. Inclusivity, in this case, means a deliberate focus on liberation from oppression that includes, but extends beyond, racism. Antiracism in educational justice work has been a popular topic over the last five years. Scholars and educators, myself included, have written prolifically on the topic. In my quest to be an antiracist scholar and teacher educator, I have read and/or assigned the following outstanding books and more:

- *How to Build Your Antiracist Classroom* by Orlene Badu
- *Anti-Racist Teaching: 8 Steps to Build a Framework for Diversity, Equity, and Inclusion in Your School* by Symone James Abiola
- *The Antiracist School Leader: What to Know, Say, Do* by Daman Harris
- *Confronting Racism in Teacher Education: Counternarratives of Critical Practice* by Bree Picower and Rita Kohli
- *The Anti-Racist Writing Workshop: How to Decolonize the Creative Classroom* by Felicia Rose Chavez
- *Getting Into Good Trouble: A Guide to Building an Antiracist School System* by Gregory C. Hutchings Jr. and Douglass S. Reed
- *What's Race Got to Do With It? How Current School Reform Policy Maintains Racial and Economic Inequality* by Bree Picower and Edwin Mayorga

- *Antiracist Pedagogy in the Early Childhood Classroom* by Miriam Tager
- *Confronting Racism in Teacher Education* by Bree Picower and Rita Kohli

Moreover, I have taught the following courses:

- Introduction to Antiracist Pedagogy
- History and Psychology of Racism
- Race in Education and Schooling

I've facilitated workshops on the following topics:

- Eradicating Anti-Black Racism
- How to Become an Antiracist Educator
- Racism in Schooling

One shortcoming in the body of scholarship, teacher education, and professional learning on racism and educational equity, mine included, is its failure to sufficiently connect racism to the multitude of ways students suffer in schools and/or its failure to recognize the broad forms of oppression that stem from white supremacy. I came to this realization partly through my students. In an Introduction to Antiracist Pedagogy course, a nonbinary undergraduate student asked if we could examine gender discrimination in addition to racial discrimination. She wasn't trying to avoid issues of race; to the contrary, she wanted to explore the connections between racism and gender binarism. Her request helped me to realize that my antiracist teaching must include the larger fight to dismantle all forms of oppression and to accept that I cannot be limited to an antiracist stance but must have an anti-oppression stance in my justice work.

Ultimately, this chapter is a call for community among different groups of justice workers, for "without community there is no liberation.... But community must not mean a shedding of differences, nor the pathetic pretense that these differences do not exist" (Lorde, 1984/2007, p. 112). We can be different, yet undivided.

Healing the Trees

Healing trees planted in white supremacist soil demands that we

1 recognize that all the -isms, along with the intersections among them, inflicted upon students can be eliminated only when we dismantle white supremacy;

2 avoid race reductionism, which is defined as reducing all injustice to racism (Reed, 2020);
3 learn from all marginalized voices in the conversation about educational justice;
4 participate in collective action by seeing others' suffering as our own;
5 realize that there is no hierarchy of oppression; and
6 hold an anti-oppression stance, or be committed to justice across dimensions.

To succeed, a reimagined 21st-century movement for educational justice cannot be fragmented. It must be radically inclusive. Activist Ella Baker's (1969) quote encapsulates my ideas about a single system of oppression and a single struggle:

> In order for us as poor and oppressed people to become a part of a society that is meaningful, the system under which we now exist has to be radically changed. This means that we are going to have to learn to think in *radical* terms. I use the term radical in its original meaning—getting down to and understanding the root cause. It means facing **a system** that does not lend itself to your needs and devising means by which you change **that system**. [emphasis mine]

Despite the differences in groups' experience with oppression, the root cause is imperialist white supremacist capitalist cisheteropatriarchy. It is only through intragroup solidarity among the oppressed that we can take down our foe. Howard's (2024, p. 178) wisdom is a call for inclusivity and solidarity:

> In this moment, there is a need for a diverse coalition of voices to speak loudly, boldly, and fiercely. For too long, it has largely been people of color who have been on the frontlines fighting for truth and inclusion. We explicitly call for white parents, practitioners, and researchers who do not agree with recent conservative attacks on education to step up and be coconspirators in the pursuit of truth in public education.

This is how we create an educational system that works for everyone, especially those in the margins (Love, 2019). Black feminist Audre Lorde (1982) cautioned about channeling our rage toward each other instead of against the power that controls our lives. She acknowledged the complexity of the movement for liberation and the dangers of an "incomplete vision." A complete vision, though complex, is essential to achieving educational justice for all.

About Identity

Although Trump conservatives are critical of identity politics (organizing and theorizing based on shared experiences of injustice), social identities have been embedded in the political system since the country's inception, underscoring the need for identity-based coalitions. Still, Anzaldua noted that social identities are outwardly imposed categories that position racialized identities (like Native American, African American, and Hispanic/Latino(x)), for example, in subordination to white identity. She encouraged rejecting these identity groups in favor of an affinity group, composed of complex identities, united in its resistance to oppression (Keating & Gonzalez-Lopez, 2011). Moreover, Anzaldua urged marginalized communities to transform differences into commonalities and create communities that can work together for change. This must be the shared agenda of justice workers: rejecting oppressive dehumanization in any form and dismantling social injustice (Espinosa-Aguilar, 2005, p. 232).

> *Questions to Ponder*
> 1. Which forms of discrimination (third column in Table 10.1) are you most/least familiar with? Explain.
> 2. Can you think of any organizations or schools whose justice work is inclusive of all marginalized students? If yes, describe their work.
> 3. What are the challenges to bringing about an "educational justice for all" movement?
> 4. Do you think inclusivity and intersectionality are important aspects of reimagining educational justice? Why/why not?

Notes

1. This idea of multiplicity and interrelatedness of oppression was also expressed by Dr. Martin Luther King Jr. Even though he is known for his fight to end racism, he recognized other forms of identity-based oppression and referred to them as the triple evils. In a report to Southern Christian Leadership Conference (SCLC) staff in May 1967, King wrote, "We must see now that the evils of racism, economic exploitation and militarism are all tied together… you can't really get rid of one without getting rid of the others… the whole structure of American life must be changed."
2. Remember that identities are complex, fluid, and intersectional.

11

Healing the Trees Through Insurgency

To heal the trees of white supremacy, justice workers must encourage insurgency in teaching and learning. The term *insurgency* might conjure images of riots, marches, and demonstrations being forcefully countered by individuals in protective gear, bearing arms, and launching tear gas. Insurgency in the classroom, however, looks different. Insurgency in the classroom is teaching and learning that centers resistance to oppression, pursuit of liberation, and challenges to white supremacist authority. The stamp of insurgency in education is criticality.

We are witnessing widespread resistance to criticality, a phenomenon I described as *anti-criticality* in an editorial for *Education Week* (Caldera, 2023). Criticality can be defined as a disposition characterized by deep, analytic, evaluative thinking that causes one to develop critical consciousness. I was introduced to the term *critical consciousness* by Paulo Freire in *Pedagogy of the Oppressed* (1970), a concept he expounded on in *Education for Critical Consciousness* (1974). Freire, in the former work, defined *critical consciousness*, or *conscientizagao*, as "learning to perceive social, political, and economic contradictions and to take action against the oppressive elements of reality" (1970, p. 35). He explained further, "The important thing is to help men (and nations) help themselves, to place them in consciously critical conversations with their problems, to make them agents of their own recuperation" (1974, p. 12). Anti-criticality, on the other hand, describes a state of shallow thinking, refusal to examine reality, and judgment based on incomplete or false information. Research has shown that attending to students' critical consciousness has several positive consequences: overall well-being, resilience, high self-esteem, better grades, and more (Seider, El-Amin, & Bott, 2025).

Building on Freire's work, I see critical consciousness as an unending journey to truth characterized by a willingness to examine, interrogate, and acknowledge the ways systems and institutions function. Integral, too, is the commitment to redress the harm that results from injustice. The journey to critical consciousness begins with observing the world and asking important questions about one's lived experiences and the lived experiences of others. It is a necessary disposition for justice workers. For many, however, the journey to critical consciousness is stalled before it even begins.

Don't Ask Questions

As a little girl growing up in the Deep South, in a region also known as the Bible Belt, questioning "why" or "how" was shunned. I remember adults admonishing one another, "Don't question God." This admonition was usually given when a tragedy struck or the inexplicable happened. The community that raised me believed that God was just and sovereign. Most importantly, God didn't make mistakes. Whatever happened in one's life had to be the will of the omnipotent God. Consequently, and maybe even inadvertently, we were taught to accept authority, not question it. Faith allowed one to believe that God's ultimate goodness would prevail. To question meant to have little faith.

Children, especially, weren't allowed to question parents—or any adults. Answers to questions like, "Why can't I go to the game?" were met with "Because I said so." We were children; they were adults. Good, well-behaved children accepted what their parents said without talking back. We were supposed to obey, not challenge. This is still true today. Questioning children are regarded as "sassy" or "disrespectful." Though I appreciate the intentions of the elders who raised me, I now realize that raising children to acquiesce, particularly children from marginalized communities like the ones I grew up in, can hinder their intellectual curiosity—a disposition that's essential to developing criticality.

These beliefs about accepting without questioning and obeying without resisting exist in schools too, particularly when it comes to behavioral expectations. Compliance continues to be the goal of student behavior in schools. After all, schools must prepare students for a society that insists that citizens be "manageable." For the most part, students have no role (or a limited one) in creating or enforcing rules. Their only role is to follow the rules—to do what they are told. Those who accept and follow the rules without questioning are rewarded with stickers, ribbons, and certificates, while students who push back, challenge, and resist are punished. Studies have shown that Black students, in particular, are often punished for what schools call "defiance" (see Forsyth et al., 2015).

Students' expected passivity is also evident in how they're expected to learn. This is especially true in schools mainly populated by students of color from low-income families, but is pervasive across U.S. schools. Black and Latino(x) students are less likely to experience high-quality teaching that is characterized by instruction that requires them to interrogate (or question), reason, problem-solve, or apply logic. Instead, these students are expected to simply remember facts, summarize details, and in some cases analyze elements (Cherng, Halpin & Rodriguez, 2022). As an example, I distinctly remember reading *The Diary of Anne Frank* in high school. Although I asked myself questions about why Anne, her family, and her community were persecuted and how the world had sat by and allowed it, I was never encouraged to ask these questions in class. Although I don't remember specifics about what we were expected to learn from reading this literature, I assume from my own secondary English teaching experience that we were likely expected to meet learning standards like determining the meaning of words and phrases as they are used in the text, examining the author's use of rhetorical language, and maybe analyzing the author's point of view. It would be much later in my adulthood that I would interrogate justice-related issues.

Zaretta Hammond (2025) calls these practices a *pedagogy of compliance.* Pedagogy of compliance is defined as a set of classroom management and instructional practices that limit student autonomy and reduce their access to rigorous instruction, creating dependent learners. Citing Martin Haberman's work, Hammond (2025) lists (1) asking low-level questions, (2) rote learning, and (3) punishing noncompliance as characteristic of pedagogies that are too often employed with historically marginalized students. A pedagogy of compliance can be linked to teacher bias, with white teachers having "lower academic perceptions" of Black and Latino students (Cherng et al., 2022). Rarely, however, are they invited to be critical thinkers and independent learners who are encouraged to challenge, imagine, disrupt, or critique. In other words, they are not allowed to develop the criticality that leads to critical consciousness. Unfortunately, many students carry this lack of critical consciousness into adulthood, leading them to accept the status quo without asking why.

In order to address and resolve the complex socio-economic-political issues that have plagued our society for centuries—issues that threaten our democracy—schools must provide a supportive structure that encourages students to engage in the kind of thinking and learning that helps them develop critical consciousness. Freire (1974) calls this form of teaching critical pedagogy. Critical pedagogues encourage and expect students to question, challenge, doubt, and justify. I recall the last line in Fanon's examination of the effects of colonization on the colonized—"My final prayer: O my body, always make me a man who questions!" (1967, p. 206). This disposition is key to insurgent teaching and learning. Pedagogical theorists have advanced several forms of critical pedagogy that encourage insurgency:

1. Liberatory pedagogy (Freire, 1970)
2. Engaged pedagogy (hooks, 1994)
3. Equity pedagogy (McGee Banks & Banks, 1995)
4. Transformative pedagogy (Nagda, Gurin, & Lopez, 2003)
5. Antiracist pedagogy (Blakeney, 2005)
6. Emancipatory pedagogy (Nouri & Sajjadi, 2014)
7. Reality pedagogy (Emdin, 2016)
8. Abolitionist teaching (Love, 2019)
9. Woke pedagogy (Caldera, 2018)

Teaching When the World Is on Fire: Reimagining the Purpose of Schooling

Lisa Delpit simply yet cogently described the work of educators during these critical times in the title of her 2019 edited book, *Teaching When the World Is on Fire*. We are living in, according to Delpit, "a time of growing division, incivility, hate, and violence" (2019, p. xxi). Interestingly, she offered this appraisal before the deluge of attacks that have occurred since

2020. I believe that our response as educators and leaders must not be to fight the fire but rather to become the fire and the fire starter, which reminds me of the oft-cited quote of unknown origin: "Education is not the filling of a pail, but the lighting of a fire."

To light students' fire, educators and lawmakers must reimagine the purpose of schooling. It might be helpful to briefly summarize these shifting, sometimes conflicting, purposes of formal education. The purpose of education in the New World (1600s) was to instill religious morals and values. For the new republic to be effective, the country needed "upstanding" citizens whose faith was rooted in the Christian Bible. Only white boys were allowed to attend these early schools. In 1848, Horace Mann, an early proponent of free public education, saw a need to expand this purpose and access. He declared to the Massachusetts State Board of Education, "Education, then, beyond all other devices of human origin, is the great equalizer of the conditions of men, the balance-wheel of the social machinery" (as cited in Education and Social Inequity, n.d.). The purpose of public education offered through common schools, according to Mann, was to bring about economic equality. In other words, common schools were needed to reduce the gap between the rich and the poor, preventing the rigid social class structure of European society.

Beliefs about the purpose of education continued to evolve in the 20th century to include the following:

1. Economics/jobs: education should enable individuals to contribute to a strong economy by working competitive jobs.
2. Citizenship: education should equip individuals to become responsible citizens who contribute meaningfully to a democratic society.
3. Individual potential: education should enable individuals to maximize their potential and pursue their dreams.
4. Global competitiveness: education should equip citizens to help the U.S. maintain its positioning as a global leader through an emphasis on STEM education.
5. Well-being: education should cultivate the well-being of students, ensuring that they have everything they need to grow into adults who are well.

Perhaps the strongest message over the last two decades regarding the purpose of education is expressed by neoliberal politicians in both of the major political parties—global workforce development. Like many school systems, this emphasis on workforce preparedness and career readiness was reflected in the mission of the now mostly defunct U.S. Department of Education: "Our mission is to promote student achievement and preparation for global competitiveness by fostering educational excellence and ensuring equal access" (U.S. Department of Education, 2025c). Many school districts echo these sentiments in missions and goals that indicate a need to prepare students for the "global marketplace," "global economy," "global competitiveness," and "changing workforce." These missions echo the spirit of nationalism. They believe that for the United States to remain economically competitive, we need schools to develop a pipeline of workers, mainly in STEM fields. Virtually absent from the discussion about the purpose of schooling is social justice. Schooling for social justice would require creating environments "in which students can acquire, interrogate, and produce knowledge and envision new possibilities for the use of that knowledge for societal change" (McGee Banks & Banks, 1995). I wrote the following mission based on my beliefs about the purpose of schooling.

> The purpose of schooling is to prepare students to dissent, disrupt, disturb, and dismantle. To this end, our mission is to develop students' awareness of the ways that long-standing systems of oppression impact their lives and to equip students to critique and ultimately destroy these systems. Our students are insurgents and change agents who think critically about the issues that impose upon their humanity.

This mission encapsulates what it means to teach for insurgency and is inspired by Black feminist Angela Davis (as cited in Beahm, 2017): "Education should spur people toward activism… to ask questions." Schooling for insurgency is grounded in one of the five major philosophies of education—social reconstructionism. Social reconstructionism in education is based on the belief that schools have a responsibility for transforming, or reconstructing, society for the benefit of all citizens. The philosophy of social reconstructionism is attributed to George Counts, who wrote in his 1932 book, *Dare the School Build a New Social Order?*, "Teachers must abandon much of their easy optimism, subject the concept of education to the most rigorous scrutiny, and be prepared to deal much more fundamentally, realistically, and positively with the American social situation than has been their habit in the past" (p. 2). Nearly a hundred years later, this call is even more pressing. Reconstructionist educators are committed to dealing with "the American social situation." They make way for critical examinations of societal structures to make them more just. Though individual social justice–oriented teachers and groups can be found in some cities like Chicago's Teachers for Social Justice and DC-area Educators for Social Justice, U.S. public schools have never broadly adopted this philosophy.

Former President Barack Obama frequently espoused a neoliberal education philosophy characterized by nationalism and global competitiveness, so I found it shocking when he seemed to have recognized the importance of preparing students for justice work. At a 2008 NAACP National Convention, he declared, "The fight for social justice and economic justice begins in the classroom" (Obama, 2008). This is a rare stance for a national elected official, regardless of political party. Other Black leaders, however, have pointed out the role of schools in cultivating critically conscious students. Nineteenth-century Black educator and civil rights activist Septima Clark urged truth and interrogation:

> The greatest evil in our country today is not racism, but ignorance. I believe unconditionally in the ability of people to respond when they are told the truth. *We need to be taught to study rather than to believe, to inquire rather than to affirm.*
>
> (Clark, 1975; emphasis added)

Civil rights leader Martin Luther King Jr. gave a nod to critical consciousness in a 1947 campus newsletter:

> Education must enable one to sift and weigh evidence, to discern the true from the false, the real from the unreal, and the facts from the fiction. The function of education, therefore, is to teach one to think intensively and to think critically.
>
> (King, 1947)

Similarly, James Baldwin, in a 1963 speech to teachers, takes this idea further:

> The purpose of education, finally, is to create in a person the ability to look at the world for himself, to make his own decisions, to say to himself this is black or this is white, to decide for himself whether there is a God in heaven or not. To ask questions of the universe, and then learn to live with those questions, is the way he achieves his own identity. But no society is really anxious to have that kind of person around. What societies really, ideally, want is a citizenry which will simply obey the rules of society. If a society succeeds in this, that society is about to perish. The obligation of

anyone who thinks of himself as responsible is to examine society and try to change it and to fight it—at no matter what risk. This is the only hope society has. This is the only way societies change.

(Baldwin, 1963)

Baldwin's quote offers support for critical consciousness in education, but, more importantly, it sheds light on why it has never become a significant goal of education—because of its potential to bring about social change. bell hooks (1994) said it best: "The classroom remains the most radical space of possibility." Critical pedagogy is teaching that will change the world. I go back to Freire (1975) as a reminder of why there is such anti-criticality among education policymakers:

> It is not education which forms society in a certain way, but society which, having structured itself in certain directions, establishes an educational system to fit the values which guide the society... a society which structures its education system to meet the interest of those who hold power, finds a means to preserve power in the process of education. The power which creates an educational system in its image will never allow education to be used against it and therefore a radical transformation of the education system can never take place unless society itself is transformed. (p. 16)

At this point in my twenty-five-year career as an educator, I've come to believe that good students aren't the ones who know all the answers, but the ones who ask challenging, provocative, uncomfortable questions. But educators and policymakers, like the adults I grew up around in my Alabama community, discourage question asking. They do this through limiting access to ethnic studies, employing teaching methods that silence student voice, overemphasizing standardization, and passing anti-CRT and anti-DEI legislation that restricts teachers from interrogating race and racism. They know that when students are encouraged to develop critical consciousness, they will ask the right questions, demand answers, imagine solutions, and change the world. They will become insurgent.

Schooling as it is performed presently leaves many graduates, even high-achieving ones, uninformed about our country's complicated history because teachers are often forbidden from teaching "divisive subjects" or they lack the racial literacy necessary to guide students' learning around oppression. It is no wonder, then, that high-ranking elected officials like former South Carolina Governor Nikki Haley, who, in 2023, was seeking the Republican nomination for president, equivocated when asked, "What was the cause of the Civil War?" Instead of answering directly and factually, she at first evaded answering in a way that showed her knowledge of racial oppression and white supremacy. Only after coming under fire did she add, "Of course, slavery was the cause of the Civil War" (Kerr, Cruz, Harper, and Walsh, 2023). Rather than civics courses prioritizing knowledge and skills related to citizens' responsibility to make society more equitable, students are taught loyalty and obedience. If students are to study the founding documents, they should do so with criticality. Without teachers leading students in this work, we will continue to have a citizenry who does not have critical literacy, meaning they are unprepared to evaluate information for truth, analyze texts for bias, and consider multiple perspectives. Through *critical* approaches to civics education, students can develop critical consciousness instead of learning blind patriotism. Critical consciousness does not mean that we arrive at the same answers or draw the same conclusions, but it does mean that we are willing to do the hard but necessary work of examining systems and institutions to recognize socioeconomic inequities. Critical pedagogy, then, encourages radical insurgency, not radical indoctrination, as right-winged nationalists accuse. (See Ending Radical Indoctrination in K-12 Schooling, Executive Order 14190.)

In their description of multicultural education, pioneers in the field McGee Banks and Banks (1995) explain that *equity pedagogy* is an essential component of multicultural education. A defining aspect of equity pedagogy is the construction and production of knowledge:

> Instead of focusing on the memorization of knowledge constructed by authorities, students in classrooms where equity pedagogy is used learn to generate knowledge and create new understanding... students relate ideas and perspectives and make judgments and evaluations. Instead of looking for the single answer to a problem, students are encouraged to generate multiple solutions and perspectives. They also explore how problems arise and how they are related to other problems, issues, and concepts.
>
> (McGee Banks & Banks, 1995)

These ideas underlying a critical education, coupled with the diversity and equity pedagogies outlined in Chapter 3, paint a picture of the kind of education all students deserve. This is not to suggest that insurgency should be the sole focus of education. However, it should be among its key functions. I return to the "freedom from" and "freedom to" analysis from Chapter 2 to describe the education that we must demand. This is education as the act of freedom.

Healing the Trees

Healing the soil of white supremacy demands that we embrace insurgency as a fundamental purpose of schooling. Insurgent education is outlined in Table 11.1.

Insurgent teaching and learning require higher-order thinking (increased cognitive demand), like analyzing, evaluating, and creating. As an example of what teaching for insurgency might look like in a middle school English classroom, consider doing a novel study. The teacher assesses students' ability to ask meaningful questions about the text, not just their ability to provide answers to questions constructed by the teacher. The teacher emphasizes the importance of asking questions about voice, perspective, power, justice, representation, and more. Students are discouraged from simply asking questions that assess understanding

Table 11.1 Insurgent Education

Freedom from	Freedom to
deculturalized instruction	learn through instruction that respects the ways that culture and language impact learning
Eurocentric, heterosexist instructional materials	see many cultures reflected in instructional materials
inaccurate, whitewashed history	learn broad historical truths about race, racialized peoples, and racism
book bans that limit access to knowledge about diverse cultures	access books that offer multicultural perspectives and experiences
education that ignores important social issues	critically examine social issues
restrictions that limit dialogue about race/gender/sexuality	engage in thoughtful, civil dialogue about diverse social identities
education that encourages blind patriotism	engage in patriotism that is enlightened by truth, which may include dissent
accepting unjust systems and institutions as they are	substantively critique systems and institutions
passive knowledge consumption	actively co-construct knowledge
agreement with widely accepted truths	question and challenge taken-for-granted truths

of plot, naming of characters, or descriptions of setting. Teaching can provide scaffolds like question starters and modeling, but should shift the cognitive load to students, allowing learners sufficient practice to develop these skills (Hammond, 2025).

Students educated for insurgency will be prepared to be justice workers, regardless of their chosen career paths. Love (2019, p. 102) advocated for schools to be places that encourage students to "give the world hell." This is how we nourish existing trees and start saplings. Educational justice beckons us to not only ensure that school systems are fair for all students, but also challenges us to transform schools into liberatory places where marginalized students are empowered to create a just society. The resistance to a critical education is part of a broader movement of anti-intellectualism, which can be defined as antagonism toward and distrust for knowledge developed through academic studies, scientific research, and other scholarly pursuits. Even when quick sound bites and short, catchy phrases are preferred to thinking deeply about complex ideas, we must insist on intellectualism, which includes critical education, as a path to justice. We must continue to demand access to free public education as a device that allows everyone to become full citizens who, through engaging in criticality, will be free to imagine a just society, and who will accept nothing less. Education must be dangerous to white supremacy—a constant threat.

> *Questions to Ponder*
>
> 1. Reflecting on your schooling experience, what seemed to be the purpose of education?
> 2. How might you take a critical approach in your teaching? What does insurgency look like in your discipline?
> 3. What do you see as links between insurgency and democracy?
> 4. Do you think insurgency is an important aspect of reimagining educational justice? Why/why not?

12

Healing the Trees Through (Radical) Imagination

In order to heal the trees of white supremacy, we must first imagine it. I recently learned that Walt Disney's research and development division is called Walt Disney Imagineering. I love the word *imagineers*, a portmanteau combining the words imagine and engineers. The umbrella term is used for the designers, illustrators, architects, engineers, and other creatives who are the brains behind Disney's magical experiences. I thought about the importance of having radical imagineers in education, creatives who envision a school system sans white supremacy. What if schools had chief imagineers instead of school leaders? Love (2019) reminded readers of the importance of "freedom dreaming." Freedom dreams, as described by Love, are not whimsical or unattainable. They are critical and imaginative. This combination of critical analysis and radical imagination is integral to reimagining the movement for educational justice. In her second book, *Punished for Dreaming*, Love (2023) insisted that dreams are key to liberation but are intentionally stifled by education reforms that offer only cosmetic changes. In other words, temporary fixes only serve momentary appeasement; they prevent us from imagining lasting change. Radical imagination licenses us to see educational justice as a very real possibility, not just an aspiration. Chicano feminist thinker Gloria Anzaldúa (in Anzaldúa & Keating, 2015) explained that to reinvent reality, we must cultivate a pretend reality and act as though we're already living in it, and eventually that reality becomes the real one. She cautioned that "without imagination, transformation would not be possible" (in Anzaldúa & Keating, 2015, p. 44).

I draw upon adrienne maree brown's (2017) work time and again for inspiration:

> Imagination is one of the spoils of colonization, which in many ways is claiming who gets to imagine the future for a given geography. Losing our imagination is a symptom of trauma. Reclaiming the right to dream the future, strengthening the muscle to imagine together as Black people, is a revolutionary decolonizing activity.
>
> (163–164)

Reclaiming the right to dream of a world that seems worlds away is a radical act that must exist outside the white supremacist imaginary, including its modes of thinking and expression. Brown (2017, p. 4) quoted Angela Davis's definition of *radical*, which, according to Davis, means "grasping things at the root," an idea that is a recurring theme of this book.

As a consultant, scholar, and teacher educator, I devote most of my energies to critically analyzing schooling as an oppressive institution and helping others in their examinations. I'm guilty of overrelying on the left side of my brain—the side that enables me to reason, analyze, and process—and neglecting the side that allows creativity, imagination, and intuition. My challenge, then, is to allow the critical part of my mind to fuel my creative side so that my brain can work in unison. Writer Toni Morrison's explanation of the function of racism is useful in understanding what hinders us from venturing into the creative: "The function, the very serious function of racism is distraction. It keeps you from doing your work." We must not continue to allow the work we do to deconstruct white supremacy to distract us from the next step in the work—imagining and constructing a liberatory school system for all children.

To be transparent, I am often too grounded in reality. I only watch movies that feature actions that can *actually* happen. When reading fiction, I always select realistic fiction. I reject fantasies and science fiction because these genres seem too far-fetched, too distant from reality. I'm challenged by the work of scholars like Imarisha (2023), who introduced the idea of visionary fiction, a means of imagining and constructing just futures. Brown (2017, p. 163) listed the forms of visionary fiction that can be tools for justice—"sci-fi, speculative fiction, fantasy, magical realism, myth, all of it." I believe that my narrow preferences for the seemingly possible and conceivable had limited my ability to imagine educational

Table 12.1 Improvement or Justice?

Improvement	Justice
What is a win that is possible and realistic?	What is the world (school system) we want?
• A system with more winners • Competition	• A system that doesn't require losers • Collaboration

justice. I realize now that I was in the school improvement camp. My prior imaginations were of a vastly improved school system making steps toward justice, not a transformed one that is truly liberatory. I also recognized my shortsighted thinking when reading Ruha Benjamin's (2022) *Viral Justice*: "The point is not simply to ensure there are more winners. We have to step outside the game to build an entirely new set of social relations that does not require losers" (p. 277). Imarisha offered two questions that illustrate a key difference in envisioning improvement instead of radically imagining justice. These two questions can be answered with Benjamin's aforementioned analogy, as demonstrated in Table 12.1.

It was only after learning from experts that I came to believe that radical imagination is integral to healing the trees whose roots were planted in white supremacist soil.

Afrofuturism

One example of how imagination can transform schools draws upon the concept of *Afrofuturism*, which can be seen as a genre and a movement that centers Black history and culture and incorporates futuristic elements into literature, music, and the arts (Womack, 2013). S. R. Toliver (2025), a teacher education scholar and Afrofuturist, detailed the functions of Afrofuturism on her website devoted to "reading Black futures." Significantly, she included the following Afrofuturism functions, among others:

1. reclaims the past to imagine a future;
2. combats oppression; and
3. envisions new, utopian worlds.

These three functions summarize what it means to radically imagine. Paige Duggins-Clay (2024) drew upon Afrofuturism to imagine safe and supportive schools where Black students belong and thrive. She believes that Afrofuturism, when applied to education, provides an opportunity to "re-think current strategies for envisioning and manifesting equal educational opportunity." In her imagining, she described schools free from bullying, filled with diverse books, guided by an inclusive curriculum, and free from hyper-surveillance and policing. Brown (2017) explained:

> Afrofuturism is not just the coolest look that ever existed. The future is not an escapist place to occupy. All of it is the inevitable result of what we do today, and the more we take it in our hands, imagine it as a place of justice and pleasure, the more the future knows we want it, and that we aren't letting go.
>
> (p. 164)

These capabilities of Afrofuturism can inform a "justice for all" ethic.

A Radical Imagination

In Ruha Benjamin's 2024 book *Imagination: A Manifesto*, she teaches that radical imagining

1. can be done individually and collectively;
2. can inspire us to push beyond what we are told is politically possible (idealism) while at the same time tending to our existing material conditions (pragmatism);
3. can be both fantastical and mundane;
4. can help us envision who we want to be and the world we want to live in; and
5. requires us to know what from the past to discard and what to take into the future.

Perhaps most importantly, Benjamin cautions that we should consider the fact that imagination does not guarantee that the way forward is better than the present and warns that imagination is not inherently ethical.

Radical imagination leads to a new social order that exists outside of imperialist white supremacist capitalist cisheteropatriarchy. What is the school system we want? The collective answer to this question can only be reached when we create space for radical imagination. Healing the trees means imagining what the following aspects of schooling might look like under this new social order.

- Funding: how schooling is paid for
- Research: what knowledge is valuable and how it is produced
- Curricula: what students learn
- Pedagogy: how teachers teach (instructional methods)
- Resources: materials teachers use
- Discipline: behavioral expectations of students
- Assessment: how teachers measure learning
- Languaging practices: communication standards
- Philosophy: the purpose of schooling
- Lifestyle expectations: ideal teachers, parents, and families

Using Artificial Intelligence to Imagine

Imagineers in education may utilize technological tools, including artificial intelligence[1] (AI), to aid in the creation of a just school system. I asked a friend to make the following request of ChatGPT:

> Imagine a school system that is diverse, equitable, and inclusive for all students. This school system resists white supremacy and aims to ensure that all students are treated justly and have what they need to thrive. The school system reflects the diversity of the country, and it prepares students to be members of a democratic society. Consider curricula, materials, teachers, instructional strategies, discipline, and all other aspects of schooling. What might a school like this look like in its everyday operations?

The response sheds light on the possibilities and limitations of AI.

> *A diverse, equitable, inclusive, and justice-oriented school system would exhibit the following characteristics in its everyday operations:*
> **1. Curricula and Materials**

- *Representative and Inclusive Content: Curricula reflect the histories, cultures, contributions, and perspectives of diverse racial, ethnic, linguistic, LGBTQIA+, religious, disability, and socioeconomic groups.*
- *Critical Consciousness: Students engage critically with historical and contemporary issues related to race, racism, white supremacy, and other forms of oppression.*
- *Culturally Responsive Pedagogy: Materials validate students' identities, promote empathy, and build understanding across difference.*

2. Teachers and Staff

- *Diverse Faculty and Staff: Recruitment, hiring, and retention practices prioritize racial, ethnic, linguistic, gender, and other forms of diversity among teachers and administrators.*
- *Continuous Professional Development: Regular, mandatory training on antiracism, cultural responsiveness, implicit bias, trauma-informed practices, and restorative justice approaches.*
- *Reflective Practice: Teachers regularly evaluate their practices for bias and work collaboratively to improve.*

3. Instructional Strategies

- *Differentiated Instruction: Teachers employ strategies that honor the learning styles, backgrounds, and unique strengths of each student.*
- *Cooperative Learning: Classroom practices emphasize collaboration, dialogue, community building, and social-emotional learning.*
- *Student Voice and Agency: Students are active participants in their learning, encouraged to engage in inquiry, critical questioning, and democratic processes within the classroom.*

4. Discipline and Behavioral Supports

- *Restorative Justice: Discipline focuses on understanding, repairing harm, relationship building, accountability, and community rather than punishment or exclusion.*
- *Bias Awareness: Policies and practices are regularly reviewed to ensure equitable treatment, especially for historically marginalized students.*
- *Social and Emotional Learning (SEL): Explicit SEL practices support students in managing emotions, developing healthy relationships, and resolving conflict constructively.*

5. Family and Community Engagement
- *Partnership with Families: Schools actively partner with families of all backgrounds, respecting cultural practices, languages, and knowledge, and inviting meaningful participation.*
- *Community Involvement: Schools engage with local communities as active partners in education, inviting community wisdom, resources, and input.*

6. Assessment and Accountability
- *Holistic Assessments: Schools prioritize formative, authentic, and culturally responsive assessments that reflect diverse knowledge and skills.*
- *Transparent Data Use: Assessment data disaggregated by race, ethnicity, gender, socioeconomic status, disability, and language proficiency guides ongoing improvements toward equity.*

7. Environment and Climate
- *Inclusive School Culture: Physical and social environments reflect respect, validation, and celebration of diverse identities, experiences, and voices.*
- *Equitable Resource Allocation: Schools ensure fair distribution of resources, support staff, and opportunities, especially toward communities historically marginalized or underserved.*

8. Everyday Examples of Operation:
- *Morning meetings featuring diverse voices and perspectives.*
- *Instructional materials regularly audited for bias and representation.*
- *Student-led community forums or projects addressing real-world issues related to social justice.*
- *Teachers trained in restorative circles to handle conflicts constructively and equitably.*
- *School-wide events explicitly celebrating cultural heritage and diversity.*
- *Active dialogue with students about democratic participation and citizenship in classroom activities.*

By embedding equity, diversity, inclusion, and antiracist practices into every aspect of the school's operations, such a school system prepares students to be critical thinkers, engaged citizens, and empathetic community members.

As this response shows, generative AI is limited in its imaginative capacity and can only reproduce existing knowledge (data), risking the reproduction of social inequities. (See Ruha Benjamin's Race After Technology: Abolitionist Tools for the New Jim Code.) Justice workers might use this ChatGPT-generated response to guide dialogues that expand our thinking. The following questions could lead to more substantive radical imaginations:

1. Who/what was included?
2. Who/what was excluded?
3. How can the AI-generated response be made truly radical?
4. In what way does/doesn't this response reflect a "justice for all" philosophy?
5. What traces of white supremacy are evident in the response?

Healing the Trees

Healing the trees demands that we radically imagine just schooling.

1. Radical imagining exists outside the white supremacist imaginary.
2. Radical imagining should make use of art, music, literature, technology, and more.
3. Radical imagining requires designated time for freedom dreaming.
4. Radical imagining demands that the vision, movement, and liberation be shared among all historically oppressed groups.

As a reminder, "The more people who cocreate the future, the more people whose concerns will be addressed from the foundational level in the world" (brown, 2017, p. 158). Likewise, Lorde (1982) believed that "any future vision which can encompass all of us, by definition, must be complex and expanding." This wisdom must be the hallmark of our work. Imarisha's (2023) words seem an appropriate reminder to end this chapter:

> This is the challenge of true liberatory movements—we critique and fight against what exists, but we take on the responsibility of stretching beyond the now, beyond what we have seen and felt and held, to root in a shared vision of true liberation. And then we do the work of building that into existence.
>
> (p. 59)

> Questions to Ponder
>
> 1. In what ways did this chapter challenge your thinking about educational justice?
> 2. What kind of school system do you imagine? What steps can you begin to take to move this school system from imagination to reality?
> 3. What is the connection between individual imagining and collective imagining?
> 4. Do you think radical imagination is an important aspect of reimagining educational justice? Why/why not?

Note

1 Justice workers who use artificial intelligence (AI) must do so responsibly, being cognizant of the impact it has on the environment and marginalized communities. When AI is used, it should be used in ways that lead to social transformation.

Conclusion: Make a Career of Humanity

The six principles in Part III of this book have a shared goal—to "tek cyear a de root fa heal de tree," so that human beings can attend schools defined by justice. Introspection is human work. Institutionalizing is human work. Inclusivity and intersectionality are human work. Insurgency is human work. Imagining is human work. We do this human work until differences in cultural identities have no power to determine access and opportunities, until all students are seen for what they are—human.

On Differences

A great deal of this book focuses on differences in the human experience because of socially constructed identities. My goal in doing so is to illustrate how white supremacy infringes upon the rights of students who are marginalized in any of a multitude of ways. Identity differences matter only because institutions are governed by policies and practices that restrict the freedom of those in the margins. Too often in education, though, we portray students from marginalized populations as problems to be fixed. I have been guilty of doing this too, often describing my work as preparing teachers to better serve students of color. This wording is problematic because it conveys that students of color are different from other students, when the truth is that they, and other marginalized students, are simply, beautifully human. When we acknowledge differences, we must be careful that we don't suggest that these differences render them sub- or superhuman. Said differently, there's great danger in *othering*, a term that means to regard individuals and communities as intrinsically different and oftentimes inferior. Before we see them as *others*, we must first see them as they are—human beings. In his postcolonial classic *Black Skin, White Masks*, Fanon (1967) introduced the concept of a "zone of non-human space" to describe the space created by white colonizers and occupied by colonized people who are pushed to the margins of humanity. In this space live the inferior, the others, the racialized, the inhuman, who are constantly trying to assert their humanity. Colonized peoples have been denied the right to simply be seen as human. The anecdote that follows is illustrative of the extent to which white people tried to convince themselves that enslaved Black people were nonhuman.

Enslaved humans often tried to escape captivity. In search of freedom, they'd risk their lives by attempting to run away from slave owners. To explain why enslaved humans would want to run away instead of acquiescing to the most extreme human degradation imaginable, in 1851 a white physician theorized that enslaved Black humans wanting to be free suffered from a mental illness he named "drapetomania" (Willoughby, 2018). Dr. Samuel A. Cartwright refused to see Black individuals as humans whose inherent desire was to be free. Instead, he saw enslaved Black individuals with this desire as abnormal, deviant (Willoughby, 2018). This basic human desire was reserved for white individuals, suggesting that to be human and desirous of freedom meant to be white.

It is important to remember an essential truth: historically marginalized individuals, despite their humanity having been under assault for centuries, are humans with the same desires and needs as other humans. I'm reminded of the poem "Human Family" by Maya Angelou (1990), in which she declared,

> I note the obvious differences
> between each sort and type,
> but we are more alike, my friends,
> than we are unalike. (p. 4)

To Humanize?

Some might use the term *humanize* when speaking of this need to see historically marginalized individuals as humans first. However, I'm hesitant to use the words *humanize* or *humanizing* to describe the work I do to advance educational justice. *Humanize* reminds me of a word that I first encountered as an English major, *personify*, meaning, in literature, to give human characteristics to nonhuman objects, as in "my heart danced." *Anthropomorphize* has a similar denotation. *Humanize*, with the *-ize* suffix, literally means to make human or to give human qualities. All three words—*humanize, personify*, and *anthropomorphize*—suppose that a nonhuman thing can become humanlike. Most times when I've encountered the term *humanizing*, it has been used to describe equity work with students of color, such as *humanizing pedagogy, humanizing relationships*, or *humanizing education*. Although I believe that those who use the word don't mean to suggest that students of color need to be made human, I'm afraid that the frequent association between *humanizing* work and students of color might inadvertently convey a harmful belief: that students of color lack what they already have—humanity.

Even more problematic is when *humanize* means to civilize or refine. Europeans have historically used language to characterize people of African descent and Indigenous peoples of the Americas as being sub- or superhuman and have portrayed themselves as the quintessential human (and distinctly citizens). Specifically, people of African descent have been described in animalistic terms—beasts and apelike—which justified colonizers' enslavement of Africans and their descendants. The insistence on rendering Black people as animals reveals the oppressor's own need to be seen as human. Ta-Nahesi Coates, in the foreword to Toni Morrison's (2017) brilliant work *The Origin of Others*, sheds light on this need:

> The necessity of rendering the slave a foreign species appears to be a desperate attempt to confirm one's own self as normal. The urgency of distinguishing between those who belong to the human race and those who are decidedly non-human is so powerful the spotlight turns away and shines not on the object of degradation but on its creator.
>
> (p. xiii)

White colonizers distinguishing themselves as "normal" and others as "abnormal" didn't just happen with Europeans' treatment of Black folks. Colonizers described Native Americans as savages and barbarians. In 2022, the Anthropology Association apologized for its 20th-century mischaracterizations of Native Americans as "savage" and "sub-human species in every aspect" (cited in Parsons, 2022).

These attempts at othering can also be seen in the language used to describe immigrants to the United States, especially those at the southern border. They are viewed as illegals. Outsiders. In 2018, then-President Trump derogatorily called immigrants "aliens" in a speech seven times (Trump,

2018). The term *aliens* is used by some to define immigrants or noncitizens. Viewing humans as aliens allows one to distance and disregard instead of connect and commune. Human beings are not aliens. The belief that all humans—regardless of their race, ethnicity, age, nationality, gender, sexuality, socioeconomic status, religion, citizenship status, ability, or language—have the same value reflects one of our country's espoused values: egalitarianism.

Even though Europeans have abused their power by enacting abhorrent physical and psychic violence upon disenfranchised communities, colonizers and white supremacists mustn't be attributed the power to *dehumanize*. They did not make individuals human, or humanize them, so they cannot take away humanity, or dehumanize them. In *Caste: The Origin of Our Discontents*, Wilkerson (2020) described what it means to dehumanize:

> To dehumanize another human being is not merely to declare that someone is not human, and it does not happen by accident. It is a process, a programming. It takes energy and reinforcement to deny what is self-evident in another member of one's own species.
>
> (p. 141)

Since marginalized peoples' humanity is "self-evident," the most oppressors can do is to deny this truth. The power to dehumanize is beyond their grasp. What they have done for centuries, however, is to treat colonized peoples inhumanely.

To perceive historically marginalized individuals as anything but human supports white supremacist notions around who deserves to be human and whose humanity matters. It is important to remember that human beings are at the heart of educational justice work. Coupled with our pursuit of civil rights must be a commitment to basic human rights, which the United Nations (2025) defines thus:

> Human rights are rights inherent to all human beings, regardless of race, sex, nationality, ethnicity, language, religion, or any other status. Human rights include the right to life and liberty, freedom from slavery and torture, freedom of opinion and expression, the right to work and education, and many more.

By seeing students as human before we acknowledge differences, we lay claim to their human rights. Throughout my writing of this book, the African concept of *ubuntu* lingered in my mind and pulsed in my heart. *Ubuntu* is a philosophy based on the belief in a common humanity. Its literal translation is "I am because you are." I am only free because you

Conclusion: Make a Career of Humanity

are free. Or, in Hamer's words, "Nobody's free until everybody's free" (in Brooks & Houck, 2011, p. 136). It is the refrain of Wall Kimmerer's (2013) book, "All flourishing is mutual" (p. 15). Similarly, Fanon's (1967) questions in *Black Skin, White Masks* provide direction for justice workers: "Superiority? Inferiority? Why not simply try to touch the other, feel the other, discover each other?" (p. 206). Justice work requires touching, feeling, and discovering the other. We owe it to each other to work for justice in the spirit of *ubuntu*, because reimagining the movement for educational justice will require a concerted effort to ensure that all human beings are treated humanely. In all of our tree healing, we must remember that we are working to heal and liberate humans—work that we must do *until everybody's free*. Black feminist leader Anna Julia Cooper wrote, in 1892, that "the cause of freedom is not the cause of a race or a sect, a party or a class—it is the cause of human kind, the very birthright of humanity" (1988, p. 121).

I end this book with a quote from a speech that Dr. Martin Luther King Jr. gave during the March for Integrated Schools on April 18, 1959:

> Make a career of humanity. Commit yourself to the noble struggle for equal rights. You will make a better person of yourself, a greater nation of your country, and a finer world to live in.

Questions to Ponder

1. How are you making a career of humanity?
2. When do you think it's important to see humans as the same? When do differences matter?
3. How will your justice work be impacted by reading this book?

References

ABC News. (2016, August 31). *What Donald Trump has said about Mexico and vice versa.* https://abcnews.go.com/Politics/donald-trump-mexico-vice-versa/story?id=41767704

Abrams, Z. (2023, September 1). *Teaching social-emotional learning is under attack.* American Psychological Association. https://www.apa.org/monitor/2023/09/social-emotional-learning-under-fire

Abreu, R. L., Audette, L., Mitchell, Y., Simpson, I., Ward, J., Ackerman, L., Gonzalez, K. A., & Washington, K. (2022). LGBTQ student experiences in schools from 2009–2019: A systematic review of study characteristics and recommendations for prevention and intervention in school psychology journals. *Psychol Schs, 59,* 115–151. https://doi.org/10.1002/pits.22508

ACLU. (2024, December 6). *In 2024, the ACLU tracked 533 anti-LGBTQ bills in the U.S.* https://www.aclu.org/legislative-attacks-on-lgbtq-rights-2024

ACLU. (2025, July 11). *The ACLU is tracking 598 anti-LGBTQ bills in the U.S.* https://www.aclu.org/legislative-attacks-on-lgbtq-rights-2025.

Alfonseca, K. (2024, January 5). *The forces behind Harvard president Claudine Gay's resignation.* ABC News. https://abcnews.go.com/US/forces-harvard-president-claudine-gays-resignation/story?id=106071191

Al Jazeera. (2025, May 15). *Who are the students Trump wants to deport?* https://www.aljazeera.com/news/2025/3/27/who-are-the-students-trump-wants-to-deport#:~:text=On%20March%2010%2C%20Trump%20posted,war%20on%20Gaza%20broke%20out

Altman, N. (2006). Whiteness. *The Psychoanalytic Quarterly, 75*(1), 45–72.

Alvarez, B. (2015, July 27). How one educator is taking ethnic studies mainstream. *NEA Today.* https://www.nea.org/nea-today/all-news-articles/how-one-educator-taking-ethnic-studies-mainstream

Anzaldua, G. (2009). To(o) Queer the Writer—Loca, escritora y chicana. In A. *Keating* (Ed.), *The Gloria Anzaldúa Reader* (pp. 163-175). Duke University Press.

Anderson, C. (2017). *White Rage: The Unspoken Truth of Our Racial Divide.* Bloomsbury.

Anderson, J. (2022, February 23). *The state of critical race theory in education.* Harvard Graduate School of Education Edcast. https://www.gse.harvard.edu/ideas/edcast/22/02/state-critical-race-theory-education

Angelou, M. (1990). *I shall not be moved.* Random House.

Ansley, F. L. (2015). White supremacy (and what we should do about it). In G. Anzaldúa & A. Keating (Eds.), *Light in the dark/Luz en lo oscuro: Rewriting identity, spirituality, reality*. Duke University Press. (Original work published 1997)

Anzaldúa, G. E. (2015). *Light in the dark/luz en lo oscuro: Rewriting identity, spirituality, reality* (A. Keating, Ed.). Duke University Press. https://doi.org/10.2307/j.ctv1220hmq

Atkins, J. D. C. (1887). *Barbarous dialects should be blotted out....* Excerpts from the 1887 Report of the Commission of Indian Affairs. https://www.languagepolicy.net/archives/atkins.htm

Attaya, M. K., & Hilliard, L. J. (2023). Applying critical race theory to social and emotional learning programs in schools. *Social and Emotional Learning: Research, Practice, and Policy, 1*, 1–9. https://doi.org/10.1016/j.sel.2023.100005

Au, K., & Jordan, C. (1981). Teaching reading to Hawaiian children: Finding a culturally appropriate solution. In H. Trueba, G. Guthrie, & K. Au (Eds.), *Culture and the bilingual classroom: Studies in classroom ethnography* (pp. 139–152). Newbury House.

Austin Daily Herald. (2021, January 23). Our opinion: Journalism can't be painted broadly. https://www.austindailyherald.com/2021/01/our-opinion-journalism-cant-be-painted-broadly/

Baker, E. (1969). *The Black woman in the civil rights struggle*. https://awpc.cattcenter.iastate.edu/2019/08/09/the-black-woman-in-the-civil-rights-struggle-1969/

Baldwin, J. (1963). *A talk to teachers*. Zinn Education Project. https://www.zinnedproject.org/materials/baldwin-talk-to-teachers

Banks, S. (2019, Fall). The birth of Chicano Studies. *Cal State, LA Magazine*. Retrieved from https://www.calstatelamagazine.com/features/the-birth-of-chicano-studies

Ball, S. J. (2021). *The education debate*. The Policy Press.

Banks, J. A. (2013). The construction and historical development of multicultural education, 1962–2012. *Theory into Practice, 52*, 73–82. https://doi.org/10.1080/00405841.2013.795444

Banks, J. A. (2014). *An introduction to multicultural education* (5th ed.). Pearson.

Beahm, M. (2017, January 19). Angela Davis: "No liberation without education." *Kitsap Daily News*. https://www.kitsapdailynews.com/news/angela-davis-no-liberation-without-education/#:~:text=Just%20as%20racism%20and%20sexism,drives%20us%20to%20ask%20questions.%E2%80%9D

Beal, F. M. (2008). Double Jeopardy: To Be Black and Female. *Meridians, 8(2)*, 166–176. http://www.jstor.org/stable/40338758

References

Beauboeuf-Lafontant, T. (2005). Womanist lessons for reinventing teaching. *Journal of Teacher Education, 56*(5), 436–445. https://doi.org/10.1177/0022487105282576

bell hooks Center. (2023). Dissident feminisms. Berea College. Retrieved from https://www.berea.edu/centers/the-bell-hooks-center/symposium.

Benjamin, R. (2019). *Race After Technology: Abolitionist Tools for the New Jim Code*. Polity.

Benjamin, R. (2022). *Viral justice: How to grow the world we want*. Princeton University Press.

Benjamin, R. (2024). *Imagination: A manifesto*. W. W. Norton & Company.

Bestor Townsend, C., & Zagger, Z. V. (2025, March 3). *Iowa governor signs law making state the first to remove gender identity protections from civil rights code*. Ogletree Deakins. https://ogletree.com/insights-resources/blog-posts/iowa-governor-signs-law-making-state-the-first-to-remove-gender-identity-protections-from-civil-rights-code/

Beykont, Z. F. (2002). *English-only language policies in the United States*. Linguapax International. https://www.linguapax.org/wp-content/uploads/2015/09/CMPL2002_T1_Beykont.pdf

Black Lives Matter in Schools. (2025). *The demands*. https://www.blacklivesmatteratschool.com/the-4-demands.html

Black Past. (2007). (1857) Frederick Douglass, "If there is no struggle, there is no progress." https://www.blackpast.org/african-american-history/1857-frederick-douglass-if-there-no-struggle-there-no-progress/

Blakeney, A. M. (2005). Antiracist pedagogy: Definition, theory, and professional development. *Journal of Curriculum and Pedagogy, 2*(1), 119–132. https://doi.org/10.1080/15505170.2005.10411532

Booth, A. L. (2003). We are the land: Native American views of nature. In H. Selin (Ed.), *Science across cultures: The history of non-western science, vol. 4, nature across cultures* (pp. 329–349). Springer.

Brady, Thomas P., "A Review of Black Monday" (1954). Pamphlets and Broadsides. 3. https://egrove.olemiss.edu/citizens_pamph/3

Bronfenbrenner, U. (1979). *The ecology of human development: Experiments by nature and design*. Harvard University Press.

Brooker, R. (2024). *The education of Black children in the Jim Crow South*. America's Black Holocaust Museum. https://www.abhmuseum.org/education-for-blacks-in-the-jim-crow-south/

Brooks, M. P., & Houck, D. W. (Eds.). (2011). *Speeches of Fannie Lou Hamer: To tell it like it is*. University Press of Mississippi.

brown, a. m. (2017). *Emergent strategy: Shaping change, changing worlds*. AK Press.

Bryant, J., & Appleby, C. (2025, May 6). *These states' anti-DEI legislation may impact higher education.* Best Colleges. https://www.bestcolleges.com/news/anti-dei-legislation-tracker/

Bush, M. E. L. (2004). *Breaking the code of good intentions: Everyday forms of whiteness.* Bloomsbury Academic.

Caldera, A. (2018). Woke pedagogy: A framework for teaching and learning. *Diversity, Social Justice, and the Educational Leader, 2*(3), 1–11.

Caldera, A. (2020). Challenging capitalistic exploitation: A Black feminist/womanist commentary on work and self-care. *Feminist Studies, 46*(3), 707–716.

Caldera, A. (2021a). Moment, momentum, or movement? Forging paths toward racial justice for Black students. *Race and Pedagogy Journal: Teaching and Learning for Justice, 5*(2), 1–5.

Caldera, A. (2021b, May 21). Southlake community must not continue to avoid conversations about race. *Fort Worth Weekly.* https://www.fwweekly.com/2021/05/21/southlake-community-must-not-continue-to-avoid-conversations-about-race/

Caldera, A. (2023). A portrait of life at Como High School: An ethnographic study of a segregated Black high school. In V. Garry & E. P. Isaac-Savage (Eds.), *Black cultural capital: Activism that spurred African American high schools* (pp. 181–199). Information Age Publishing.

Caldera, A., & Babino-Ruiz, A. (2020). Being a conduit and culprit of white language supremacy: A duo autohistoria-teoría. *Transcontinental Human Trajectories, 8*, 1–18.

Caldera, A., Bernstein, D., Parker-Hill, K., Testen, K., Kistenbroker, C., & Theerman, J. (2023, July 25). *The case for woke education: How to resist anti-intellectualism and anti-truth in education.* https://www.edweek.org/teaching-learning/opinion-the-case-for-woke-education/2023/07#:~:text=Not%20taking%20action%20is%20just,denies%20to%20others%20certain%20rights

Calderon-Berumen, F., Babino, A., & Caldera, A. (2023). "You can't be a teacher talking like that":The shaping of identities for teachers of color. In K. Porcher, R. Ramkellawan-Arteaga, C. Hinds-Rodgers, & J. Bell (Eds.), *From being woke to doing #theWork* (pp. 48–58). Brill.

Camangian, P., & Cariaga, S. (2021). Social and emotional learning is hegemonic miseducation: Students deserve humanization instead. *Race Ethnicity and Education, 25*(7), 901–921. https://doi.org/10.1080/13613324.2020.1798374

Cancelmo, C., & Mueller, J. C. (2019). *Whiteness.* Oxford Bibliographies. https://www.oxfordbibliographies.com/display/document/obo-9780199756384/obo-9780199756384-0231.xml

Cárdenas, J. A., & Cárdenas, B. (1977). *The theory of incompatibilities: A conceptual framework for responding to the educational needs of Mexican American children*. IDRA.

Carter, S. P., Honeyford, M., McKaskie, D., Guthrie, F., Mahoney, S., & Carter, G. D. (2007). What do you mean by whiteness? *College Student Affairs Journal, 26*, 152–159.

Carver, W. (2022, May 18). Testimony of Willie Carver before the subcommittee on civil rights and civil liberties, U.S. House of Representatives. https://www.congress.gov/117/meeting/house/114793/witnesses/HHRG-117-GO02-Wstate-CarverW-20220519.pdf

Cazden, C. B., & Leggett, E. L. (1976). *Culturally responsive education: A response to LAU Remedies II. U.S. Department of Health, Education & Welfare*. National Institute of Education.

Celebrators of Diwali. (n.d.). *Designate Diwali a professional development day for Coppell School District (no classes)*. Change.org. https://www.aljazeera.com/news/2025/3/27/who-are-the-students-trump-wants-to-deport#:~:text=On%20March%2010%2C%20Trump%20posted,war%20on%20Gaza%20broke%20out

Charles, J. B. (2023, June 23). The evolution of DEI. *The Chronicle of Higher Education*. https://www.chronicle.com/article/the-evolution-of-dei

Cherng, H. S., Halpin, P. F., & Rodriguez, L. A. (2022). Teaching bias? Relations between teaching quality and classroom demographic composition. *American Journal of Education, 128*(2), 171–201.

Clark, S. P. (1975). *Septima Poinsette Clark 1898–1987: Educator & civil rights activist*. The Historical Marker Database. https://www.hmdb.org/m.asp?m=134228

Cole-Malott, D. M., & Samuels, S. (2022). Becoming a culturally relevant and sustaining educator (CRSE): White pre-service teachers: Reflexivity, and the development of self. In S. Browne & G. Jean-Marie (Eds.), *Reconceptualizing social justice in teacher education* (pp. 39–62). Palgrave Macmillan.

Colker, R. (2022). The white supremacist constitution. *Utah Law Review, 3*(4), 651–708. https://doi.org/10.26054/0d-ezsf-g1kb

Collins, C. S., Newman, C. B., & Jun, A. (2023). *Global white supremacy: Anti-blackness and the university as colonizer*. Rutgers University Press.

Collins, P. H. (1990). Black feminist thought in the matrix of domination. In *Black feminist thought: Knowledge, consciousness, and the politics of empowerment*. Unwin Hyman.

Columbia Office of the President, nd. Our resolution with the federal government. Retrieved from https://president.columbia.edu/content/our-resolution-federal-government.

The Combahee River Collective. (2014). A Black feminist statement. *Women's Studies Quarterly*, *42*(3/4), 271–280. http://www.jstor.org/stable/24365010

Connell, R. (2012). Just education. *Journal of Education Policy*, *27*(5), 681–683. https://doi.org/10.1080/02680939.2012.710022

Cooper, A. J. (1988). *A voice from the South*. Oxford University Press.

Counts, G. S. (1932). *Dare the school build a new social order?* The John Day Company.

Crenshaw, K. (1991). Mapping the margins: Intersectionality, identity politics, and violence against women of color. *Stanford Law Review*, *43*(6), 1241–1299. https://doi.org/10.2307/1229039

CRT Forward. (2024a). *CRT forward*. https://crtforward.law.ucla.edu/

CRT Forward. (2024b). *CRT forward tracking project*. https://crtforward.law.ucla.edu/map/

Davis, A. (1981). *Women, race, and class*. Vintage.

Death Penalty Information Center. (2025). *Criminalization of homosexuality in American history*. https://deathpenaltyinfo.org/policy-issues/biases-and-vulnerabilities/lgbtq-people/criminalization-of-homosexuality-in-american-history

Deliso, M., & Dwyer, D. (2025, June 27). *SCOTUS rules in favor of parents seeking to opt children out of reading LGBTQ-themed books*. ABC News. https://abcnews.go.com/Politics/scotus-rules-favor-parents-seeking-opt-children-reading/story?id=122528056

Delpit, L. (2019). *Teaching when the world is on fire*. The New Press.

Demillo, A. (2023, March 23). *Other states are copying Florida's "don't say gay" efforts*. Associated Press. https://apnews.com/article/huckabee-sanders-desantis-dont-say-gay-lgbtq-702fd5dc9633a7c93432f582de51a5fb

DiAlto, S. (2012). 3 From "Problem Minority" to "Model Minority": The Changing Social Construction of Japanese Americans. In A. Schneider & H. Ingram (Ed.), *Deserving and Entitled: Social Constructions and Public Policy* (pp. 81-103). SUNY Press.

Duggins-Clay, P. (2024, February 27). *Black students belong—The case for an Afrofuturistic education*. https://www.idra.org/resource-center/black-students-belong-the-case-for-an-afrofuturistic-education/

Duncan-Andrade, J. M. R. (2022). *Equality or equity: Toward a model of community-responsive education*. Harvard Education Press.

Duster, A. M. (2013). *Crusade for justice: The autobiography of Ida B. Wells*. University of Chicago Press.

Earnshaw, V. A., Menino, D. D., Sava, L. M., Perrotti, J., Barnes, T. N., Humphrey, D. L., & Reisner, S. L. (2020). LGBTQ bullying: a qualitative investigation of student and school health professional perspectives. *Journal of LGBT Youth*, *17*(3), 280–297. https://doi.org/10.1080/19361653.2019.1653808

Education and Social Inequality. (n.d.). https://www.trinity.edu/~mkearl/strat-ed.html

Education First/Ed Reports. (2021, June). *Culturally centered education: A primer*. https://www.education-first.com/wp-content/uploads/2021/06/Culturally-Centered-Education_-A-Primer-6.8.21-1.pdf

The Education Trust (2023, June 15). Affirmative action in higher education: Moving the conversation forward. Retrieved from https://edtrust.org/rti/affirmative-action/.

Emdin, C. (2016). *For white folks who teach in the hood—and the rest of y'all too: Reality pedagogy and urban education*. Beacon Press.

Encyclopedia Virginia. (n.d.). Nat Turner's revolt (1831). https://encyclopediavirginia.org/entries/turners-revolt-nat-1831/

Englander, T. (2023, July 27). 'The result of this policy will be homeless and dead children': Citizens address Va. Board of Education on new transgender policy. WRIC. Retrieved from https://www.wric.com/news/virginia-news/the-result-of-this-policy-will-be-homeless-and-dead-children-citizens-address-va-board-of-education-on-new-transgender-policy/

Espinosa-Aguilar, A. (2005). Radical rhetoric: Anger, activism, and change. In A. Keating. (Ed.) *EntreMundos/AmongWorlds* (pp. 227-232). Palgrave Macmillan.

Espinoza-Kulick, M. A. V. (n.d.). *Growth and expansion of ethnic studies*. LibreTexts. https://socialsci.libretexts.org/Bookshelves/Ethnic_Studies/Introduction_to_Ethnic_Studies_(Fischer_et_al.)/02%3A_The_Ongoing_Struggle_for_Ethnic_Studies/2.05%3A_Growth_and_Expansion_of_Ethnic_Studies#:~:text=In%20the%20over%20fifty%20years,and%20as%20a%20site%20of

Fanon, F. (1967). *Black skin, white masks*. Grove Press.

Federal Register. (2025). 2025 Donald J. Trump executive orders. https://www.federalregister.gov/presidential-documents/executive-orders/donald-trump/2025

Fleishman, J. (2023, January 27). School librarians vilified as the "arm of Satan" in book-banning wars. *Los Angeles Times*. https://www.latimes.com/politics/story/2023-01-27/school-librarians-vilified-as-the-arm-of-satan-in-book-banning-wars

Forsyth, C. J., Biggar, R. W., Forsyth, Y. A., & Howat, H. (2015). The punishment gap: Racial/ethnic comparisons in school infractions by objective and subjective definitions. *Deviant Behavior, 36*(4), 276–287.

Fram, A., & Lemire, J. (2018, January 12). *Trump: Why allow immigrants from "shithole countries"?* The Associated Press. https://abcnews.go.com/Politics/donald-trump-mexico-vice-versa/story?id=41767704.

Franklin, M. E. (1992). Culturally sensitive instructional practices for African-American learners with disabilities. *Exceptional Children, 59*(2), 115–122.

Freire, P. (1974). *Education for critical consciousness*. Seabury Press.
Freire (1975). Education for liberation. One World, 8, p. 16. Retrieved from https://www.acervo.paulofreire.org/items/26814f4e-e465-4186-a139-27161b2d3bc7
Freire, P. (1985). Reading the world and reading the word: An interview with Paulo Freire. *Language Arts, 62*(1), 15-21.
Freire, P. (2000). *Pedagogy of the oppressed* (30th anniversary ed.). Continuum. (Original work published 1970)
Frelick, B. (2017, March 9). *Trump's revised travel ban still mired in prejudice*. Huffington Post. https://www.hrw.org/news/2017/03/09/trumps-revised-travel-ban-still-mired-prejudice?gad_source=1&gad_campaignid=16363698676&gbraid=0AAAAADrFXchkJcFh80jItnnjS5Qr5VnOC&gclid=Cj0KCQjwyvfDBhDYARIsAItzbZHhBoj2F27oGdRtMe20_7zUFifboLg-L54I5unjGknGXGG1nKNorzQaAhmxEALw_wcB
Friends Committee on National Legislation. (2020, October 6). *The doctrine of discovery*. https://www.fcnl.org/updates/2016-09/doctrine-discovery.
Garcia, A., & O'Donnell-Allen, C. (2015). *Pose, wobble, flow: A culturally proactive approach to literacy instruction*. Teachers College Press.
Gauntt, S. (2025, July 26). *In rush for immigration arrests, a shift by ICE to "incredibly aggressive" tactics, advocates say*. Maryland Matters. https://marylandmatters.org/2025/07/26/in-rush-for-immigration-arrests-a-shift-by-ice-to-incredibly-aggressive-tactics-advocates-say/
Gay, G. (2002). Preparing for culturally responsive teaching. *Journal of Teacher Education, 53*(2), 106–116.
Gender Justice. (2025). *Get the facts: Trans inclusion in sports*. https://www.genderjustice.us/toolkits/trans-inclusion-sports/
Gillborn, D. (2005). Education policy as an act of white supremacy: Whiteness, critical race theory and education reform. *Journal of Education Policy, 20*(4), 485–505.
Gilmore, N. (2020, March 17). The unknown architect of the civil rights movement. *The Saturday Evening Post*. https://www.saturdayeveningpost.com/2020/03/the-unknown-architect-of-the-civil-rights-movement/
Givens, J. R. (2021). *Fugitive pedagogy: Carter G. Woodson and the art of Black teaching*. Harvard University Press.
Gomez, C., & Jimenez-Silva, M. (2012). Mexican American studies: The historical legitimacy of an educational program. *Journal of the Association of Mexican American Educators, 6*(1), 15–23.
Gorski, P. (1999). *The brief history of multicultural education*. EdChange. https://www.edchange.org/multicultural/papers/edchange_history.html
Gorski, P. (2010, April 4). *The challenge of defining "multicultural education."* EdChange. https://www.edchange.org/multicultural/initial.html

Greco Danaher, M., Shivers, N. L., Siegner, S. A., & Wagner, B. S. (2025, April 21). *Utah, West Virginia, and Wyoming enact laws defining male and female*. Ogletree Deakins. https://ogletree.com/insights-resources/blog-posts/utah-west-virginia-and-wyoming-enact-laws-defining-male-and-female/

Gremke, A. (1863). *Address at the women's national loyal league—May 14, 1963*. Iowa State University. https://awpc.cattcenter.iastate.edu/2017/03/21/address-at-the-womens-loyal-national-league-may-14-1863/

Grinde, D. A. (2004). Taking the Indian out of the Indian: U.S. policies of ethnocide through education. *Wicazo Sa Review, 19*(2), 25–32. http://www.jstor.org/stable/1409496

Gullah/Geechee Nation. (2021). *Hunnuh mus tek cyarce de root fa heal de tree: Gullah/Geechee Resiliency*. https://gullahgeecheenation.com/2021/07/14/hunnuh-mus-tek-cyare-de-root-fa-heal-de-tree-gullah-geechee-resiliency/

Hammond, Z. (2015). *Culturally responsive teaching and the brain: Promoting authentic engagement and rigor among culturally and linguistically diverse students*. Corwin Press.

Hammond, Z. (2025). *Rebuilding students' learning power: Teaching for instructional equity and cognitive justice*. Corwin Press.

Hannah-Jones, N. (2025, June 27). How Trump upended 60 years of civil rights in two months. *New York Times*. https://www.nytimes.com/2025/06/27/magazine/trump-civil-rights-law-discrimination.html

Hannah-Jones, N., Roper, C., Silverman, I., & Silverstein, J. (2021). *The 1619 Project: A New Origin Story*. One World.

Harper, S. (2022, October 17). Where is the $200 billion companies promised after George Floyd's murder? *Forbes*. https://www.forbes.com/sites/shaunharper/2022/10/17/where-is-the-200-billion-companies-promised-after-george-floyds-murder/

Harper, S. (2024). Ten truths and one very big lie about racial realities in K–12 schools and higher education institutions. In R. M. Johnson & S. R. Harper (Eds.), *The big lie about race in America's schools* (pp. 21–42). Harvard Education Press.

Harper, S., Chang, M. J., Patton Davis, L., Garces, L. M., Gaston Gayles, J., Jenkins, T. S., & Wolf-Wendel, L. (2024). *Truths about DEI on college campuses*. USC Race and Equity Center. https://race.usc.edu/wp-content/uploads/2024/03/Harper-and-Associates-DEI-Truths-Report.pdf

The Heritage Foundation. (2023). *Project 2025: Mandate for leadership: The conservative promise*. https://static.heritage.org/project2025/2025_MandateForLeadership_FULL.pdf

Hill Collins, P. (2000). *Black feminist thought: Knowledge, consciousness, and the politics of empowerment* (2nd ed.). Routledge.

Hillyard, V., & Marquez, A. (2024, July 11). *Trump disavows Project 2025, but he has long-standing ties to some key architects.* NBC News. https://www.nbcnews.com/politics/donald-trump/project-2025-trump-heritage-foundation-what-know-rcna161338

Hinger, S. (2023, July 12). *Moving beyond the Supreme Court's affirmative action rulings.* ACLU. https://www.aclu.org/news/racial-justice/moving-beyond-the-supreme-courts-affirmative-action-rulings

Hixenbaugh, M. (2021, January 22). *A viral video forced a wealthy Texas suburb to confront racism. A "silent majority" fought back.* NBC News. https://www.nbcnews.com/news/us-news/viral-video-forced-wealthy-texas-suburb-confront-racism-silent-majority-n1255230

Hoby, H. (2015). Toni Morrison: "I'm writing for black people… I don't have to apologise." *The Guardian.* https://www.theguardian.com/books/2015/apr/25/toni-morrison-books-interview-god-help-the-child

Hofstetter, J. (2025, March). *Shifting priorities: How the official English executive order could affect language access efforts.* Migration Policy Institute. https://www.pewresearch.org/short-reads/2024/07/22/what-we-know-about-unauthorized-immigrants-living-in-the-us/

Hollie, S. (2011). *Culturally and linguistically responsive teaching and learning: Classroom practices for student success.* Shell Educational Publishing.

hooks, b. (1994). *Teaching to transgress: Education as the practice of freedom.* Routledge.

hooks, b. (2000). *Feminism is for everybody: Passionate politics.* South End Press.

hooks, b. (2018). *All about love: New visions.* William Morrow. (Original work published 2000)

Horton, M. (1990). *We make the road by walking: Conversations on education and social change.* Temple University Press.

Horton, M., & Freire, P. (1990). *We make the road by walking: Conversations on education and social change.* Temple University Press.

Howard, J. R., & Howard, T. C. (2024). Dispelling "The Big Lie" with truth-telling for justice and democracy in US schools. In R. M. Johnson & S. R. Harper (Eds.), *The big lie about race in America's schools* (pp. 169–178). Harvard Education Press.

Howard, T. C. (2024). *Equity now: Justice, repair, and belonging in schools.* Corwin Press.

Hultgren, M. L. (1989). *To lead and to serve: American Indian education at Hampton Institute, 1878–1923.* Virginia Foundation for the Humanities and Public Policy, in cooperation with Hampton University.

Hunsaker, A. (2021, January 18). *NBC's rarely seen 1967 interview with Dr. Martin Luther King, Jr.* Primetimer. https://www.primetimer.com/quickhits/the-rarely-seen-1967-nbc-news-interview-of-dr-martin-luther-king-jr#:~:text=%22Many%20of%20the%20people%20who,the%20 realization%20of%20genuine%20equality.%22

Hurston, Z. N. (2018). *Their eyes were watching god*. Virago Press. (Original work published 1937)

IDRA. (2024). *IDRA education policy fellows program*. https://www.idra.org/education_policy/idra-education-policy-fellows-program/

Imarisha, W. (2023). To build a future without police and prisons, we have to imagine it first. In A. J. Ritchie (Ed.), *Practicing new worlds: Abolition and emergent strategies* (pp 55–62). AK Press.

Ingram Willis, A., & Lewis, K. C. (1998). A conversation with Gloria Ladson-Billings. *Language Arts, 75*(1), 61–70.

Inoue, A. (2022). *Labor-Based Grading Contracts: Building Equity and Inclusion in the Compassionate Writing Classroom*, 2nd ed. University Press of Colorado.

Institute for Education Sciences. (2025). *About IES*. https://ies.ed.gov/about

Johnson, T. (n.d.). *The Alcatraz Indian Occupation*. National Park Service. https://www.nps.gov/alca/learn/historyculture/we-hold-the-rock.htm#:~:text=This%20short%20occupation%20is%20significant,return%20later%20that%20same%20evening

Jones, R. P. (2023). *The hidden roots of white supremacy and the path to a shared American future*. Simon & Schuster.

Jordan Irvine, J. (1990). Transforming teaching for the twenty-first century. *Educational Horizons, 69*(1), 16–21.

Jordan Irvine, J. (1992). Making teacher education culturally responsive. In M. Dilworth (Ed.), *Diversity in teacher education* (pp. 79–92). Jossey-Bass.

Josephy, M. H., & Yu, A. M. (2025, May 28). The rise and fall of DEI at Harvard. *The Harvard Crimson*. https://www.thecrimson.com/article/2025/5/28/dei-rise-and-fall/#:~:text=By%20the%20time%20the%20Trump,was%20abruptly%20renamed%20in%20April

Keating, A. & González-López, G. (2011). Building Bridges, Transforming Loss, Shaping New Dialogues: Anzaldúan Studies for the Twenty-First Century. In A. Keating & G. González-López (Ed.), Bridging: *How Gloria Anzaldúa's Life and Work Transformed Our Own* (pp. 1-16). University of Texas Press.

Kendi, I. X. (2016). *Stamped from the beginning: The definitive history of racist ideas in America*. Random House.

Kerr, N., Cruz, A., Harper, A, & Walsh, K. (2023, December 28). Nikki Haley doesn't cite slavery as cause of the Civil War after question at campaign stop. ABC News. Retrieved from https://abcnews.go.com/Politics/nikki-haley-doesnt-cite-slavery-cause-civil-war/story?id=105956626#:~:text=Interest%20Successfully%20Added-,Nikki%20Haley%20doesn't%20cite%20slavery%20as%20cause%20of%20the,War%20was?%E2%80%9D%20she%20asked.

King, M. L. Jr. (1947). *The purpose of education*. The Martin Luther King, Jr. Research and Education Institute. https://kinginstitute.stanford.edu/king-papers/documents/purpose-education

King, M. L. Jr. (1959). *Address at the youth march for integrated schools on 18 April 1959*. The Martin Luther King, Jr. Research and Education Institute. https://kinginstitute.stanford.edu/king-papers/documents/address-youth-march-integrated-schools-18-april-1959

King, M. L. Jr. (1963a, August 28). *I have a dream* [Speech audio recording]. American Rhetoric.

King, M. L. Jr. (1963b). *Letter from Birmingham Jail*. Digital Public Library of America. https://dp.la/item/356f3e56d09c5a8aa3da628e6844822b

King, M. L. K. (1965). Remaining awake through a great revolution. Retrieved from https://www2.oberlin.edu/external/EOG/BlackHistoryMonth/MLK/MLKmainpage.html

Kipling, R. (1899). "The White Man's Burden." The Rudyard Kipling Foundation. Retrieved from https://www.kiplingsociety.co.uk/poem/poems_burden.htm

Kishimoto, K. (2022). Beyond teaching racial content: Antiracist pedagogy as implementing antiracist practices. In S. Browne & G. Jean-Marie (Eds.), *Reconceptualizing social justice in teacher education* (pp. 105–126). Palgrave Macmillan.

Klibanoff, E., & Priest, J. (2025, June 4). Texas' undocumented college students no longer qualify for in-state tuition. *The Texas Tribune*. https://www.aljazeera.com/news/2025/3/27/who-are-the-students-trump-wants-to-deport#:~:text=On%20March%2010%2C%20Trump%20posted,war%20on%20Gaza%20broke%20out

Kratz, J. (2024, December 29). The little known history of DEI and why it's critical to its survival. *Forbes*. https://www.forbes.com/sites/juliekratz/2024/12/29/history-of-dei-why-it-matters-for-the-future/

Ladson-Billings, G. (1995). Towards a theory of culturally relevant pedagogy. *American Educational Research Journal*, *32*(3), 465–491.

Ladson-Billings, G. (2006). *From the achievement gap to the education debt: Understanding achievement in U.S. schools*. 2006 Presidential Address—AERA Session 49.010.

Ladson-Billings, G., & Tate, W. F. (1995). Toward a critical race theory of education. *Teachers College Record*, *97*(1), 47–68.

Lalami, L. (2020). *Conditional citizens: On belonging in America*. Pantheon.

Lantz, P. M., & Carter, E. (2024, April 24). State bans on "divisive concepts" in public higher education: Implications for population health. *The Milbank Quarterly*. https://www.milbank.org/quarterly/opinions/state-bans-on-divisive-concepts-in-public-higher-education-implications-for-population-health/

Lavietes, M. (2022, June 27). *Kentucky's 2022 teacher of year quits profession citing homophobia.* NBC News. https://www.nbcnews.com/nbc-out/out-news/kentuckys-2022-teacher-year-quits-profession-citing-homophobia-rcna35224

Law, N. V., & Hollins-Alexander, S. (n.d.). *#CorwinTalks: Strategies to foster cultures of belonging in schools and classrooms.* https://corwin-connect.com/2024/03/corwintalks-strategies-to-foster-cultures-of-belonging-in-schools-and-classrooms/#:~:text=We%20cannot%20create%20equitable%20schools,By%20Crystal%20Belle

Levengood, T. W., & Hadland, S. E. (2023). Hostile laws and hospitalization: Why anti-LGBTQ+ legislation threatens adolescent lives. *Journal of Hospital Medicine, 18*(5), 449–452. https://doi.org.10.1002/jhm.13038

Library of Congress. (n.d.) 1968 East Los Angeles Walkouts. Retrieved from https://guides.loc.gov/latinx-civil-rights/east-la-walkouts

Leigh-Osroosh, K.T. & Hutchison B. (2019). Cultural identity silencing of Native Americans in education. *Race and Pedagogy Journal 4*(1), 1–33.

Light, M. T., & Miller, T. Y. (2017). Does undocumented immigration increase violent crime? *Criminology, 56* (2), 370–401.

Lipka, J., Hogan, M. P., Webster, J. P., Yanez, E., Adams, B., Clark, S., & Lacy, D. (2005). Math in a cultural context: Two case studies of a successful culturally based math project. *Anthropological and Education Quarterly, 36*(4), 367–385.

Lopez, B. (2021, September 18). How a Black high school principal was swept into a "critical race theory" maelstrom in a mostly white Texas suburb. *The Texas Tribune.* https://www.texastribune.org/2021/09/18/colleyville-principal-critical-race-theory/

Lorde, A. (1982). *Learning from the 60s.* https://www.blackpast.org/african-american-history/1982-audre-lorde-learning-60s/

Lorde, A. (2007). *Sister outsider: Essays and speeches.* Crossing Press. (Original work published 1984)

Love, B. (2019). *We want to do more than survive: Abolitionist teaching and the pursuit of educational freedom.* Beacon Press.

Love, B. (2023). *Punished for dreaming: How school reform harms Black children and how we heal.* St. Martin's Press.

Lucas D'Oyley, D. (2020, October 26). The news isn't #TeacherBae's clothing—It's the exploitation of her body. *Essence.* https://www.essence.com/news/teacher-bae-patrice-brown-exploitation/

Ma, D. (2026). *Anti-oppressive universal design for teachers: Building equitable classrooms.* Routledge.

Markovich, A. (2021, October 20). Berkeley mandated ethnic studies 30 years ahead of California. Now the district's going a step further.

Berkeleyside. https://www.berkeleyside.org/2021/10/20/ethnic-studies-berkeley-high-school

Martinez Keel, N. (2025, February 27). Oklahoma education officials pass pro-Bible social studies standards. *Oklahoma Voice*. https://oklahomavoice.com/2025/02/27/oklahoma-education-officials-pass-pro-bible-social-studies-standards/#:~:text=State%20Superintendent%20Ryan%20Walters%2C%20who,to%20Advanced%20Placement%20government%20classes

The Martin Luther King, Jr. Research and Education Institute (n.d.). Montgomery Bus Boycott. Stanford University. Retrieved from https://kinginstitute.stanford.edu/montgomery-bus-boycott.

Maxwell, A., & Shields, T. (2019). The myth of a post-racial America. In A. Maxwell & T. Shields (Eds.), *The long southern strategy: How chasing white voters in the South changed American politics* (pp. 93–124). Oxford University Press.

Mays, K.T. (2021). *An Afro-Indigenous History of the United States*. Beacon Press.

McCall, C. S., Romero, M. E., Yang, W., & Weigand, T. (2022): A call for equity-focused social-emotional learning. *School Psychology Review*, *52*(5), 586–607. https://doi.org/10.1080/2372966X.2022.2093125

McCarty, T. L., & Lee, T. S. (2014). Critical culturally sustaining/revitalizing pedagogy. *Harvard Educational Review*, *84*(1), 101–124.

McCorkle, W., & Rodriguez, S. (2021). When nationalism supersedes belief in religious freedom: An analysis of teachers' beliefs. *Educational Studies*, *57*(2), 182–201. https://doi.org/10.1080/00131946.2020.1863802

McCorkle, W., & Rodriguez, S. (2023). Levels of nationalism among middle and high school social studies teachers: Implications for promoting equity for immigrant students and with educators. *The Journal of Social Studies Research*, *47*(2), 92–107. https://doi.org/10.1016/j.jssr.2022.01.004

McGee, B. S., Germany, A. F., Phillips, R. L., & Barros-Lane L. (2022). Utilizing a critical race theory lens to reduce barriers to social and emotional learning: A call to action. *Children & Schools*, *44*(1), 39–47.

McGee, K. (2023, July 11). Texas A&M recruited a UT professor to revive its journalism program, then backtracked after "DEI hysteria." *The Texas Tribune*. https://www.texastribune.org/2023/07/11/texas-a-m-kathleen-mcelroy-journalism/

McGee Banks, C. S., & Banks, J. A. (1995). Equity pedagogy: An essential component of multicultural education. *Theory into Practice*, *34*(3), 152–158. https://www.jstor.org/stable/1476634

McKenzie-Jones, P. (2023, October 10). *"Let's raise some hell": Clyde Warrior and the red power movement*. Organization of American Historians. https://www.oah.org/process/mckenzie-jones-clyde-warrior-and-red-power/

Miller, V., Fernandez, F., & Hutchens, N. H. (2023). The race to ban race: Legal and critical arguments against state legislation to ban critical race theory in higher education. *Missouri Law Review, 88*(2), 61–106.

Mohatt, G., & Erickson, F. (1981). Cultural differences in teaching styles in an Odawa school: A sociolinguistic approach. In H. Trueba, G. Guthrie, & K. Au (Eds.), *Culture and the bilingual classroom: Studies in classroom ethnography* (pp. 105–119). Newbury House.

Molina, N. (2014). *How Race Is Made in America: Immigration, Citizenship, and the Historical Power of Racial Scripts*. University of California Press.

Moll, L. C., Amanti, C., Neff, D., & Gonzalez, N. (1992). Funds of knowledge for teaching: Using a qualitative approach to connect homes and classrooms. *Theory into Practice, 31*(2), 132–141. https://doi.org/10.1080/00405849209543534

Morgan, J. L. (1997). "Some could suckle over their shoulder": Male travelers, female bodies, and the gendering of racial ideology, 1500–1770. *The William and Mary Quarterly, 54*(1), 167–192. https://www.jstor.org/stable/2953316

Morrison, T. (2017). *The origin of others*. Harvard University Press.

Muhammad, G. (2020). *Cultivating genius: An equity framework for culturally and historically responsive literacy*. Scholastic Inc.

NAACP. (n.d.). *Affirmative action in education matters for equity, opportunity, and the nation's progress*. https://naacp.org/resources/affirmative-action-education-matters

Nadworny, E., & Owens, J. (2025, July 25). *What we know about Columbia's $221 million settlement with the Trump administration*. NPR. https://www.npr.org/2025/07/25/nx-s1-5479240/columbia-trump-administration-settlement-details

Nagda, B. (R.) A., Gurin, P., & Lopez, G. E. (2003). Transformative pedagogy for democracy and social justice. *Race Ethnicity and Education, 6*(2), 165–191. https://doi.org/10.1080/13613320308199

National Center for Education Statistics. (2024). *Racial/ethnic enrollment in public schools*. https://nces.ed.gov/programs/coe/indicator/cge/racial-ethnic-enrollment.

National Conference of State Legislators. (2025). *State legislators at work: Insights into legislator time and demographics*. https://www.ncsl.org/center-for-legislative-strengthening/state-legislators-at-work

National Education Association. (2022, September 9). *The legal and pedagogical case for culturally responsive and racially inclusive public education for all students*. https://www.nea.org/resource-library/legal-and-pedagogical-case-culturally-responsive-and-racially-inclusive-public-education-all

National Immigration Forum. (2021). *"The great replacement theory" explained.* https://forumtogether.org/wp-content/uploads/2021/12/Replacement-Theory-Explainer-1122.pdf

National Native American Boarding School Healing Coalition. (n.d.). *U.S. Indian boarding school history.* https://boardingschoolhealing.org/us-indian-boarding-school-history/

National Parks Service. (2020, July 10). *American Latino theme study: Education.* https://www.nps.gov/articles/latinothemeeducation.htm

Nawaz, A., Kopelev, S., & Okay, D. (2025, May 12). White South Africans arrive in the U.S. after receiving refugee status from Trump. *PBS News Hour.* https://www.pbs.org/newshour/show/white-south-africans-arrive-in-u-s-after-receiving-refugee-status-from-trump

Nichols, B. (2022). White supremacist capitalist patriarchy. In C. F. E. Holzhey & J. Schillinger (Eds.), *The case for reduction* (pp. 263–265). ICI Berlin Press.

Nitzberg, A. (2025, July 31). *Trump congratulates Ivy League school after $50M deal to restore federal funding: "Woke is officially DEAD."* Fox News. https://www.foxnews.com/politics/trump-congratulates-ivy-league-school-after-50m-deal-restore-federal-funding-woke-officially-dead

Nouri, A., & Sajjadi, S. (2014). Emancipatory pedagogy in practice: Aims, principles and curriculum orientation. *International Journal of Critical Pedagogy, 5*(2), 76–87.

Nunn, N., & Qian, N. (2010). The Columbian exchange: A history of disease, food, and ideas. *Journal of Economic Perspectives, 24*(2), 163–188.

Obama, B. (2008). *Barack Obama in back-to-back speeches at the 99th NAACP Convention.* https://www.ontheissues.org/Archive/2008_NAACP_Barack_Obama.htm

Obasogie, O. K. (2020, June 5). Police killing black people is a pandemic, too. *The Washington Post.* https://www.washingtonpost.com/outlook/police-violence-pandemic/2020/06/05/e1a2a1b0-a669-11ea-b619-3f9133bbb482_story.html

Office of the President, (2025, July 30). Brown and the U.S. government reach agreement. Brown University. Retrieved from https://president.brown.edu/president/brown-and-us-government-reach-agreement.

Ortiz, P. (2018). *An African American and Latinx history of the United States.* Beacon Press.

Pak, S. K., Rodriguez Kmec, I., Tynan, E., & Warren, M. R. (2022, May 19). *Caught in an educational dragnet: How the school-to-deportation pipeline harms immigrant youth and youth of color.* National Immigration Law Center. https://www.aljazeera.com/news/2025/3/27/who-are-the-students-trump-wants-to-deport#:~:text=On%20March%2010%2C%20 Trump%20posted,war%20on%20Gaza%20broke%20out

Palmer, P. J. (1997). The heart of a teacher: Identity and integrity in teaching. *Change: The Magazine of Higher Learning, 29*(6), 14–21. https://doi.org/10.1080/00091389709602343

Paris, D. (2012). Culturally sustaining pedagogy: A needed change in stance, terminology, and practice. *Educational Researcher, 41*(3), 93–97.

Parker, C. S., & Blum, R. M. (2025). Exploring the motivations of the MAGA movement. In S. Livingston & M. Miller (Eds.), *Connective action and the rise of the far-right: Platforms, politics, and the crisis of democracy* (pp. 191–206). Oxford University Press.

Parsons, R. (2022, March 28). Anthropology association apologizes to Native Americans for the field's legacy of harm. *Scientific American*. https://www.scientificamerican.com/article/anthropology-association-apologizes-to-native-americans-for-the-fields-legacy-of-harm/#:~:text=In%201901%20 the%20soon%20to,propped%20up%20arguments%20for%20eugenics

Passel, J. S., & Krogstad, J. M. (2024, July 22). *What we know about unauthorized immigrants living in the U.S.* Pew Research Center. https://www.pewresearch.org/short-reads/2024/07/22/what-we-know-about-unauthorized-immigrants-living-in-the-us/

Patterson, K., Santiago, A. M., & Silverman, R. M. (2021). The enduring backlash against racial justice in the United States: Mobilizing strategies for institutional change. *Journal of Community Practice, 29*(4), 334–344. https://doi.org/10.1080/10705422.2021.1998875

Payne, C. M. (2022). *So much reform, so little change: The persistence of failure in urban schools.* Harvard University Press.

Pierce, S. D. (2024, January 2). Cox touted his action on diversity, equity and inclusion goals. Now he says university DEI statements border on 'evil'. *The Salt Lake Tribune*. Retrieved from https://www.sltrib.com/news/politics/2024/01/02/cox-touted-his-action-diversity/.

Peña, C., Lopez, S. R., Castañeda, E., Quintero, J. M., & Askari, M. (2023). Chicana/Latina feminism: What is it and how does it define us? *New Directions for Adult and Continuing Education, 2023,* 65–75. https://doi.org/10.1002/ace.20512

PEN America. (2023, April 20). *Banned in the U.S.: State laws supercharge book suppression in schools.* https://pen.org/report/banned-in-the-usa-state-laws-supercharge-book-suppression-in-schools/

Platoff, E. (2018, May 24). Gay Mansfield ISD teacher on leave after showing students photo of her wife. KERA News. Retrieved from https://www.keranews.org/texas-news/2018-05-24/gay-mansfield-isd-teacher-on-leave-after-showing-students-a-photo-of-her-wife powell, j. a., & Menendian, S. (2024). *Belonging without othering: How we save ourselves and the world*. Stanford University Press.

Powell, T. S. (2021). Culturally-connected integrated STEM instruction. In K. Sprott, J. R. O'Connor, & C. Msengi (Eds.), *Designing culturally competent programming for PK–20 classrooms* (pp. 119–137). IGI Global.

Pratt, R.H. (1892). "Kill the Indian in him, and save the man": Pratt on the education of Native Americans. Carlisle Indian School Digital Resource Center. Retrieved from https://carlisleindian.dickinson.edu/teach/kill-indian-him-and-save-man-r-h-pratt-education-native-americans

Prichep, D. (2024, May 6). *Transgender bathroom bills are back, gaining traction after past boycotts*. NPR. https://www.npr.org/2024/05/06/1249406353/transgender-bathroom-bill-republican-states

Quilantan, B., Carballo, R., & Perez, J. Jr. (2025, July 8). *Education department dismisses thousands of civil rights complaints at an "unheard of" pace*. Politico. https://www.politico.com/news/2025/07/08/education-departments-civil-rights-complaint-dismissals-prompt-concern-from-trump-opponents-00439118

Quinn, M., & Rosen, J. (2025, September 3). *Judge rules Trump administration's funding freeze against Harvard was unlawful*. CBS News. https://www.cbsnews.com/news/judge-rules-trump-administrations-funding-freeze-for-harvard-was-unlawful/

Rector, K. (2025, May 9). Whether it's his plan or not, Trump's policies so far closely align with Project 2025. *Los Angeles Times*. https://www.latimes.com/politics/story/2025-05-09/trump-policies-closely-align-with-project-2025

Reed, T. (2020). *Toward Freedom: The Case Against Race Reductionism*. Verso.

Re'vell, M. D. (2019). Moving toward culturally restorative teaching exchanges: Using restorative practices to develop literacy across subject area-content. *International Journal of Smart Education and Urban Society*, *10*(2), 53–69.

Richardson, H. (2020, December 16). Utah Compact on Racial Equity, Diversity and Inclusion. Utah Policy. Retrieved from https://utahpolicy.com/archive/25771-utah-compact-on-racial-equity-diversity-and-inclusion-2.

Riechmann, D., & Tang, T. (2020, March 18). *Trump dubs COVID-19 "Chinese virus" despite hate crime risks*. https://apnews.com/article/donald-trump-ap-top-news-asia-crime-virus-outbreak-a7c233f0b3bcdb72c06cca6271ba6713

Riley, G. (1984). Some European (mis)perceptions of American Indian women. *New Mexico Historical Review*, *59*(3), 237–266. https://digitalrepository.unm.edu/nmhr/vol59/iss3/2

Ritchie, A. J. (2023). *Practicing new worlds: Abolition and emergent strategies.* AK Press.

Roberts, K. (2021, July 1). *How will you know if critical race theory is taught in your child's school?* Texas Public Policy Foundation. https://www.texaspolicy.com/how-will-you-know-if-critical-race-theory-is-taught-in-your-childs-school/

Ross, H. J. (2014). *Everyday bias: Identifying and navigating unconscious judgments in our daily lives.* Rowman & Littlefield.

Runnels, A. (2023, December 28). Diversity offices on college campuses will soon be illegal in Texas, as 30 new laws go into effect. *The Texas Tribune.* https://www.texastribune.org/2023/12/28/texas-new-laws-dei-ban-colleges-universities/

Russell, S. T., Bishop, M. D., Saba, V. C., James, I., & Ioverno, S. (2021). Promoting School Safety for LGBTQ and All Students. *Policy insights from the behavioral and brain sciences, 8(2),* 160–166. https://doi.org/10.1177/23727322211031938

Ryan, T. (2025, October 9). Federal courts rule ten commandments displays in public schools unconstitutional. IDRA. Retrieved from https://www.idra.org/resource-center/federal-courts-rule-ten-commandments-displays-in-public-schools-unconstitutional/

Saad, L. F. (2020). *Me and white supremacy: Combat racism, change the world, and become a good ancestor.* Sourcebooks.

San Francisco State University. (n.d.). *Africana studies.* https://bulletin.sfsu.edu/colleges/ethnic-studies/africana-studies/

Santoro, N. (2009). Teaching in culturally diverse contexts: What knowledge about self and others do teachers need? *Journal of Education for Teaching: International Research and Pedagogy, 35*(1), 33–45.

Schultz, E. (2021, June 18). Yes, Virginia—there is critical race theory in our schools. *Fairfax County Times.* https://www.fairfaxtimes.com/articles/yes-virginia-there-is-critical-race-theory-in-our-schools/article_ba449c18-cf99-11eb-a719-4bfc9103236c.html

Sciarra, D. G. (2023). *Equity and diversity: Defining the right to education for the 21st century.* Education Law Center. https://edlawcenter.org/assets/uploads/ELC_50th_Anniversary_Report.pdf

Seidel, A. L. (2019). *The founding myth: Why Christian nationalism is un-American.* Union Square.

Seider, S., El-Amin, A, & Bott, J. (2025). *Educating for Justice: Schoolwide Strategies to Prepare Students to Recognize, Analyze, and Challenge Inequity.* ASCD.

Serverian-Wilmeth, K. (2018). *Culturally mediated instruction.* Brown University. https://wacharters.org/wp-content/uploads/2019/12/Culturally-Mediated-Instruction-_-Teaching-Diverse-Learners.pdf

Shulman, L. E. (1987). Knowledge and teaching: Foundations of the new reform. *Harvard Educational Review, 57*(1), 1–12.

Smith, B. (1982). Racism and women's studies. In G. T. Hull, P. Bell Scott, & B. Smith (Eds.), *All the women are white, all the blacks are men, but some of us are brave: Black women's studies* (pp. 48–51). The Feminist Press.

Smith, G. A., Cooperman, A., Alper, B. A., Mohamed, B., Rotolo. C., Tevington, P., Nortey, J., Kallo, A., Diamant, J., & Fahmy, D. (2025, February 26). *Decline of Christianity in the U.S. has slowed, may have leveled off*. Pew Research Center. https://www.pewresearch.org/religion/2025/02/26/decline-of-christianity-in-the-us-has-slowed-may-have-leveled-off/

Spector, C. (2025, June 17). *Student absences increased under threat of deportation efforts, study finds*. Stanford Institute for Economic Policy and Research. https://siepr.stanford.edu/news/student-absences-increased-under-threat-deportation-efforts-study-finds#:~:text=Beyond%20learning%20loss&text=Dee%20pointed%20to%20past%20research,levels%20of%20anxiety%20and%20depression

Starker Glass, T., & Carter Berry, L. (2022). *Teaching for justice & belonging: A journey for educators and parents*. John Wiley & Sons.

Stelter, B. (2020, September 6). *Analysis: Fox news segment prompts Trump to target diversity training*. CNN. https://www.cnn.com/2020/09/06/media/donald-trump-fox-news-critical-race-theory

Stolberg, S. G. (2021, July 27). Coronavirus and police brutality roil black communities. *The New York Times*. https://www.nytimes.com/2020/06/07/us/politics/blacks-coronavirus-police-brutality.html

Thomas, M., & Wendling, M. (2024, September 15). *Trump repeats baseless claims about Haitian immigrants eating pets*. BBC News. https://www.bbc.com/news/articles/c77l28myezko

Thompson, A., & Cuseo, J. (2020). *Infusing equity & cultural competence into teacher development*. Kendall Hunt.

Tintiangco-Cubales, A., Kohli, R., Sacramento, J., Henning, N., Agarwal-Rangnath, R., & Sleeter, C. (2014). Toward an ethnic studies pedagogy: Implications for K–12 schools from the research. *The Urban Review, 47*, 104–125.

Toliver, S. R. (2025). *Defining Afrofuturism*. https://readingblackfutures.com/defining-afrofuturism/

Trans Legislation Tracker. (2025). *2025 anti-trans bills tracker*. https://translegislation.com/

Trethan, P. (2025, June 9). Demographics of Los Angeles show its a fertile ground for anti-ICE protests. USA Today. Retrieved from https://www.

usatoday.com/story/news/nation/2025/06/09/la-immigrants-population-demographics-protest/84114134007/

The Trevor Project. (2023). *2023 U.S. national survey on the mental health of LGBTQ+ young people.* https://www.thetrevorproject.org/survey-2023/

The Trevor Project. (2024, August 21). *Anti-LGBTQ+ school policies and LGBTQ+ young people.* https://www.thetrevorproject.org/research-briefs/anti-lgbtq-school-policies-and-lgbtq-young-people/

Trump, D. (2018, November 1). *Remarks by President Trump on the illegal immigration crisis and border security.* https://trumpwhitehouse.archives.gov/briefings-statements/remarks-president-trump-illegal-immigration-crisis-border-security/

Tsu, C.M. (2013). '5 From Menace to Model: Reshaping the "Oriental Problem."' *Garden of the World: Asian Immigrants and the Making of Agriculture in California's Santa Clara Valley* (2013; online edn, Oxford Academic, 26 Sept. 2013).

Tyler, A. (2024). *How to end Christian nationalism.* Broadleaf Books.

UCLA Center X. (2016, July 20). Ethnic studies K–12: Introduction. *XChange: Publications and Resources for Public School Professionals.* https://centerx.gseis.ucla.edu/xchange/ethnic-studies-k-12/introduction/

Ukpokodu, O. (2006). Essential characteristics of a culturally conscious classroom. *Social Studies and the Young Learner, 19*(2), 4–7.

United Nations. (2025). *What are human rights?* https://www.un.org/en/global-issues/human-rights

U.S. Department of Education. (2025a). *About OCR.* https://www.ed.gov/about/ed-offices/ocr/about-ocr

U.S. Department of Education. (2025b). *Federal role in education.* https://www.ed.gov/about/ed-overview/federal-role-in-education

U.S. Department of Justice Office of Public Affairs. (2025a, July 30). *Justice department releases guidance for recipients of federal funding regarding unlawful discrimination.* https://www.justice.gov/opa/pr/justice-department-releases-guidance-recipients-federal-funding-regarding-unlawful

U.S. Department of Education. (2025c). *Mission of the U.S. Department of Education.* Retrieved from https://www.ed.gov/about/ed-overview/mission-of-the-us-department-of-education

U.S. Department of Justice Office of Public Affairs. (2025b, July 14). *Justice department releases guidance on implementing president Trump's executive order designating English as the official language of the United States.* https://www.justice.gov/opa/pr/justice-department-releases-guidance-implementing-president-trumps-executive-order

Uyematsu, A. (1969). The emergence of yellow power in America. *Gidra, 1*(7), 8–11.

Uyematsu, Amy "The Emergence of Yellow Power in America," (reprinted from Gidra, October, 1969), , eds., Amy Tachiki, Eddie Wong, Franklin Odo, Buck Wong (UCLA Asian American Studies Center, 1971), pp. 9–13.

Uyematsu, A. (1971). The emergence of yellow power in America. In A. Tachiki, E. Wong, F. Odo, & B. Wong (Eds.), *Roots: An Asian American reader* (pp. 9–13). Continental Graphics.

Uyematsu, A. (2022). Remembering Amy Uyematsu (1947–2023). *Amerasia Journal, 48(3)*, 259–271. https://doi.org/10.1080/00447471.2023.2279031

Vaught, S. E. (2011). *Racism, public schooling, and the entrenchment of white supremacy: A critical race ethnography.* State University of New York Press.

Vázquez Ríos, E., (2013). *The little school of the 400: A Mexican-American fight for equal access and its impact on state policy.* Dissertations, Theses, & Student Research, Department of History, 58. https://digitalcommons.unl.edu/historydiss/58

Villegas, A. M. (1988). School failure and cultural mismatch: Another view. *The Urban Review, 20*, 253–265.

Villegas, A. M., & Lucas, T. (2002). Preparing culturally responsive teachers: Rethinking the curriculum. *Journal of Teacher Education, 53*(1), 20–32.

Viner, M., & Murphy, B. (2021). *Promoting educational success through culturally situated instruction.* Lexington Books.

Virginia, M. E. (2023). *Pontiac's resistance.* EBSCO. https://www.ebsco.com/research-starters/history/pontiacs-resistance

Vogt, L. A., Jordan, C., & Tharp, R. G. (1987). Explaining School Failure, Producing School Success: Two Cases. *Anthropology & Education Quarterly, 18*(4), 276–286. http://www.jstor.org/stable/3216657

Wallace-Wells, B. (2021). How a conservative activist invented the conflict over critical race theory. *The New Yorker.* https://www.newyorker.com/news/annals-of-inquiry/how-a-conservative-activist-invented-the-conflict-over-critical-race-theory

Wall Kimmerer, R. (2013). *Braiding sweetgrass: Indigenous wisdom, scientific knowledge, and the teaching of plants.* Milkweed Editions.

Walker, T. (2025, February 4). How dismantling the Department of Education would harm students. *NEA Today.* Retrieved from https://www.nea.org/nea-today/all-news-articles/how-dismantling-department-education-would-harm-students

Wamsley, L. (2021, July 6). *After tenure controversy, Nikole Hannah-Jones will join Howard faculty instead of UNC.* KERA. https://www.npr.org/2021/07/06/1013315775/after-tenure-controversy-nikole-hannah-jones-will-join-howard-faculty-instead-of#:~:text=Agostini/Invision/AP-,Nikole%20Hannah%2DJones%2C%20seen%20here%20 in%202016%2C%20will%20join,her%20tenure%20with%20her%20 appointment.&text=Less%20than%20a%20week%20after,crisis%20 our%20democracy%20is%20facing.%22

Ward, I. (2024, January 3). *We sat down with the conservative mastermind behind Clasy's ouster*. Politico. https://www.politico.com/news/magazine/2024/01/03/christopher-rufo-claudine-gay-harvard-resignation-00133618/

Warren, M. R. (2014). Transforming public education: The need for an educational justice movement. *New England Journal of Public Policy, 26*(1), 1–16.

Washington, B. T. (1901). *Up from slavery: An autobiography*. New York: Doubleday, Page.

The Washington Post. (2025, July 23). The antisemitism task force carrying out Trump's anti-DEI agenda. https://www.washingtonpost.com/podcasts/post-reports/the-antisemitism-task-force-carrying-out-trumps-antidei-agenda/

Watkins, N. A. (2022). The role of teachers in educational policymaking. *Literature Reviews in Education and Human Services, 1*(1), 1–23.

West, C. (1993). *Race matters*. Beacon Press.

Wilkerson, I. (2020). *Caste: The origins of our discontents*. Random House.

Willoughby, C. D. E. (2018). Running away from drapetomania: Samuel A. Cartwright, medicine, and race in the antebellum South. *The Journal of Southern History, 84*(3), 579–614. https://www.jstor.org/stable/26536293

Wilson, J., & Flanagan, A. (2022). *The racist "great replacement" conspiracy theory explained*. SPLC. https://www.splcenter.org/resources/hatewatch/racist-great-replacement-conspiracy-theory-explained/?gad_source=1&gad_campaignid=1359746550/

Wise, T. (2010). *Colorblind: The rise of post-racial politics and the retreat from racial equity*. City Lights Books.

Wohlleben, P. (2015). *The hidden life of trees: What they feel, how they communicate*. Greystone Books.

Womack, Ytasha. (2013). *Afrofuturism: The world of black sci-fi and fantasy culture*. Chicago Review Press.

Woodson, C. G. (1921). Fifty years of Negro citizenship as qualified by the United States Supreme Court. *Journal of Negro History, 6*(1), 1–53.

Woodson, C. G. (1933). *The mis-education of the Negro*. The Associated Publishers.

Zinn Education Project. (2025). *Oct. 30, 1956: Texas school district found guilty of discriminating against Mexican-American students*. https://www.zinnedproject.org/news/tdih/texas-school-discriminating-against-mexican-american-students/

Index

Bold page numbers indicate tables, *italic* numbers indicate figures.

ability
 and disability, critical introspection and **142**
 physical, identities privileged/victimized by white supremacy **163**
ableism 25
Abreu, R.L. 108
academic job market, author's experience of 72–3
affirmative action, repeal of 98–9, 120–1
African Americans
 civil rights era 34–6
 Covid-19 pandemic and 75
 use of term 6
 see also Black Americans
Africana Studies 59
Afrofuturism 183–4
age, identities privileged/victimized by white supremacy **163**
Age Discrimination in Employment Act 1967 41, **43**
ageism 25
All About Love: New Visions (hooks) 149
Altman, N. 137
American Dream, myth of 122–3
American Indian Movement (AIM) 39–40
American Indian Religious Freedom Act 42, **44**
Americans with Disabilities Act (ADA) 42, **44**

Angelou, Maya 192
Ansley, F.L. 15
anti-Asian racism 27
anti-atheism 25
anti-Black racism 27
anti-Christian bias, conservative claims of 109–10
anti-criticality 169
anti-CRT legislation 83–7, 125, 162
 purpose of this book 1–2
 Trump administration 1
anti-CRT movement 81–7, *86*
anti-DEI legislation 93–8, 120–1, 125, 162
anti-ICE protests 157–8
anti-intellectualism 179
anti-Latino(x) racism 27
anti-LGBTQIA+ legislation 103–9, *106*
anti-literacy laws, enslaved Black Americans and 53
anti-Native American racism 27
anti-racism, intersectionality and 164–6
anti-SEL legislation 89–90
anti-Semitism
 defined 25
 pro-Palestinian protests seen as 96–7, 114
 unfounded accusations of 94–5
anti-trans legislation *106*, 106–8
Anzaldúa, Gloria 181
aporophobia 25
art about indigenous peoples, colonizers' 14

Index

artificial intelligence
  radical imagination and 185–8
  use of, caution and 189n1
Asian Americans
  civil rights era 38
  white supremacy, early schools and 56–7
Asian American Studies 59
Asian/Pacific American Heritage Month 45
Asiatic Exclusion League 57
Atkins, John DeWitt Clinton 52
attacks on racial equity
  in 2020/2025 76–8
  affirmative action, repeal of 98–9
  critical race theory (CRT) 81–7, *86*
  diversity, equity and inclusion (DEI) 92–9
  effectiveness of 100
  judicial decisions against DEI 98–9
  motivation for 100
  Project 2025, Trump and 77
  social and emotional learning (SEL) 88–9

Babino, A. 144
backlash against racial equity
  in 2020/2025 76–8
  affirmative action, repeal of 98–9
  critical race theory (CRT) 81–7, *86*
  diversity, equity and inclusion (DEI) 92–9
  effectiveness of 100
  judicial decisions against DEI 98–9
  motivation for 100
  Project 2025, Trump and 77
  social and emotional learning (SEL) 88–9
Baker, Ella 167
Baldwin, James 175–6
Ball, S.J. 147, 153
Banks, J.A. 34, 60, 61, 177

banning of books with LGBTQIA+ content 104, 105, 107, 162
Beal, F.M. 23
Beauboeuf-Lafontant, T. 149
belief systems, conservative
  Black inferiority 125–7
  Eurocentrism 123–5
  meritocracy 122–3
  racial colorblindness 120–2
  understanding of, need for 119
  white nationalism 127–31
Benjamin, Ruha 18, 76, 118, 145, 183, 184
biases 138–9
Bilingual Education Act (BEA) 1968 41, **44**, 112
bilinguals, emergent 112–15
Bill of Rights of the US Constitution 20, **21**
birth of United States
  period of 16
  white supremacy and 17–19
birthright citizenship 22
Black Americans
  capitalistic violence inflicted on 18
  civil rights era 34–6
  Covid-19 pandemic and 75
  higher education 55
  legalization of citizenship **22**
  National Black (Afro-American) History Month 45
  use of term 6
  white supremacy, early schools and 53–5
  work, schooling as competing with 54
Black codes **21**
Black feminist movement 39
"A Black Feminist Statement" (Combahee River Collective) 161
Black feminist theory 160–2
Black hair 126

Black history and culture, Afrofuturism and 183–4
Black inferiority, conservatives' belief in 125–7
Black lesbians 39
Black Lives Matter in Schools movement 74
Black Lives Matter movement 73–5
Black power movement 36
Black Skin, White Masks (Fanon) 191–2, 194–5
Black students' bodies, schools' attempts to control 126
Black Studies 59
Black women, race and gender 23
blighting of the fruit 2–3, 71–8
blood quantum laws 128
bodies, Black students', schools' attempts to control 126
books with LGBTQIA+ content, banning of 104, 105, 107, 162
brown, adrienne maree 165, 182–3, 184, 188
Brown University 97
Brown v. Topeka Board of Education 34, 54, 126
bus boycott 34
Bush, M.E.L. 12

Caldera, A. 92, 138, 144
Calderon-Berumen, F. 144
Cancelmo, C. 12
capitalism 24
  imperialist white supremacist capitalist cisheteropatriarchy 25, 27–9, *28*, 161, 167
Cárdenas, B. 62
Cárdenas, J.A. 62
Carlisle School 53
Carroll Independent School District 85
Carter, E. 85
Carter, S.P. 12

Carter Berry, L. 138, 152
casteism 25
caste system
  continuous resistance to 31–2
  in US 18
Catholic faith sanctioned colonization 13–14
Charles, J.B. 91
Charleston church shooting 74, 162
Chavez, Cesar 37
Chicano movement 36–8
Chicano Studies 59
Chinese Americans
  legalization of citizenship **22**
  white supremacy, early schools and 56–7
Chinese Exclusion Act (1882) 57
Christchurch mosque attacks 129, 162
Christian faith sanctioned colonization 13–14
Christian hegemony 110
Christian nationalism 130–1
cisgenderism 25
cisheteropatriarchy, imperialist white supremacist capitalist 25, 27–9, *28*, 161, 167
citizenship 22–3, **22**
  birthright 22
  Black 22
  civil rights era, struggle to achieve full 33
  critical introspection and **141, 142**
  identities privileged/victimized by white supremacy **163**
  racialization of 32–3
  Reconstruction Era 32–3
Civil Rights Act of 1957 35
Civil Rights Act of 1964 41, **43,** 55
civil rights era
  African Americans 34–6
  Asian Americans 38
  Black feminist movement 39

Chicano feminists 39
citizenship, struggle to achieve full 33
  common goal as not achieved 33
  gay liberation movement 39
  Mexican Americans 36–8
  Native Americans 38–9
  resistance to white supremacy 33–9
  solidarity between movements, lack of 39–40
  women's rights movement 39
Clark, Septima 175
class, critical introspection and **141**, **142**
classism 25
classrooms
  culturally conscientious 64
  discussion of LGBTQIA+ topics 104–5
Coates, Ta-Nahesi 193
Colker, R. 20
Collaborative for Academic, Social, and Emotional Learning (CASEL) 88
Collins, C.S. 10, 13–14, 15
colonialism
  European 24
  settler 24
colonization
  Christian faith sanctioned 13–14
  contamination through 11
  infectious diseases, role of 14, 18
  white supremacy and 15–16
  writing and art about indigenous peoples 14
colorblindness 120–2
colorism 26
The Color Purple (Walker) 160
Columbia University 96
Combahee River Collective 161
common school movement 124
compliance, pedagogy of 171–2
conditional citizens 23

Congress for Racial Equality (CORE) 35
congruence/incongruence, critical introspection and **140**
conservative attacks on racial equity in 2020/2025 76–7
  affirmative action, repeal of 98–9
  critical race theory (CRT) 81–7, *86*
  diversity, equity and inclusion (DEI) 92–9
  effectiveness of 100
  judicial decisions against DEI 98–9
  motivation for 100
  Project 2025, Trump and 77
  social and emotional learning (SEL) 88–9
Constitution
  right to education and 50
  white supremacy and 20
Cooper, Anna Julia 23, 195
Coppell Independent School District 109
Counts, George 174
Covid-19 pandemic, racial disparities in access and outcomes 75
Cox, Spencer 95
Craven, Morgan 151
Crenshaw, Kimberlé 24, 161
critical consciousness 169–70
critical culturally sustaining and revitalizing pedagogy 65
critical introspection
  biases 138–9
  defined 135
  ethnic self/ethnic other, teachers' knowledge of 137–45
  framework for in teacher preparation and development 139–43, **140**, **141**, **142**
  healing the trees 145
  self-knowledge, importance of for teachers 136–8
  white supremacy and 143–5

criticality
    compliance, pedagogy of 171–2
    critical consciousness 169–70
    critical pedagogy 172
    educational justice and 179
    equity pedagogy 177
    novel study example 178–9
    purpose of schooling, reimagining 173–7
    questioning, discouragement of 170–1, 176
critical pedagogy 172
critical race theory (CRT)
    attacks on 81–7, *86*
    education, use in 80
    education policy and practices 81
    legislation, anti-CRT 1, 83–7, *86*, 125
    purpose of this book 1–2
    studying 80–1
    as target for conservative attacks 77
Crystal City, Texas 37
cultural assimilation 12
cultural difference studies 58, 61–7
cultural identity, critical introspection and **140**
culturally affirming education 65
culturally and historically responsive education 65
culturally and linguistically responsive teaching 64
culturally appropriate pedagogy 63
culturally based education 64
culturally compatible education 63
culturally congruent instruction 63
culturally connected instruction 65–6
culturally conscientious classroom 64
culturally inclusive pedagogy 65
culturally mediated instruction 64
culturally proactive teaching 65
culturally relevant and sustaining education 66

culturally relevant pedagogy 63
culturally responsive education 62
culturally responsive pedagogy 63
culturally responsive teaching 64
culturally restorative teaching 65
culturally sensitive instruction 63
culturally situated instruction 66
culturally sustaining pedagogy 64
culture wars 1
curricula
    Ethnic Studies 58–60, 75–6
    white supremacy and 118
Curriculum Studies (CS) xv

Davis, Angela 174, 182
Declaration of Independence, white supremacy and 18
Deferred Action for Childhood Arrivals (DACA) 43, **44**
dehumanizing 194
Delgado-Bernal, Dolores 59
Delpit, Lisa 172
Department of Education 110–12
deportation of immigrants 113, 157–8
DeSantis, Ron 132
desegregation of schools 34–5, 36–7, 54
Diaz, Danna xvii
digital divide 75
disability, critical introspection and **142**
disaggregated data, requirement for schools 79
diversity
    in DEI 90
    justice worker, author's development as xiv–xix
    purpose of this book 1–2
diversity, equity and inclusion (DEI)
    anti-DEI legislation 93–8, 120–1, 125
    attacks on 92–9
    attacks on by Trump administration 1, 3

Index

commitment to 92
diversity 90
equity 90
higher education 91–2
inclusion 90–1
judicial decisions against 98–9
myths about 92–3
origins 91–2
Doctrine of Discovery 13
"Don't Ask, Don't Tell" policy 43, **44**
"Don't Say Gay" law 105
Douglass, Frederick 100
DREAM Act 114
Driscoll Consolidated Independent School District 37
Duggins-Clay, Paige 184
Duncan-Andrade, J.M.R. 47, 50, 67, 68

Earnshaw, V.A. 108
ecosystems, schools and society 47
education
  big lie about educators 118–19
  civil rights in 34
  control over 117
  culturally affirming 65
  culturally and historically responsive 65
  culturally based 64
  culturally compatible 63
  culturally relevant and sustaining 66
  culturally responsive 62
  purpose of schooling, reimagining 173–7
  societal policies and 46–7
  white supremacy, early schools and 49–58
  see also policy/ies, education
Educators for Excellence 153
elitism 26
Elk v. Wilkins 32
El Movimiento 36–8
El Paso Walmart shooting 74, 129

emergent bilinguals 112–14
English-only movement, California 124
enslaved Black Americans, anti-literacy laws and 53
Equal Employment Opportunity Act 1972 41–2, **44**, 91
equality
  manipulation by Trump conservatives 41
  resistance to real 68
Equal Pay Act 1963 41, **43**
equity
  conservative attacks on 76–7
  in DEI 90
  pursuit of, resistance to 68
  simulation, Marcy Paul's xvii
equity pedagogy 177
ethnic self/ethnic other, teachers' knowledge of 137–45
Ethnic Studies 58–60, 75–6
ethnocentrism 26
Eurocentrism 26
European colonialism 24
European imperialism 24
Evers, Medger 35
exceptionalism, American 17
exclusion of LGBTQIA+ youth 103–9, *106*
Executive Orders
  14173 95
  14168 107
  14201 107
  14202 109–10
  14224 112
  14159 113
  14188 114, **114**
  14224 **114**
  14159 **114**
  14242 **114**
  14202 **115**
  14168 **115**
  14201 **115**

13985 **115**
14173 **115**
Department of Education, closure of 110–12
schooling, impact on **114–15**
experiences, critical introspection and **140**
explicit biases 138

faith
　critical introspection and **141, 142**
　and hope in tree planting xiii–xiv
faith sanctioned colonization 13–14
family, critical introspection and **141, 142**
family structure 26, 105
　identities privileged/victimized by white supremacy **164**
Fanon, F. 172, 191–2, 194–5
farmworker activism 37–8
fatphobia 26
federal land giveaways **22**
feminism
　Black feminist theory 160–2
　civil rights era 39
Fernandez, F. 85
Filipino farmworkers 38
Floyd, George, murder of 73–4
forced sterilization 128
For Harriet (author's blog) xv
freedom, Hamer on 5
freedom dreaming 181
Freedom Rides movement 35
Freire, Paulo 143, 169, 172, 176

Gauntt, S. 113
Gay, Claudine 94–5
Gay and Lesbian Pride Month 46
gay liberation movement 39
gender
　binarism 26
　critical introspection and **141, 142**
　identities privileged/victimized by white supremacy **163**
　and race, Black women and 23
G.I. Bill **21**
Gillborn, D. 15, 152
Givens, Jarvis 53
Gorski, P. 60
great replacement theory 128–9
Gremke, Angela 130

Haberman, 171
hair
　harassment 126
　identities privileged/victimized by white supremacy **164**
Hamer, Fannie Lou 5, 195
Hammond, Zaretta 46–7, 171
Hannah-Jones, Nikole 16, 45, 75, 94
Harper, S. 92, 118, 119
Harris, Kamala 32
Harvard University 96
　Implicit Association Test 139
healing the trees 3, 135
　inclusivity 157
　intersectionality 166–7
　see also critical introspection; insurgency in teaching and learning; policy/ies, education; radical imagination
Hernandez v. Driscoll 37
heterosexism 26
higher education
　anti-CRT legislation 85–6
　anti-DEI legislation 93–8, 121
　Black Americans 55
　Chinese Americans 57
　colorblindness and 121
　diversity, equity and inclusion (DEI) 91
　Ethnic Studies 58–60
　immigrant students 114
　Native American 52–3

Higher Education Act of 1965 41, **43,** 55
Hill Collins, P. 24
Hispanic Heritage Month 45
Hispanic/Latino(x), use of term 6
Hispanic/Latino(x) students, white supremacy, early schools and 55–6
history
　importance of looking back 2
　justice work, evolution of 2
　soil, and roots 10–11
　white supremacy, origins of 13–15
Hixenbaugh, M. 85
homelessness, LGBTQIA+ youth and 108–9
Homestead Act 1862 **22**
homophobia 26
homosexual youth 103–9, *106*
hooks, bell 24–5, 28, 117, 149, 161
hope in tree planting xiii–xiv
Howard, J.R. 137, 167
Howard, T.C. 137, 162, 167
How to End Christian Nationalism (Tyler) 130–1
Huerta, Dolores 37
"Human Family" (Angelou) 192
humanity 191–5
humanize/humanizing, use of terms 192–3
human rights 194
Hurston, Zora Neale 71
Hutchens, N.H. 85

identity
　as built around race 18–23
　social, whiteness as 11–12
ideologies, conservative
　Black inferiority 125–7
　Eurocentrism 123–5
　meritocracy 122–3
　racial colorblindness 120–2
　understanding of, need for 119
　white nationalism 127–31

"I Have a Dream" speech (King) 121, xiii
Imagination: A Manifesto (Benjamin) 184–5
imagination, radical 181–3, 184–5
　Afrofuturism 183–4
　artificial intelligence used for 185–8
imagineers 181
Imarisha, W. 182, 183, 188
immigrant students 112–14
Immigration and Customs Enforcement (ICE) 113, 157–8
Immigration and Nationality Act 1965 41, **43**
imperialism
　American 17
　European 24
imperialist white supremacist capitalist cisheteropatriarchy 25, 27–9, *28*, 161, 167
imperialist white supremacist capitalist patriarchy 24
Implicit Association Test, Harvard University 139
implicit biases 138–9
inclusivity
　all students, justice for 162, **163–4**
　anti-racism and 164–6
　author's educational journey 158–60
　Black feminist theory 160–2
　culturally inclusive pedagogy 65
　defined 157
　in DEI 90–1
　deportations/anti-ICE protests 157–8
　healing the trees 157, 166–7
incompatibilities, theory of 62
incongruence, critical introspection and **140**
Indian Civilization Fund Act (1819) 51
Indian Civil Rights Acts of 1968 39, 41, **44**
indigenous peoples

civil rights era 38-9
colonizers' writing and art about 14
infectious diseases, colonizers' 14
land, connections to 11
National American Indian Heritage Month 45
Individuals with Disabilities Education Act (IDEA) 42, **44**
inequity simulation, Marcy Paul's xvii
infectious disease. colonization and 14, 18
Institute for Education Sciences 111
instruction
　culturally congruent 63
　culturally connected 65-6
　culturally mediated 64
　culturally sensitive 63
　culturally situated 66
insurgency in teaching and learning
　compliance, pedagogy of 171-2
　criticality 169-70
　critical pedagogy 172
　educational justice and 179
　equity pedagogy 177
　freedoms from/to **178**
　novel study example 178-9
　purpose of schooling, reimagining 173-7
　questioning, discouragement of 170-1, 176
intellectualism 179
Intercultural Research Development Association (IDRA) 151
interrelatedness, King on 5
intersectionality
　all students, justice for 162, **163-4**
　anti-racism and 164-6
　author's educational journey 158-60
　Black feminist theory 160-2
　deportations/anti-ICE protests 157-8
　healing the trees 157, 166-7
Islamophobia 26

Jim Crow laws **21**
Johnson v. McIntosh 15
Jones, R.P. 13
Jun, A. 10, 13-14, 15
justice work, purpose of this book 3-5
justice workers
　author's development as xiv-xix
　identification as 4
　use of term 2

Kendi, Ibram X. 16
King, Coretta Scott 155
King, Martin Luther 5, 195
　on commitment to genuine equality 67
　critical consciousness 175
　"I Have a Dream" speech 121, xiii
　"Letter from a Birmingham Jail" 5
　on love and justice 149
　multiplicity of oppression 168n1
Kishimoto, K. 62
knowledge
　self-knowledge, importance of for teachers 136-8
　types of needed for teaching 136

Ladson-Billings, Gloria 80, 137
Lalami, Laila 23
land, indigenous peoples' connection to 11
Land Back Movement 11
language(s)
　critical introspection and **141**, **142**
　culturally and linguistically responsive teaching 64
　identities privileged/victimized by white supremacy **164**
　Native American 52
Lantz, P.M. 85
La Raza Unida Party 38
Lau v. Nichols 42, **44**, 57, 112
League of United Latin American Citizens (LULAC) 36

legislation
    anti-CRT 83–7, *86*
    anti-DEI 93–8, 120–1
    anti-LGBTQIA+ 103–9, *106*
    anti-SEL 89–90
    anti-trans 105–6, *106*
    citizenship and **22**
    DEI and 91
    justice-oriented milestones 40–5, **43–4**
    white nationalism and 131
    white supremacy and 20, **21–2**
lesbians, Black 39
"Letter from a Birmingham Jail" (King) 5
LGBTQIA+ youth 103–9, *106*
LGBTQ Pride Month 46
lies told by conservatives
    big lie about educators 118–19
    Black inferiority 125–7
    Eurocentrism 123–5
    ideologies behind 119–31
    meritocracy 122–3
    to others 118–19
    racial colorblindness 120–2
    to themselves 119–31
linguicism 26
literacy, racial 86
Lorde, Audre 166–7, 188
Love, Bettina L. 29, 67, 125, 179
love and justice 149–50
Loving v. Virginia 41, **43**

Malcolm X 154
Manifest Destiny 14–15
Mann, Horace 173
March on Washington for Jobs and Freedom 35
Marriage, critical introspection and **141, 142**
Martin, Trayvon, murder of 73
Matthew Shepard and James Byrd, Jr., Hate Crimes Prevention Act 42, 44

Mays, Kyle T. 52
McCorkle, W. 130
McElroy, Kathleen 94
McGee Banks, C.S. 177
McLaurin v. Oklahoma State Regents for Higher Education 34
McMahon, Linda 97
Meachum, John Berry 53
media, educational policymaking and 154
Mendez et al. v. Westminster 36–7
Menendian, S. 22
mental capacity, identities privileged/victimized by white supremacy **163**
mental health of LGBTQIA+ youth 108–9
meritocracy 122–3
Mexican Americans
    civil rights era 36–8
    legalization of citizenship **22**
    white supremacy, early schools and 55–6
Mexican American Studies 60
Miller, V. 85
misogynoir 26
misogyny 26
Mitchell, Koritha 164
Moll, L.C. 62
Montgomery bus boycott 34
months of observation 45–6
Morrison, Toni 182
Mueller, J.C. 12
multicultural education, emergence of 60–1
multilingual services, minimization of 112

National American Indian Heritage Month 45
National Association for the Advancement of Colored People (NAACP) 35, 99

National Association of Multicultural Education (NAME) 60–1
National Black (Afro-American) History Month 45
National Day of Remembrance for U.S. Indian Boardings Schools 52
national identity 20–3, 127–31
National Immigration Forum 128–9
National Immigration Law Center 113
National Indian Youth Council 39
nationalism, white/Christian 127–31
nationality
   critical introspection and **141**, **142**
   identities privileged/victimized by white supremacy **163**
National Native American Boarding School Healing Coalition 52
Native American Languages Act 42, **44**
Native Americans
   boarding schools 51–3, 124
   capitalistic violence inflicted on 18
   civil rights era 38–9
   infectious diseases, colonizers' 14
   land, connections to 11
   legalization of citizenship **22**
   National American Indian Heritage Month 45
   National Native American Boarding School Healing Coalition 52
   white supremacy, early schools and 51–3
Native American Studies 59
nativism 26
Naturalization Act of 1790 20, **21**
neuroablism 26
neuronormativity 27
Newman, C.B. 10, 13–14, 15
Nichols, B. 24
No Child Left Behind Act 79

Obama, Barack 32, 72, 175
Obasogie, Osagie K. 75
Office for Civil Rights 111–12

one drop rule 128
oppression, systemic
   imperialist white supremacist capitalist cisheteropatriarchy 24, 27–9, *28*, 161, 167
   interlocking forms of 23–5
Orlando nightclub shooting 74
Ortiz, P. 53–4
othering 193–4
   danger in 191
   victims of 22, **22**
outcomes for racially minoritized students 67

Palestine, US students' protests against Israel 96–7, 114
Palmer, Parker J. 136
"Parents Rights in Education" law 105
Paris, D. 66
Parker, C.S. 138
Parks, Rosa 34
partus sequitur ventrem 128
patriarchy 24
   imperialist white supremacist capitalist cisheteropatriarchy 27–9, *28*, 161, 167
Patterson, K. 71–2
Paul, Marcy xvii
Payne, 67
pedagogy
   of compliance 171–2
   critical culturally sustaining and revitalizing 65
   culturally appropriate 63
   culturally inclusive 65
   culturally relevant 63
   culturally responsive 63
   culturally sustaining 64
   resource pedagogies 66
Pedagogy of the Oppressed (Freire) 143
people of color, use of term 5
people of the global majority (PGM) 19

physical ability, identities privileged/victimized by white supremacy **163**
Pittsburgh synagogue shooting 74, 129, 162
planting trees 2, 9, xiii–xiv
  see also resistance to white supremacy
Plessy v. Ferguson 32–3
Plyler v. Doe 42, **44**
policy/ies, education
  defined 148–9
  educators role in creating 153
  engagement with, author's experience of 150–2
  love and justice 149–50
  policymaking, involvement in 152–5
  power of 147
  shaping of by teachers 151–2
  white men as controlling 148
powell, j.a. 22
Preamble to the U.S. Constitution xiii
professional associations 59
Project 2025
  Department of Education, closure of 111
  LGBTQIA+ students 106–7
  Trump and 77
pro-Palestinian protests 96–7, 114
protests, student
  1968 37
  pro-Palestinian protests 96–7, 114
public restroom ban for transpeople 105
Punished for Dreaming (Love) 181
purpose of schooling, reimagining 173–7

queer youth 103–9, *106*
questioning, discouragement of 170–1, 176

race
  citizenship and 32–3
  critical introspection and **141**, **142**
  and gender, Black women and 23
  identities privileged/victimized by white supremacy **163**
  identity in the US built around 18–22
"The Race to Ban Race" (Miller, Fernandez, and Hutchens) 85
racial capitalism 24
racial colorblindness 120–2
racial literacy **86**
racial transcendence 72
racism
  anti-racism, intersectionality and 164–6
  forms of 27
  function of 182
  justice worker, author's development as xiv–xix
  white supremacy, early schools and 49–58
radical imagination 181–3,**183**, 184–5
  Afrofuturism 183–4
  artificial intelligence used for 185–8
Randolph, A. Philip 35
Reconstruction Era, resistance to white supremacy 32–3
redlining **21**
Regents of the University of California v. Bakke 42, **44**, 55, 91, 98
religion
  colonization sanctioned by 13–14
  critical introspection and **141**, **142**
  identities privileged/victimized by white supremacy **163**
religious intolerance 130–1
religious minority students 109–10
replacement theory 128–9
resistance to white supremacy
  civil rights era 33–9
  as continuous, by victims 31–2
  justice-oriented milestones 40–5, **43–4**
  months of observation 45–6

Reconstruction Era 32–3
see also white supremacy
resource pedagogies 66
Respect for Marriage Act 43, **44**
restrictive housing covenants **21**
Reynolds, Sherrie 159–60
Rodriguez, S. 130
Roe v. Wade 42, **44**
roots 10–11
    white supremacy as contaminating 15–16
Ross, Howard J. 138
Rufo, Christopher 81–2, 95
Russell, S.T. 108
Rustin, Bayard 35, 149

Saad, Layla F. 17, 119, 143
sanism 27
Santiago, A.M. 71–2
Santoro, N. 136, 137
SB 17/HB 5127 93
schools
    return to early, desire for 117–18
    societal policies and 46–7
    white supremacy, early schools and 49–58
"school to deportation pipeline" 114
Scott v. Sandford 32
segregation/desegregation of schools 34–5, 36–7, 54, 126
Seidel, A.L. 110, 130
Self-Determination Era 39
self-knowledge, importance of for teachers 136–8
Selma-to-Montgomery marches 35
settler colonialism 24
sex, identities privileged/victimized by white supremacy **163**
sexism 27
sexuality
    critical introspection and **141**, **142**
    identities privileged/victimized by white supremacy **164**

sexual orientation 103–9
SFFA v. Harvard 96, 120
SFFA v. UNC 120
sharecropping 21
Shulman, L.E. 136
Silverman, R.M. 71–2
sit-in movement 35
The 1619 Project (Hannah-Jones) 16, 75, 94
skin color
    critical introspection and **141**, **142**
    identities privileged/victimized by white supremacy **164**
slavery
    Black inferiority, belief in 125
    partus sequitur ventrem 128
social and emotional learning (SEL) 77, 87–8
social class, critical introspection and **141**, **142**
social identity
    race and 18–22, **21–2**
    whiteness as 11–12
social positionality, critical introspection and **140**
social reconstructionism 174
social reproduction
    schools of 49–50
    theory 160
societal institutions, critical introspection and **140**
sociocultural competence of teachers 67
socioeconomic status, identities privileged/victimized by white supremacy **163**
soil, and roots 10–11
    solidarity between civil rights movements, lack of 39–40
    white supremacy as contaminating 15–16
solidarity between civil rights movements, lack of 39–40

Southeast Asians in Coppell Independent School District 109
Southern Poverty Law Center 128
sports, trans women and 107
Stamped from the Beginning (Kendi) 16
Standard North American Family (SNAF) 26
Starker Glass, T. 138, 152
state education policies, anti-DEI sentiments in 97
state-sanctioned violence 73–4
sterilization, forced 128
Stonewall riots 39
structural inequities, Marcy Paul's simulation xvii
struggle, need for 101
student protests
   1968 37
   pro-Palestinian 114
systemic oppression
   imperialist white supremacist capitalist cisheteropatriarchy 25, 27–9, *28*, 161, 167
   interlocking forms of 23–5, *28*

Tate, William F. 80
teacher education, author's experience of job market and 72–3
teachers, sociocultural competence of 67
Teachers for Social Justice 153
teaching
   culturally and linguistically responsive 64
   culturally proactive 65
   culturally responsive 64
   culturally restorative 65
Teaching to Transgress (hooks) 117
Teaching When the World Is on Fire (Delpit) 172
TeachPlus 153
Teach Truth campaign 119

tenant farming **21**
terminology 5–6
Texas, anti-DEI legislation 93–4
Texas Public Policy Foundation 83
texturism 27
14th Amendment 32
   right to education 50, 54
Their Eyes Were Watching God (Hurston) 71
Third World Liberation Front 58–9
Till, Emmett, murder of 34
Tintiangco-Cubales, A. 58
Title IX of the Education Amendments 42, **44**
Toliver, S.R. 183
transformative SEL 88
transgender students 105–6, *106*, 107, **115**
Trans Legislative Tracker 106, *106*
trees
   analogy, use of as xiii, xix
   blighting of the fruit 2–3, 71
   planting 2, 9, xiii–xiv
   soil, and roots 10–11
   white supremacy as contaminating soil 15–16
   see also healing the trees
Trevor Project 104, 108–9
Trump, Donald
   Executive Order 14159 113
   Executive Order 14168 107
   Executive Order 14173 95–6
   Executive Order 14188 114
   Executive Order 14201 107
   Executive Order 14202 109–10
   Executive Order 14224 112
   Project 2025 and 77
   white nationalist behavior 129
Trump administration
   attacks on educational justice 1
   Harvard University, pressure on 96
Tyler, A. 130–1

ubuntu 194, 195
United Farm Workers (UFW) 37–8
United States
   birth of, period of 16
   as colonizer 17–18
unity in justice movement, importance of 46
University of North Texas (UNT) Diversity and Equity Conference xvii–xviii
Utah Compact on Racial Equity, Diversity and Inclusion 95
Uyematsu, A. 38

Vaught, Sabina E. 49–50
Vaught S.E. 19
Villegas, 67
violence, state-sanctioned 73–4
Viral Justice (Benjamin) 183
visionary fiction 182–3
voting as civil rights issue 35
Voting Rights Act 1965 41, **43**

Wagner Act 1935 **22**
Walker, Alice 160
Wall Kimmerer, Robin 10, 11, 33, 46, 195, xiii
Warren, Earl 34
Warren, M.R. 29
Washington, Booker T. 124
Watkins, N.A. 153
Watts riots, California 35–6
West, Cornell 99, 121, 149, 159
Western culture 123–5
white anxiety 82–3
white extinction, fear of 128–9
white language supremacy 26
white nationalism 127–31
whiteness
   invisibility of 121–2, 137
   as social identity 11–12
   use of term 12

white normativity 12
white people, use of term 6
white proximity 12
white racial purity, desire for 127–8
white supremacy
   all races as sustaining 15
   binaries resulting from 19
   birth of US rooted in 17–19
   Christian faith sanctioned colonization 13–14
   Christian hegemony 110
   Christian nationalism 130–1
   colonization and 15–16
   critical introspection and 143–5
   curriculum and 118
   defined 15–17
   Doctrine of Discovery 13
   early schools 49–58
   educational injustice and 29
   forms of systemic oppression rooted in 25–9, *28*
   as global phenomenon 15
   great replacement theory 128–9
   identities privileged/victimized by **163–4**
   imperialist white supremacist capitalist cisheteropatriarchy 25, 27–9, *28*, 161, 167
   imperialist white supremacist capitalist patriarchy 24
   influence on schools 51
   institutionalization of 14–15
   internalized 143
   legislation **21–2**
   Manifest Destiny 14–15
   meritocracy and 123
   oppression, interlocking forms of 23–4
   origins of 13–15, 16
   racial colorblindness and 120–2
   use of term 12

whiteness used synonymously with 12
see also resistance to white supremacy
Whitfield, James 84–5
Wilkerson, Isabel 18, 31, 194
Wohlleben, P. 10, 33
woke, meaning of 80
Women's History Month 45
women's rights movement 39
Woodson, Carter G. 22, 54
work, schooling as competing with 54

workforce development, education and 174
writing and art about indigenous peoples, colonizers' 14

X, Malcolm 154
xenophobia 27

yellow power movement 38

"zone of non-human space" 191–2

Author's Biography

Dr. Altheria Caldera is Adjunct Senior Professional Lecturer in the School of Education at American University in Washington, DC; and CEO/Principal Consultant at Caldera and Associates Educational Consulting. Her research focuses on how to make schooling just for all students. She has published approximately two dozen peer-reviewed articles and book chapters, and has coedited a book, *Ourselves in Our Work: Black Women Scholars of Black Girlhood* (2024). Altheria is a first-generation college graduate student who attributes much of her success to the support she received as an undergraduate at a historically Black college.